DESTINATION EARTH

A HISTORY OF ALLEGED ALIEN PRESENCE

Alan Baker

BLANDFORD

A BLANDFORD BOOK

First published in the UK 1998 by Blandford
a Cassell imprint

Cassell plc
Wellington House
125 Strand
London WC2R 0BB

Distributed in the United States by Sterling Publisher Co., Inc.,
387 Park Avenue South, New York, NY 10016–8810

A Cataloguing-in-Publication Data entry for this title is available from
the British Library.

ISBN 0-7137-2719-5

Designed by Chris Bell
Printed and bound in Great Britain by MPG Books Ltd, Bodmin,
Cornwall

Contents

Introduction

A S WE APPROACH the year 2000, public interest in the paranormal is increasing at a dramatic (some would say a
positively alarming) rate. While the skeptics (see below)
maintain their exasperated and adamantine opposition to
every aspect of what is loosely labelled 'the unexplained', people
in all walks of life on every continent are increasingly turning their
attention to subjects they perhaps would have ignored or derided
only a few years ago.

These developments have, of course, been noticed by the
media, and little time has been lost in responding to this potentially highly lucrative state of affairs. The phenomenal success of
television programmes like *The X Files* has spawned so many imi-
tations that the image of two government agents investigating the
paranormal is now widely seen in advertisements for everything
from mobile phones to floor mops.

Likewise, 'fact-based' programmes, such as *Strange But True?* in
the United Kingdom, and *Sightings* and *Paranormal Borderline* in the
United States, are satisfying a growing appetite among the general
public for reports of the bizarre and unexplained. The media attention sparked by public interest has itself rebounded and fuelled yet
further interest in a kind of paranormal chain reaction, which has
had more than one skeptic foaming at the mouth.

The difference between skeptics (with a 'k' – US spelling from
the Greek) and sceptics (with a 'c' – from the Latin) is so subtle as

to be negligible, but, to the ufologist, it is a fundamental one. While a skeptic denies the reality of *any* anomalous phenomena, or at best maintains that all such events are ultimately amenable to explanation within current scientific parameters, a sceptic prefers to tread lightly the middle ground between total denial and total credulity, willing to accept (provisionally) the reality of a paranormal event if the evidence is sufficiently impressive, while keeping an eye open for new information. Charles Fort, the reclusive explorer of the vast field of anomalous phenomena, called the skeptics 'Exclusionists' (in his first published book, *The Book of the Damned*, he says that, by 'Damned', he means data that have been 'excluded' by orthodox science). It is a measure of his importance that today, when we speak of the more open-minded group of sceptics, we call them 'Forteans'.

Hence the subtitle of this book: *A History of Alleged Alien Presence*. The 'Alleged' should not be taken as implying that I disbelieve *all* reports of encounters with strange beings. It will become quite clear, I hope, that I believe there is definitely a core mystery, a small minority of cases that represent the presence on Earth of a genuine, non-human intelligence (wherever its origin may ultimately lie). The reader should thus bear in mind that by 'alien' I do not necessarily mean extra-terrestrial; I simply mean an intelligence that is profoundly *other*.

Neither will I be looking exclusively at cases where direct contact was reported. The history of alleged alien presence includes many events that hold bizarre or otherworldly *implications* rather than representing explicit one-to-one contacts. A case in point is that of Zygmunt Adamski, who, on 11 June 1980, left his home to buy a bag of potatoes. His corpse, burned by an unidentified corrosive substance, was discovered five days later.

Adamski was 56 when he died. A Pole who had fled to England when the Nazis invaded his country, he lived with his wife Lottie in the Tingley suburb of Leeds, West Yorkshire. Five days after Adamski's mysterious disappearance, his body was discovered by Trevor Parker, who was loading his truck at his father's coal yard in Todmorden. Parker was preparing for the last delivery of the day when he came upon Adamski's corpse. Parker later reported:

> It was just lying there in plain sight. I didn't know whether the man was dead or alive, so I called the police and an

ambulance. I was very frightened, I didn't want to be out
there myself. The body gave me a very eerie feeling. I have no
idea how the man got in the yard, but I know one thing for
absolute certain – there was no body on that coal pile when I
loaded my truck earlier in the day.

According to consultant pathologist Dr Alan Edwards' report to the
police, Zygmunt Adamski had died of a heart attack. His scalp,
neck and the back of his head had been burned by a strange corrosive substance, which had not damaged his face and clothes. The
implication was that the substance had been applied carefully,
while the top of the body was naked. Although his watch and wal-
let were missing, there was £5 in his pocket.

The police were unable to make any headway whatever with
their inquiries, in spite of the coroner postponing the inquest three
times to give them more time. According to Mrs Adamski, her husband had no reason to be in Todmorden; nor did he drink or have
any enemies.

The UFO connection was established when one of the two
policemen, who had been dispatched to the coal yard when the
body was found, claimed that he had seen an unidentified object a
few hours previously.

At the inquest, James Turnbull the coroner said:

As a trained lawyer, I have to rely on facts. Unfortunately,
we have not been able to uncover any facts which may have
contributed to this death. I tend to believe that there may be
some simple explanation.

However, I do admit that the failure of forensic scientists to
identify the corrosive substance which caused Mr Adamski's
burns could lend some weight to the UFO theory. As a
coroner, I cannot speculate. But I must admit that if I was
walking over Ilkley Moor tomorrow and a UFO came down, I
would not be surprised. I might be terrified, but not surprised.

I cannot believe that all the thousands of reports of this
sort of phenomenon, covering almost every country in the
world, and going back through the ages, result from human
error.

UFO investigator Graham Birdsall commented: 'There is world-
wide interest in this case – it is the biggest UFO story for many

years. The fact that the police have even considered the possibility of UFO involvement is unique.'

Whatever the true nature of Zygmunt Adamski's fate, the shadow of alien activity hangs over many more injuries, deaths and disappearances, providing further evidence of a genuine mystery at the heart of alleged alien encounters. My own provisional acceptance of this fact is what prompted me to write this book. It is an attempt to examine the events, stories and rumours that have, by means of the paranormal chain reaction mentioned above, influenced and fed off each other over the years (and indeed centuries), to produce a modern mythological system, one that has continued to grow and change, almost like a living organism mutating to ensure its survival in a constantly shifting environment.

So, in the pages that follow, there are stories from the dawn of civilization, of fish-bodied deities who taught humanity the fundamentals of art and science; reports of encounters with non-human intelligences from medieval through to modern times; encounters with beings claiming to have come from other worlds, and others claiming always to have been native to this one. We shall also examine how the public attitude to the concept of alien presence has altered over the years, moving inexorably from fascination and hope to mistrust and fear, and we shall make the acquaintance of some of those who have been responsible for influencing that attitude.

With regard to the concept of alien presence, it seems to me that we are in a no-lose situation, in spite of the fulminations of the Exclusionists. If such encounters are no more than delusions and hallucinations, they are eminently worthy of study in psychological and sociological terms for that reason alone. If, on the other hand, there really is something 'out there' which decided, perhaps millennia ago, to come here, then a small minority of alleged UFO and alien-related incidents are, without doubt, the most momentous events in the history of our species.

This possibility is what first attracted me to ufology, and its related fields. The implication that much of this material represents events that currently exist beyond our present scientific parameters should in no way discourage our examination of it. We should remember the problems that the quantum theory gave Einstein, and how it took another great genius, Niels Bohr, to carry the work on and through the necessary paradigm shift.

Total skepticism is just as dangerous and unhealthy as total credulity. If we can keep our minds open long enough to examine new evidence as and when it appears, we may just be in a position to answer some of the fundamental questions about the universe and our relationship to it that have haunted us since the earliest days of humanity.

PART ONE

FROM ANTIQUITY TO THE PRESENT

ONE

Sirius, the Iron Sun

T HE BRIGHT STAR SIRIUS holds a pre-eminent position in the history of the human imagination, its significance stretching back to the dawn of history. The main reason it inspires wonder today is the belief that it is home to a race of spacefarers that made contact with humanity in the distant past, and perhaps maintain that contact even today.

THE DOG STAR AND ITS COMPANION

The brightest star in the heavens, Sirius is actually a binary system in the constellation Canis Major, and is approximately 8.7 light years from Earth. Around Sirius A (which can be seen with the naked eye) revolves Sirius B, an example of what is known as a 'white dwarf', a star which was once similar to our own Sun, but is believed to be nearing the end of its life. Unlike its companion, Sirius B is totally invisible to the naked eye, and was seen for the first time only in 1862, by the American astronomer Alvin Clark. Since Sirius B is 100,000 times fainter than Sirius A, it was not possible to photograph it until 1970.

White dwarfs are incredibly dense objects, so dense that a cubic metre of Sirius B weighs about 20,000 tons. Like all celestial bodies, Sirius B follows an elliptical orbit around the larger star, which takes 50 Earth years to complete.

SIRIUS IN ANTIQUITY

In classical mythology, the Dog Star is closely associated with the constellation Orion, at whose heel it lies. In Greek myth, Orion's ascent into the sky was the result of his death at the hands of the goddess Artemis. There are a number of versions of how this occurred. One has it that Artemis shot Orion by accident at Apollo's instigation; another that he had incurred her wrath by boasting that he had killed all the wild beasts in Crete; yet another that, after he had attempted to ravish her, she produced a scorpion from the earth, which killed both Orion and his dog, Sirius, both of whom were subsequently transported into the sky.

The Greeks were not the first people to be fascinated by Sirius. The ancient Egyptians identified the star with Isis, the wife and sister of Osiris, and mother of Horus. Isis was identified by the Greeks with Demeter, Hera, Selene and Aphrodite, and eventually she absorbed all the qualities of the other goddesses. She is also credited with performing the rites of embalmment for the first time in history, upon the corpse of her husband, who had been assassinated by their violent brother, Set. The murdered god was thus restored to eternal life.

In *Fingerprints of the Gods: A Quest for the Beginning and the End*, Graham Hancock quotes from a translation of the Giza Pyramid Texts, which dates back to around 2450 BC (the passage is addressed to Osiris):

Thy sister Isis cometh unto thee rejoicing in her love for thee.
Thou settest her upon thee, thy issue entereth into her, and
she becometh great with child like the star Sept [Sirius, the
Dog Star]. Horus-Sept cometh forth from thee in the form of
Horus, dweller in Sept.

Like Robert Temple before him, Hancock finds this imagery intriguing because of the duality that is implied with regard to the double star Sirius. According to Hancock:

Many interpretations of this passage are, of course, possible.
What intrigued me, however, was the clear implication that
Sirius was to be regarded as a *dual entity* in some way
comparable to a woman 'great with child'. Moreover, after
the birth (or coming forth) of that child, the text makes a

special point of reminding us that Horus remained a 'dweller in Sept', presumably suggesting that he stayed close to his mother.

While both Hancock and Temple are interested in the apparent anachronism that ancient cultures might have been aware that Sirius was a double star, they disagree over the possible explanation for this. Hancock suggests there may have been an unknown prehistoric civilization whose knowledge of science (including astronomy) was equal to and perhaps greater than our own. Temple, on the other hand, attributes this knowledge to the intervention in antiquity of an altogether stranger group of individuals.

THE DOGON, THE NOMMOS AND THE MYSTERY RELIGIONS

Between 1946 and 1950, two French anthropologists, Marcel Griaule and Germaine Dieterlen, lived with the Dogon tribe of Mali, West Africa. During that time, four of the Dogon head priests were persuaded to share their most secret traditions with the scientists, who were astonished by what they were told.

Central to the Dogon traditions was the star Sirius, about which they knew far more than seemed possible. For instance, they knew that Sirius has a twin – the white dwarf Sirius B, invisible from Earth – and also that Sirius B is extremely heavy. According to the Dogon priests, it is made of a substance 'heavier than all the iron on Earth'. In addition to this, not only did they know that the white dwarf's orbit around Sirius A takes 50 years, but also that the orbital path is elliptical; they even knew the position of Sirius A within the ellipse.

Griaule and Dieterlen were also astounded to learn that the Dogon knew of Saturn's ring system, the four main moons of Jupiter, the revolution of the planets around the Sun, and the spiral shape of the Milky Way.

What is yet more astonishing, however, is the explanation given by the Dogon themselves for this knowledge: they believe that their ancestors were visited in antiquity by spacefarers from a planet in the Sirius star system. According to Robert Temple in his book *The Sirius Mystery*, the Dogon are the last people on Earth to worship this race of amphibians, who landed in the Persian Gulf at the dawn of human civilization. Memories of this event are represented not only in the culture of the Dogon, but also in the legends and art of Babylonia, Egypt and Greece.

The Dogon priests told the two French anthropologists that they called the alien visitors 'Nommos'. These creatures, they said, needed to spend most of their time submerged in water, a trait they shared with the Babylonian god Oannes. The priests described 'the spinning and whirling of the descent of the ark' (the Nommos' spacecraft), and the noise of thunder it made upon landing. Reference is also made in the legends to the ark 'spurting blood' – perhaps a rocket exhaust. The Dogon spoke of an additional star-like object that remained in the sky while the ark descended to Earth, which may imply the presence of a larger mother ship.

> The whole body of the animal was like that of a fish; and it
> had under a fish's head another head, and also feet below,
> similar to those of a man, subjoined to the fish's tail. His voice,
> too, and language, were articulate and human; and a
> representation of him is preserved even to this day. . . . When
> the sun set, it was the custom of this Being to plunge again
> into the sea, and abide all night in the deep; for he was
> amphibious.

This is not a Dogon description of a Nommo, but an extract from the surviving fragments of the *Babylonian History* of the priest Berossus. It refers to Oannes, the ancient civilizer-god who taught the Sumerians mathematics, astronomy, agriculture, social and political organization, and written language.

In *The Sirius Mystery*, Temple argues beyond this initial connection between the Nommos of the Dogon and the Oannes of the ancient Sumerians, and demonstrates a connection between Oannes and Sirius and the Classical 'mystery religions', which were recorded in a coded form that represented an arcane system of knowledge available only to initiates of the mysteries. There are, however, occasional clues pointing to the connection with Sirius, including the repeated motif of the number 50, representing the orbital period of Sirius B, and a dog-headed deity, representing Sirius A, the Dog Star.

There is a large amount of material within the mythology of the ancient world to support Temple's theories concerning Sirius. Aside from the Annedoti ('Repulsive Ones'), of whom Oannes was the most famous, there are Dagon and Atargatis, who were worshipped by the Philistines, and had fishes' tails and human bodies. At the Pharos off Alexandria resided the amphibian god Proteus, known as 'The Old Man of the Sea', who used to rest in a cave, sheltering 'from the heat of the star Sirius'. Lake Triton in North Africa was the home of another amphibian god, Triton, who helped the Argonauts (of whom there were, perhaps significantly, 50).

The Aegean Sea was home to Nereus (like Proteus, a shapechanger), who had 50 daughters, half human, half fish. At Phigalia on the Mediterranean there was an ancient sanctuary described by Pausanias, where an image of Artemis was kept. The representation of the goddess was that of a woman down to the waist, and below that, a fish. The amphibian gods known as the Telchines lived on the island of Rhodes. After they were scattered from the island by Zeus, some of them fled to Greece, where they became the 50 'hounds of Actaeon'. According to Robert Graves, the Telchines had dogs' heads and flippers in place of hands.

SIRIUS CALLING!

There is some evidence to suggest that whoever lives at Sirius may be capable of communicating across the light years with certain human beings.

Anyone familiar with the work of the American writer Robert Anton Wilson will know that he says his being is home to 24 selves, each with differing beliefs and agendas, and any of which can be brought into play in order to deal with a particular stimulus. In *Cosmic Trigger: Final Secret of the Illuminati*, he describes how he 'entered a belief system, from July 1973 until around October 1974, in which [he] was receiving telepathic messages from entities residing on a planet of the double star Sirius'.

Unwilling wholeheartedly to accept the idea that he was literally in contact with extra-terrestrials, Wilson, after a meeting with the world-famous computer scientist and ufologist Dr Jacques Vallée, began to formulate a new belief system based on the theory that 'otherworldly communication' has been going on for centuries, and in the end may well *not* turn out to be the result of an extra-terrestrial presence.

However, no sooner had Wilson begun to think of his Sirius experiences as merely a modern interpretation of a phenomenon that has always been with us, than he came across Temple's *The Sirius Mystery*, which seemed to lend considerable weight to his initial feeling that he really was in contact with Sirians.

On 23 July 1973, Wilson awoke from a dream that he could not quite remember; the only piece of information he had retrieved from his dream state he quickly scribbled down. The message was: 'Sirius is very important.' He proceeded to look through his library of occult books and, on pages 15 and 50 of Kenneth Grant's *The Magical Revival*, came across the following:

> *Phoenix* was [Aleister] Crowley's secret name in the Ordo Templi Orientis . . . The Phoenix was also an ancient constellation in which Sothis, or Sirius, was the chief star . . .
>
> Crowley identified the heart of (his magical) current with one particular Star. In Occult Tradition, this is 'the Sun behind the Sun', the Hidden God, the vast star Sirius, or Sothis . . .

The component of his being that Wilson calls 'the Skeptic' was intrigued but unconvinced by this, so he went to the public library, and made another intriguing discovery: 'this very day, July 23 [the number 23 is of very great significance to Wilson and others, including William Burroughs], when I had received the message "Sirius is very important," is *the day when, according to Egyptian tradition, the occult link (through hyperspace?) is most powerful between Earth and Sirius.*' (Wilson's emphasis.) In Egypt, the Sirius celebrations began on 23 July and continued through to 8 September. This is the origin of the expression 'dog days' (from 'Dog Star days'), since it is in this period that Sirius rises and sets with the Sun.

According to Wilson, even the Skeptic was impressed by this, and he found himself wondering whether the Crowley invocation he had been using had opened up a channel of communication between Earth and Sirius, a channel used by 'adepts since ancient Egypt'.

SIGNALS FROM THE STARS?

Is it at all feasible that Robert Anton Wilson, and other occult adepts, have actually been in contact with intelligent entities in the Sirius star system? In *Cosmic Trigger*, he draws our attention to a Norwegian radio engineer called Jorgen Hals who, in 1927, received signals 'which have never been explained; in the 1950s, various Russian scientists tried to prove that the Hals signals were of interstellar origin, but this theory is still being debated and no consensus has emerged.'

However, in 1971 an American electronics engineer called L. George Lawrence was investigating 'the Backster effect' (telepathy in plants) near Mount Palomar in California. Using his own special equipment, Lawrence apparently picked up signals that seemed to be emanating from the sky in the region of the Big Dipper. After checking his equipment for bugs, he wrote a report to the Smithsonian Institution in Washington:

> An apparent train of interstellar communication signals of unknown origin and destination has been observed. Since interception was made by *biological* sensors, a biological-type signal transmission must be assumed. Test experiments were conducted in an electromagnetic deep-fringe area, the equipment itself being impervious to electromagnetic radiation. Follow-up tests revealed no equipment defects. Because interstellar listening experiments are not conducted on a routine basis, the suggestion is advanced that verification tests should be conducted elsewhere, possibly on a global scale. The phenomenon is too important to be ignored.

As Wilson states, these findings do imply that there is a certain amount of interstellar communication going on that does not use radio, on which the proponents of SETI (Search for Extraterrestrial Intelligence – an attempt to listen in on any radio transmission from space) are relying, but rather utilizes the '"biological" or cellular level of consciousness'.

OTHER TONGUES, OTHER FLESH

Wilson cites the story of a UFO contactee called George Hunt Williamson, who describes his experiences in a book entitled *Other Tongues, Other Flesh*, published in 1953. The 'other tongues' of the title refers to the language used by the aliens, who hailed from Sirius. Wilson was somewhat surprised to discover that some of the alien words were 'almost identical with some words in the "angelic" language used by Dr John Dee, Aleister Crowley and other magi of the Illuminati tradition. For instance, Williamson transcribes one of the words he received as *leshtal*; Crowley has "lashtal".' According to Williamson, the Sirians have been in contact with Earth for several thousand years, and those humans who know of them use as their insignia the Eye of Horus, which, as any conspiracy buff will tell you, is the symbol of the Illuminati.

Few, if any, contactees are taken seriously, but Wilson does ask some interesting questions concerning Williamson's claims. How, for instance, could he have used words in the angelic language which was known only to a small number of Cabalistic occultists? While he could, of course, have read up on the Cabala, he surely could not have known in 1953 that Crowley was connected with Sirius, since Kenneth Grant was the first to demonstrate that connection, in 1973. It is also strange that Williamson chose the eye in the triangle (connected with Crowley and the Illuminati) as the symbol of a secret society in contact with Sirius.

With Robert Shea, Robert Anton Wilson wrote the *Illuminatus* trilogy, perhaps the most famous conspiracy-inspired novel of them all. Many of the motifs and allusions in *Illuminatus* (including the number 23 and the eye in the triangle) were conceived *before* Wilson became aware of their significance with regard to the Illuminati and Sirius. This, along with Robert Temple's evidence about the Dogon, has led him to believe that 'the most obvious and economical explanation . . . seems to be that an Earth – Sirius communication has occurred, at least once, probably several times.'

SUPERLUMINAL COMMUNICATION AND THE COSMIC TRIGGER

Although he tried to maintain a healthy skepticism about the true nature of his Sirius experiences, Wilson admits that in the end he couldn't help wondering if it were all literally true, if there were, after all, some 'strange cosmic link' between Earth and the Dog Star. He quotes Temple thus:

I would even venture that we may be under observation or surveillance at this very moment, with an extra-terrestrial civilisation based at the Sirius system monitoring our development to see when we will *ready ourselves* for their contacting us. . . . Would they think that [*The Sirius Mystery*] was their cue? If what I propose in this book really is true, then am I pulling a cosmic trigger?

At one point, Wilson turns to quantum physics in an attempt to explain scientifically the synchronicitous nature of his knowledge of the 23 enigma and the Sirius – Illuminati link. This can be made acceptable in theory by virtue of the Einstein-Rosen-Podolsky (ERP) demonstration, which indicates that, if quantum mechanics is true, 'some particles are in instantaneous contact even if at opposite ends of the universe'. There is a serious problem with the ERP, however, namely, that instantaneous contact implies action at a speed that is faster than light, which is forbidden by Special Relativity.

A possible solution to this problem has been put forward by Dr Jack Sarfatti. Wilson states:

> [Dr Sarfatti] assumes that ERP transmissions (faster than light) are *information without transportation*. Limiting our view to a local universe – to transmissions at, or less than, the speed of light – is 'electromagnetic chauvinism' . . . *Information without transportation* is information without energy, without 'signals' in the ordinary sense. The rule of Special Relativity is, thus, not challenged but merely reduced to a definition of locality; it applies only to *signals* and *energy systems*. Pure *information* can take the form of ERP transmissions not limited by signals or the speed of light. [Wilson's emphases.]

I will leave it to the reader to decide just what all of this means: whether there is an alien civilization at Sirius, and whether its representatives have visited us in the past and maintain contact with some of us today. The subject is both immensely intriguing and, given the apparent connections between the Sirians and the Illuminati – assuming they all exist – rather sinister.

On the third anniversary of his original Sirius experience (23 July 1976), Robert Anton Wilson attempted to repeat it through occult means, using the invocation of Hadit (the Intelligence identified with Sirius in Aleister Crowley's symbology). The following week, *Time* magazine ran a full-page review of Temple's *The Sirius Mystery*.

TWO

Miracles Old and New

ANCIENT ASTRONAUTS: A TENABLE THEORY?

WHILE THE IDEA that spacefarers from the Sirius star system arrived on Earth at the dawn of human civilization is little more than an intriguing possibility, it does carry a certain amount of intellectual weight, thanks mainly to the scholarly approach Robert Temple took with his material. Notwithstanding the large amount of additional evidence pointing to the importance of Sirius to the ancient world (discussed in Chapter 1), the most impressive aspect of the subject remains the anachronistic knowledge held by the Dogon tribe, concerning the orbital path and composition of Sirius B.

The theory of so-called 'ancient astronauts' is not a new one, and was not new even when Erich von Daniken wrote his vastly successful *Chariots of the Gods?* which was published in 1967. The enormous popularity of that book, and those that followed, illustrates how the public imagination can be galvanized by unusual theories, whatever their quality.

Francis Hitching, in his *World Atlas of Mysteries* quotes the magazine *Encounter* (XLI:2 – August 1973), which summarized the five central assertions of von Daniken and other like-minded writers:

1. Alien beings from a distant galaxy visited the Earth about 10,000 years ago, possibly after an intergalactic battle;

2. These 'sons of the stars' created 'intelligent man' by altering the genes of monkeys 'in their image';
3. The alien astronauts were 'worshipped as gods' by mankind because of their unfathomable technology;
4. Many hitherto unidentified archaeological finds may be relics of the astronauts' visit;
5. Myths, the Bible, and other 'sacred books' are really accounts of the sojourn on earth of 'gods'.

Fascinating stuff, and it is easy to see how such theories could catch on with a public that has always been amenable to the idea that the world is vastly more intriguing and mysterious than dry academia would have it believe. However, the purveyors of such theories tend to be somewhat wanting in their knowledge of archaeology, as Francis Hitching coolly demonstrates in his *World Atlas of Mysteries*. Since he does this so splendidly, I shall draw rather heavily on his analysis of a number of 'proofs' of ancient astronauts, culled from books by von Daniken and other writers of his ilk.

The Olmec sculptures are said to be so heavy that they will never be removed from their places of discovery and put on show in any museum. This is untrue: three are on display in Mexico City, and another in the Metropolitan Museum of Art in New York. The Olmec sculptures are undeniably beautiful objects, and are artefacts of the 'mother culture' of Central America, so called because it is the oldest thus far identified. While they certainly have an earthly origin, they do seem to depict a racial type that is not indigenous to the Americas. In his book *Fingerprints of the Gods*, Graham Hancock (a writer far superior to von Daniken) suggests that their apparently Negroid features imply contact between the Olmecs and a seafaring African civilization 3,000 years ago. As Hancock reminds us, this date was arrived at through the carbon dating of charcoal fragments found in the same pits as the carved heads, which proved the age of the charcoal while only implying the age of the heads themselves. However, even if the Olmec heads are relics of an ancient and unknown civilization, as Hancock suggests (placing its centre of operations in a temperate, pre-ice age Antarctica), there is still nothing whatsoever to suggest that their creation required anything more than human skill and ingenuity.

The 'Palenque astronaut' discovered in southeastern Mexico is an old favourite of ancient astronaut theorists, turning up with depressing regularity in just about every book on the subject. The image is carved on a stone slab, and shows a man in profile, surrounded by complex designs. According to von Daniken and others, this man is a space pilot of some kind, manipulating the controls of a rocket ship, and surrounded by complex machinery. The man's headdress is said to contain 'tubes, and something like antennae on top'.

The truth of the matter is rather more mundane, although still fascinating from an archaeological point of view. The man in the carving is the Mayan King Pacal, who died in AD 683. All of the surrounding images can be found elsewhere in Mayan art, and their meaning can be discovered by anyone willing to read a decent book on the Mayan civilization. The 'rocket' is actually a sacred maize tree, which is the Mayan symbol of rebirth. Pacal is not manipulating the controls of a spaceship, but plucking a fruit. His curious sitting position is not the result of the confines of a cockpit, but represents his suspension between life and death. Similarly, the carvings said to depict the aft or engine section of the craft in fact represent the jaws of death itself, the entrance to the underworld.

The most spectacular accomplishment of ancient engineers is undoubtedly the Giza necropolis, comprising the Great Pyramid of Cheops (Khufu), the Pyramid of Chephren (Khafre) and the Pyramid of Mycerinus (Menkaure), together with their much smaller satellite pyramids and numerous other structures. The main contention of the ancient-astronaut theorists is that these structures could not have been built with the technology extant at the time (c. 2500 BC). Without ropes and rollers, and without grain to feed the work-force, the construction of the Giza necropolis could not have been achieved, and could not even be achieved *today* with the combined resources of every continent.

Again, the facts are somewhat different. Ropes and rollers *were* available in the Fourth Dynasty, and while archaeologists are unsure as to exactly what lifting devices were used to haul the blocks to the upper reaches of the pyramids, they have one or two theories which do not require the presence of advanced extra-terrestrials. It is most probable that a ramp of reed and mud bricks, either linear or spiralling up around the rising form of the pyramid, was used. As to there not being enough grain available to feed a large work-force, the highly fertile Nile valley would have been well able to satisfy their requirements.

The Piri Re'is map is one of the most impressive documents in the field of historical anomalies. According to the ancient-astronaut theorists, its accuracy could not have been achieved without the aid of high-altitude photographs, probably taken by a spacecraft in low orbit, particularly since it appears to show Antarctica centuries before the continent was officially discovered in AD 1818.

The map focuses on the western coast of Africa, the eastern coast of South America and the northern coast of Antarctica. It was drawn on gazelle skin by the Turkish admiral Piri Re'is in 1513. He himself wrote of the map: 'I made use of about twenty old charts and eight Mappa Mundis', by which he meant the charts called *Jaferiye* by the Arabs, and drawn at the time of Alexander the Great. In *Fingerprints of the Gods*, Graham Hancock points out the enormous implications of the map, implications that were first explored by Professor Charles Hapgood of Keene State College, New Hampshire, in his 1966 book *Maps of the Ancient Sea Kings*. The coast of Queen Maud Land is shown free of ice; geological evidence confirms that the latest date it could have been charted in such a condition is 4000 BC. This would require a sophisticated maritime civilization to have been in place at that time, which is hotly denied by archaeologists.

The reader will note that, highly controversial as these claims are, they still do not require the presence of visiting extra-terrestrials: one does not need a high-altitude camera to make a map.

In a letter dated 6 July 1960, Lieutenant-Colonel Harold Z. Olmeyer, then serving with a Reconnaissance Technical Squadron of the United States Air Force, wrote to Professor Hapgood with his opinion of the Piri Re'is map (the italics are his):

> Your request for evaluation of certain unusual features of the Piri Re'is World Map of 1513 by this organization has been reviewed.
>
> The claim that the lower part of the map portrays the Princess Martha Coast of Queen Maud Land Antarctica, and the Palmer Peninsula, is reasonable. We find this is the most logical and in all probability the correct interpretation of the map.
>
> The geographical detail shown in the lower part of the map agrees very remarkably with the results of the seismic profile made across the top of the ice-cap by the Swedish-British Antarctic Expedition of 1949.

This indicates *the coastline had been mapped before it was covered by the ice-cap*.

The ice-cap in this region is now about a mile thick.

We have no idea how the data on this map can be reconciled with the supposed state of geographical knowledge in 1513.

In notes written on his map, Piri Re'is tells us that the information is derived from earlier source maps. Some of these were the work of contemporary or near-contemporary explorers, but others dated back to the fourth century BC or earlier. According to Hapgood, those fourth-century BC sources were based on even older sources, which were in turn based on sources going back to the deepest antiquity (Hapgood, page 5).

Astounding as these implications are with regard to the dating of the origin of human civilization, they do not support the ancient-astronaut hypothesis. While the Piri Re'is map does include data that could not possibly have been known in 1513 (not only the presence of a continent that had not been officially 'discovered' until 1818, but also its coastal outline *before* the onset of ice around 4000 BC), the general accuracy of the map leaves rather a lot to be desired. In other words, while it does seem to display the knowledge of an ancient seafaring civilization capable of mapping coastlines, it does *not* display sufficiently accurate information to imply the use of low-orbiting spacecraft with their cameras pointed down, as von Daniken maintains in *Chariots of the Gods?*

Another old favourite of von Daniken and his colleagues is the Nazca plain, with its curious figures which include a hummingbird, a monkey and a spider, as well as vast lines criss-crossing the rough, pebble-strewn surface. The ancient-astronaut theorists' contention is that these figures constitute a landing field for alien spacecraft, which were drawn to the 'ideal' terrain.

The reader may be aware that the United States National Aeronautics and Space Administration (NASA) is currently attempting to develop a reusable vertical take-off and landing space vehicle, an attempt which will undoubtedly succeed within a few years. Why, therefore, would a civilization untold centuries in advance of ourselves, capable of crossing the light years to visit our ancestors, need runways for their spacecraft to land? The German mathematician and archaeologist Maria Reiche, who spent decades investigating the Nazca lines, dismissed the extra-terrestrial notion by pointing out the unsuitable nature of the terrain, which is far too soft to support a working landing field: 'The ground is quite soft; I'm afraid the spacemen would have gotten stuck.'

The vision of the Old Testament prophet Ezekiel by the River Chebar in Mesopotamia has been touted for years as impressive evidence for the presence on Earth of extra-terrestrial visitors in biblical times. In the first chapter of the Book of Ezekiel, we read:

> A whirlwind came out of the north, a great cloud, and a fire
> unfolding itself, and a brightness was about it, and out of the
> midst thereof as the colour of amber, out of the midst of the
> fire. Also out of the midst thereof came the likeness of four
> living creatures. And this was their appearance; they had the
> likeness of a man. And every one had four faces, and every
> one had four wings. And their feet were straight feet; and the
> sole of their feet was like the sole of a calf's foot and they
> sparkled like the colour of burnished brass.

Is this a description of the arrival of strange beings from another world? The answer is clearly 'yes', but not quite in the literal, objective sense that von Daniken and friends would have us believe. In the final verse of Chapter 1, Ezekiel states: 'This was the appearance of the likeness of the glory of the Lord.' Elsewhere, the prophet describes his experiences as 'visions of God' and says that 'the hand of the Lord' was upon him. As Francis Hitching reminds us, this phrase is consistently used in the Old Testament to denote a state of altered consciousness. In fact, Ezekiel even describes the creatures he 'saw' as cherubim.

MYTHOLOGY REINVENTS ITSELF

So much for evidence of ancient astronauts; but, as proponents of alien abductions are wont to say, absence of evidence is not evidence of absence. It may well be that the Earth was visited in the distant past by spacefarers from far-flung worlds (the Sirius connection indicates this), but it is not sensible to present the achievements of our ancestors as categorical proof. They were far more capable people than many give them credit for.

In examining the history of alleged alien presence on Earth, it is thus advisable to leave remote history to the archaeologists, who can convincingly counter virtually every assertion made by the ancient-astronaut theorists. Writers on the paranormal are fond of quoting Sherlock Holmes in *The Sign of Four*: 'When you have eliminated the impossible, whatever remains, however improbable, must be the truth.' The main problem with most ancient astronaut theorizing is that the eminently probable is eliminated, leaving the extremely *improbable* as 'truth'. For this reason, I think we should travel forward in time to the centuries after Christ, and on into the Middle Ages. Here we will be able to see the development of a belief in non-human intelligences that forms a direct line through to the present, and still influences our attitudes towards (and even our encounters with) those entities.

It is during those centuries that the relationship between the human and the non-human underwent two profound alterations. The first was the demonization of pagan mythological polytheism by Christianity. In his fascinating book *Daimonic Reality: A Field Guide to the Otherworld*, Patrick Harpur illustrates this with a quote from the epistles of St Paul: 'the things which the gentiles sacrifice, they sacrifice to the devils, and not to God' (1 Cor. 10:20; Harpur, page 54.) Harpur goes on to remind us that the complex realm of non-human intelligence revered by pagan peoples all over the world was assimilated into the Christian world-view, becoming part of the angelic realm, or, more precisely, the realm of *fallen* angels, cast out of Heaven along with Satan.

And yet, in spite of this attempt to organize the realm of the supernatural into sharply demarcated regions of good and evil, of angels and demons, there remained an intermediate realm whose denizens were not content to be so ignominiously pigeonholed. These entities are, of course, the fauns, satyrs, and nymphs; the good people; the gentry; the fairies.

The connection between the mythology of the fairies and modern accounts of alien beings has been made before, most notably by Jacques Vallée. Since any examination of alleged alien encounters would be incomplete without its inclusion, I will return to and elaborate upon it later in this chapter.

The second profound alteration in the relationship between the human and non-human involved not assimilation but exclusion, at the hands of the seventeenth-century rationalists. The world-view of thinkers such as Descartes and Spinoza was scientific and secular, relying upon the exercise of reason, rather than empiricism, as the only valid source of knowledge. Thus the world of the supernatural was simply not recognized: supernatural events could not exist within the contemporary rationalist world-view, and therefore they did not exist.

Cartesian philosophy was the chief cause of this state of affairs; since Descartes founded his philosophy upon the one premise he held to be indisputable, his existence as a thinking subject ('I think, therefore I am'), the result was the separation of the world into subjective consciousness and the objective, external world (see Harpur, page 61). To attempt this total denial of the mythical and supernatural (what today we call the paranormal) was not only unhealthy and dangerous, but doomed to failure. In denying even the subjective reality of non-human intelligence, the rationalists were trying to deny the very processes that had driven human civilization onward from neolithic times, through the founding of the first cities at Sumer, the architectural triumphs of the ancient Egyptians, the Greek and Roman civilizations, and, ultimately, to their own invention of rationalism. For it was through mythopoeic processes that the great civilizations came to know themselves and their place in the cosmos, giving rise to their phenomenal success in the fields of art, social philosophy and science.

It is quite amusing to consider the importance placed by orthodox science upon the empirical verification of phenomena today. This view – that experience, especially of the senses, is the only source of knowledge – was the very thing the rationalists rejected in favour of reason. Thus the rationalists' denial of the supernatural was based upon the opposing view to that of twentieth-century empirical science. Of course, orthodox science denies the paranormal today because of what it sees as an absence of empirical evidence, but it is ironic that it has actually inherited its dismissive attitude from an opposing philosophical doctrine. (The absence – or otherwise – of empirical evidence for alien presence is something we shall return to in Chapters 5 and 7).

As I mentioned above, Jacques Vallée has probably done more than any other ufologist to promote the idea that there are profound connections between modern reports of encounters with UFOs and their alleged occupants, and reports from previous centuries regarding the entities commonly called 'fairies'. Before going into particular cases, it is worth looking at the 16 conclusions arrived at by The Rev. Robert Kirk, who lived in Aberfoyle, Scotland, in the seventeenth century. Rev. Kirk spent much of his life pondering the nature of the numerous entities that were believed to interact with human beings in remote regions of Europe. He called this society of non-human entities 'The Secret Commonwealth'. Here is Jacques Vallée's summary of Kirk's conclusions:

1. They have a nature that is intermediate between man and the angels.

2. Physically, they have very light and fluid bodies, which are comparable to a condensed cloud. They are particularly visible at dusk. They can appear and vanish at will.

3. Intellectually, they are intelligent and curious.

4. They have the power to carry away anything they like.

5. They live inside the earth in caves, which they can reach through any crevice or opening where air passes.

6. When men did not inhabit most of the world, the creatures used to live there and had their own agriculture. Their civilisation has left traces on the high mountains; it was flourishing at a time when the whole countryside was nothing but woods and forests.

7. At the beginning of each three-month period, they change quarters because they are unable to stay in one place. Besides, they like to travel. It is then that men have terrible encounters with them, even on the great highways.

8. Their chameleon-like bodies allow them to swim through the air with all their household.

9. They are divided into tribes. Like us, they have children, nurses, marriages, burials, etc., *unless they just do this to mock our own customs* or to predict terrestrial events [Vallée's emphasis.]

10. Their houses are said to be wonderfully large and beautiful, but under most circumstances they are invisible to human eyes. Kirk compares them to enchanted islands. The houses are equipped with lamps that burn forever and fires that need no fuel.

11. They speak very little. When they do talk among themselves, their language is a kind of whistling sound.

12. Their habits and their language when they talk to humans are similar to those of local people.

13. Their philosophical system is based on the following ideas: nothing dies; all things evolve cyclically in such a way that at every cycle they are renewed and improved. Motion is the universal law.

14. They are said to have a hierarchy of leaders, but they have no visible devotion to God, no religion.

15. They have many pleasant and light books, but also serious and complex books dealing with abstract matters.

16. They can be made to appear at will before us through magic.

The parallels between the two orders of being (fairy and alien) are so striking that I shall make my way through all 16 conclusions, illustrating each one in turn with examples of our current information regarding alleged non-human visitors.

1. The gradual secularization of twentieth-century society is both undeniable and understandable, in view of the huge advances made in science and in our comprehension of the universe. Our alien visitors, therefore, fulfil a profound need on our part for an order of being that is both vastly superior to us, and acceptable within the current secular context. Like 'the good people' of past centuries, they occupy an intermediate position between mortal, fallible humanity, and an immortal, omniscient Creator. Taken in isolation, this would seem to militate in favour of a purely mythological origin for non-human entities; however, viewed in a wider context, the nature of the aliens is exactly parallel to that of the fairies of folklore.

2. The majority of reports suggest a certain physical type for the aliens. They are frequently described as being thin and frail-looking, though apparently strong. This is especially true of the so-called Greys, whose spindly limbs and large, featureless eyes have reminded more than one witness of insects. Ufologists who subscribe to the extra-terrestrial hypothesis for the origin of these beings suggest that this physical structure might enable the aliens to withstand the enormous pressures resulting from the spectacular performance characteristics of their vehicles. These craft have also been reported on frequent occasions to appear and vanish without trace, as if suddenly becoming invisible, or simply winking out of existence.

3. The aliens are also, of course, highly intelligent. Certain testimonies, by people such as Robert Lazar (see page 131), place their average IQ at 200.

4. If the thousands of reported alien abductions are to be believed as representing objective reality, the Greys certainly have the power to carry away anything (and anyone) they like. And, like our ancestors' encounters with the good people, these meetings are sometimes quite enjoyable, sometimes terrifying.

5. The interior of the Earth has been put forward increasingly in recent years as the main centre of operations – if not, in some cases, the ultimate origin – of the various alien groups present on Earth. Like abductions, this is an increasingly important idea, which will be dealt with in its own section in Chapter 6.

6. With the idea that the aliens were around 'when men did not inhabit most of the world' to use Vallée's phrase, we find ourselves on shaky ground as far as parallels with modern encounters go, mainly because the idea refers to their history, rather than their direct attributes. However, the belief that the good people have a long history, one that might pre-date humanity, would seem to support the assertion, made by Vallée and others, that what we now call 'UFO' and 'alien' encounters have occurred throughout recorded history.

7. If the ultimate origin of the non-humans is elsewhere than the Earth, the very fact that they are here proves their liking for travel, whether for reasons of exploration, research or whatever. However, here we once again enter the territory of mythology, of our own psychological and cultural history. It would seem that the non-humans' liking for highways is significant in this respect. Just as travellers of previous centuries frequently encountered members of the fairy race (with varying consequences) on lonely highways, contemporary sightings often occur on isolated stretches of road. The anthropologist Victor Turner called such locations 'liminal' zones. They are places of transition, of travel in terms of both space and time. Highways, crossroads, bridges and shores are liminal zones; the hours of dusk and dawn – the boundaries between day and night – are liminal times; so is the turn of the year. Patrick Harpur reminds us that caravan sites or trailer parks are often haunted by strange creatures and flying objects, perhaps because, as he says, they are 'liminally situated between town and country, habitat and wilderness' (*Daimonic Reality*, page 53). It is easy to understand why such locations were (and are) regarded as places where strange things could happen: like the forest, the roads spanning the open country between the safety of habitats were seen as harbouring a host of potential dangers, both natural and supernatural. In these places, the traveller of centuries past kept a wary eye open for both robbers and vampires, sinister vagabonds as well as werewolves. It is an apprehension that has been carried through to contemporary urban life, an apprehension that prompts me, for instance, always to lock the doors when I am in a car, day or night. Merely common sense, in these violent times? Of course. Just as it was common sense for our ancestors to regard their highways and other avenues of travel with caution. It may be, as Harpur thinks, that this is the reason for the high incidence of strange encounters in liminal zones, where 'the laws of time and space, matter and causality seem attenuated; and we glimpse for an instant an unseen order of things'. Perhaps our heightened sense of our surroundings – the modern versions of predator-haunted forests – at these times forces a subtle alteration in our consciousness, making us more amenable to interaction with a hitherto invisible non-human intelligence. After all, they do like to travel.

8. In the majority of alleged alien encounters, and especially the modern abductions, the entities are described as moving in a variety of abnormal ways. Some shuffle their feet awkwardly; others move without any walking motion whatsoever, gliding gracefully across the floor; while others are so bizarre as to be downright ludicrous, such as the entities encountered in Brazil in 1977 by Antonio La Rubia, who described creatures having a single leg, like a pogo stick. One of the most striking motifs of the modern alien-abduction experience is the way in which the Greys frequently move, especially at the beginning and end of the episode. They are described as floating into the victims' homes through windows or even walls, subduing their targets and then floating them up through the air out of the room and into the UFO. This strange mode of locomotion subtly echoes the chameleon-bodied fairies described by the Revd Kirk.

9. Just as the fairies are divided into tribes, so, it seems, are our current alien guests. The aliens allegedly visiting us now can be broken down into the following groups or species: Greys (of which there are several subgroups); humanoid Nordics (again, in several subgroups); reptilians and monsters (which include Bigfoot-type creatures and the so-called 'bellicose hairy dwarfs').

10. Fairy houses are said to be wonderfully large and beautiful enchanted places from which there is occasionally no return. This imagery of beauty, light and wonderful, sometimes colossal, architecture is frequently encountered in descriptions of UFO interiors. Indeed, the lamps that burn forever and the fires that need no fuel have their counterparts in the soft, ubiquitous light with no obvious source which is often noticed by UFO abductees.

11. In common with the fairies of past centuries, the Greys speak very little, at least verbally, preferring to communicate with their unwilling guests via telepathy (when they deign to communicate at all). Occasionally, a witness will describe the aliens' native language as resembling whistles or chirps, which sound rather like the 'whistling sound' of the fairy language.

12. One of the attributes of the Greys, which has led many researchers to postulate that they have spent considerable time eavesdropping on our culture, perhaps by monitoring our radio and television broadcasts, is their apparent mastery of our language structures and idioms. They are reported to use phrases such as 'Don't worry,' 'We're not going to hurt you' 'Everything's going to be all right.' Again, we can see a connection between this behaviour and that of the fairies, whose language, when they talk to humans, is similar to that of local people.

13. One of the defining characteristics of the contactee cases of the 1950s and 1960s was the aliens' propensity to ramble on about their system of ethics and philosophy. They constantly reiterated their concern regarding humanity's irresponsible use of nuclear energy, saying that we were disrupting the balance of the universe and threatening the safety of the other inhabited planets. This concern with balance, harmony and the cyclic nature of time echoes the philosophy of the good people, who believe that nothing dies, that all things evolve cyclically.

An example of the aliens' interest in the concept of time is a case described by researcher John Keel in his book *UFOs: Operation Trojan Horse*. In November 1966, two Minnesota women had an encounter with a strange flying object. During the encounter, one of the women fell to her knees in a trancelike state. A strange, metallic voice came from her lips, asking: 'What . . . is . . . your . . . time . . . cycle? What . . . constitutes . . . a day . . . and . . . what . . . constitutes . . . a . . . night?' 'A day is approximately 12 hours long, and a night is 12 hours long,' replied the woman's friend. After a few more questions, the woman came out of her trance, and the object departed.

14. The aliens' attitude to 'God' has also, on occasion, featured in encounter reports. Like the good people, they often display a lack of devotion to any god. In 1952 a Peruvian man, known simply as C.A.V., met UFO entities described as looking like mummies with joined legs, or one double leg. They wanted to speak to his 'chief' about (once again) the danger to the universe posed by our nuclear weapons tests. C.A.V. said:

> I asked them who their God was and I noticed a sort of mockery. 'God?' they said. 'What God?' 'Well, the Supreme Creator,' I said, 'who made the universe.' 'Well, we are like gods,' they said. 'How can you be gods?' I asked. And they said that we were very backward.

15. The fairies have pleasant and light books, and also serious and complex books. Likewise the aliens: there are many reports of communication taking the form of strange writings passed on to contactees. The most famous contactee, George Adamski, met a Venusian on 20 November 1952 in the California desert. The spaceman asked for one of Adamski's photographic plates, which he took away. On 13 December, the plate was returned to Adamski, who discovered some strange writing on it.

On 2 March 1965, John Reeves, who lived near Weeki Wachee Springs, Florida, encountered a Martian spacecraft and occupant while he was walking in the woods. After apparently taking a photograph of Reeves, the entity returned to its craft and departed. Reeves discovered two pieces of folded paper at the landing site, which bore strange symbols like 'oriental writing or shorthand writing'. The message was later deciphered. It read: 'Planet Mars – Are you coming home soon – We miss you very much – Why did you stay away too long'.

During the alleged abduction of Barney and Betty Hill in New Hampshire in 1961, Betty asked the leader of the group of entities if she could take something from the UFO, as proof of her experience. He gave her a 'book' containing strange writing, but then changed his mind, evidently having decided that it would be better if she had no proof.

16. It is difficult to see how any parallel can be drawn between the fairies' appearance through the use of magic, and modern aliens. However, an admittedly tenuous link can be found if we look at the problem in terms of culture and imagination. Magic, as defined by Aleister Crowley, is the alteration of natural processes in accordance with human will; and this extends to the processes governing the activities of the good people, who could be forced to appear before a sufficiently powerful magician. However, it could be claimed that modern humanity possesses its own form of magic, its own method of altering natural processes (at fundamental levels) in accordance with its will.

Nuclear physics fits the bill rather neatly, and the reader will probably be aware that what is called the modern era of ufology began in the 1940s, when nuclear weapons were first tested, and used. Ufologists are keen to remind us that strange objects are frequently sighted in the vicinity of military bases and nuclear power stations, probably because these are the places where our latest technology is developed, tested and deployed. It could thus be argued that our manipulation of the atom is the 'magical process' which summons the technological equivalent of the non-human entities of folklore.

The reader may have noticed that, in listing the connections between fairies and ufonauts, I have referred to the accounts of contactees as well as those of abductees. This will cause serious problems for most ufologists, who look upon the claims of contactees with contempt. In order to understand why, we must remind ourselves of the differences between a contactee and an abductee. This difference can be described in terms of time and motive.

As mentioned above, the wave of contactee reports occurred mainly in the 1950s and 1960s. Their claims centred on the arrival on Earth of gentle, entirely human-looking beings, usually from planets within our own solar system, who dispensed glib pearls of cosmic wisdom and made polite requests that humanity cease its nuclear tests forthwith. As we shall see in the next chapter, they chose the unlikeliest people to pass on these messages, casting serious doubt on their judgement of character.

This is entirely at odds with the more recent wave of supposed alien abductions, which centre on the activities of an altogether more unpleasant bunch of entities, the Greys. This group are fond of taking people into their craft against their will, (rather than issuing polite invitations), and performing hideous physical and psychological experiments on them. The abduction scenario is treated with a good deal more respect by ufologists than the contactee scenario, probably because it fits more neatly with modern ideas about the nature of highly advanced beings, and because their motives (selfish, materialistic, geared to their own well-being at the expense of ours) seem eminently understandable and plausible to a humanity that is capable of the same arrogance and disregard for others. (A Grey is reported to have asked one victim why she was so indignant at her treatment, when human beings behave in the same way towards animals and even other humans.)

Whatever the relative merits of contactee and abduction scenarios, for our immediate purposes we must place them side by side, since they are elements in a coherent progression from the supernatural beings of traditional folklore through to the present. This can be seen from the parallels between the attributes of folkloric beings, as summarized by Vallée, and those of the non-humans reported throughout the latter half of the twentieth century.

There are thus grounds for suggesting, as Vallée does most convincingly in his books (notably *Passport to Magonia* and *Dimensions*), that we are witnessing the activities of a genuine non-human intelligence, an intelligence that is constantly reshaping itself in order to correspond to the prevailing world-view in any particular period. They have appeared to human eyes as angels and demons, as fairies, as brilliant men of science (during the Great Airship flap of the last few years of the nineteenth century – see pages 161–2), and as the pilots of extra-terrestrial space vehicles. They are the harbingers of a reinvented mythology, a psychic process by which we may bridge the gap between a dangerous and uncertain present and the boundless potential of our future.

THREE

Springtime on Venus

ADAMSKI OPENS THE FLOODGATES

ALTHOUGH, AS WE have seen, the weaving of the tapestry of non-human encounters began well before the twentieth century, it displayed a new pattern with the claims of George Adamski. Born in Poland on 17 April 1891, Adamski emigrated with his family to the United States when he was one year old. His early manhood was rather eventful: from 1913 to 1916 he was a member of the US cavalry, and was stationed on the Mexican border. Afterwards, he took a variety of jobs, including maintenance man at the Yellowstone National Park, flour-mill worker in Portland and concrete contractor in Los Angeles. In 1926 he began teaching philosophy, and a few years later founded a monastery in Laguna Beach, California, called 'The Royal Order of Tibet'. He called himself 'Professor' Adamski, even though he possessed no qualifications.

An extremely enterprising individual, Adamski managed to obtain the special licence needed during Prohibition to make wine for religious purposes. He later told two followers: 'I made enough wine for all of Southern California. I was making a fortune.' Adamski doubtless found the repeal of Prohibition somewhat inconvenient, for he said that otherwise, 'I wouldn't have had to get into this saucer crap'. This is, of course, a damning statement to have made, especially for all those who still believe in his claims.

During the late 1940s, Adamski and his wife, Mary, ran a hamburger stand on the slopes of Mount Palomar, not far from the 200-inch (5-metre) Hale telescope. It was on the night of 9 October 1946 that, while watching a meteor shower with some friends, Adamski saw what he described as 'a large black object, similar in shape to a gigantic dirigible' hanging motionless in the night sky.

Late in 1949, two men stopped at the hamburger stand for lunch. Adamski later claimed that Joseph P. Maxfield and Gene L. Bloom of the Naval Electronics Laboratory at Point Loma, near San Diego, asked him to help photograph the flying saucers that had started to overfly the region in large numbers (a procession of 184 had flown above Mount Palomar in August 1947). Adamski attached a camera to his 6-inch (15.2 cm) telescope – he was a keen amateur astronomer – and soon 'succeeded in getting what I deemed at the time to be two good pictures of an object moving through space'. He claimed to have turned them over to Bloom.

However, after Adamski had given a lecture on the subject of flying saucers to the Everyman's Club in La Mesa, in which he mentioned the photographs he had given the Navy, a reporter with the *San Diego Journal* contacted the Naval Electronics Laboratory. They denied knowing anything about them. According to Bloom, he and Maxfield had stopped at Adamski's hamburger stand for lunch while on their way to the Palomar Observatory, but they did not ask for Adamski's help, and did not even know of his interest in flying saucers. Bloom said: 'Everything Adamski wrote about us was fiction, pure fiction.'

Adamski made frequent trips into the desert east of Mount Palomar, hoping to make contact with one of the saucers that had been sighted in the region. On 20 November 1952 he made another such trip, in the company of 'Dr' George H. Williamson (whom we met in Chapter 1) and his wife, Betty, Al and Betty Bailey, Alice Wells and Lucy McGinnis. Around midday they stopped for lunch near Desert Center, California. Suddenly, in the sky above them they saw 'a gigantic cigar-shaped silvery ship'. Adamski said: 'Someone take me down the road, quick! That ship has come looking for me and I don't want to keep them waiting!' Lucy McGinnis and Al Bailey drove Adamski about 800 metres (half a mile) down the road. He told them not to return for him for an hour, unless he signalled. His friends complied and retreated to watch from a distance.

Adamski then noticed a figure standing in a ravine about 400 metres (a quarter of a mile) away. The figure beckoned to him. He approached, and found himself face to face with what he later described as 'a man from space – A HUMAN BEING FROM ANOTHER WORLD!' The man was handsome, and wore a loose single-piece suit of a brown, shimmering material that fitted closely about the neck, wrists and ankles. His hair was sandy-coloured and touched his shoulders, and his tanned face was smooth and hairless; Adamski had the impression that the man didn't need to shave.

All the time Adamski was with the man, he experienced 'a feeling of infinite understanding and kindness, with supreme humility' that seemed to radiate from the visitor. Using a combination of English, hand gestures and telepathy, Adamski was able to learn that the visitor hailed from Venus. The spaceman was here to voice the concerns of many races, both within and beyond the solar system, regarding radiation from nuclear testing, which could not only destroy all life on Earth, but contaminate the rest of space as well. (In view of the amount of cosmic radiation from supernovae, stars and planets, etc., which is naturally floating around space, the Venusian's fears about a few atom bomb tests on Earth seem a little out of proportion.)

The encounter lasted about an hour. After the Venusian had left and Adamski's friends had rejoined him, they took a plaster cast of one of the visitor's footprints. (It was rather convenient that they had some plaster to hand, as more than one writer has commented.)

In the months that followed, Adamski had further adventures with his new-found space friends. He met with them in Los Angeles, where they were wearing business suits, and was invited to visit a large 'mother ship' in orbit above the Earth. He spoke with men and women from Venus, Mars and Saturn. He was also taken on a trip to the Moon, parts of which had 'vegetation, trees and animals', and where 'people live in comfort'. There were snow-topped mountains, timber-clad slopes and lakes and rivers. There were also cities with people walking the streets and travelling in aerial vehicles. Similar conditions prevailed on Venus, where a balanced life-style, good (vegetarian) diet and a cloud canopy that shielded then inhabitants from the harmful rays of the Sun ensured a life expectancy of about a thousand years.

Adamski wrote a 60-page account of his experiences and sent

it to the British writer Desmond Leslie, who added it to a book he had just completed. Published as *Flying Saucers Have Landed* in September 1953, it sold over 100,000 copies and made Adamski world-famous.

How much credence should we give to the claims of George Adamski? The short answer is: not much. After his encounter with the Venusian spaceman, he was visited at his burger stall by Captain Edward J. Ruppelt of the US Air Force's Project Blue Book. Ruppelt later described the contactee:

> To look at the man and to listen to his story you had an
> immediate urge to believe him. Maybe it was his appearance.
> He was dressed in well worn, but neat, overalls. He had
> slightly greying hair and the most honest pair of eyes I have
> ever seen. (*Report on Unidentified Flying Objects*, pages 263–26)

Adamski may have had an honest pair of eyes, but his subsequent antics belie the impression he gave. He began a speech before the Corona, California, Lions Club (reported in the 12 March 1953 issue of Riverside *Enterprise*) by claiming that his material 'has all been cleared with the Federal Bureau of Investigation and Air Force Intelligence'. The FBI decided to pay him a visit to remind him that the Bureau did not endorse individuals, and that it was not advisable to make false claims to this effect. He wrote a statement confirming that he understood this, and a copy was left with him.

Adamski subsequently showed this statement to an interviewer, and said that he had been 'cleared' by the FBI, who, not amused, sent more agents who 'read the riot act to him in no uncertain terms'. They also warned him that legal action would be taken if he continued. Adamski later said that the FBI had warned him to keep quiet. (See Curtis Peebles, *Watch the Skies! A Chronicle of the Flying Saucer Myth*, pages 117–18.)

Further doubt was cast on Adamski's claims by James W. Moseley in January 1955. Moseley talked with Al Bailey, who had been with Adamski on the day of his contact. Bailey denied seeing the spacecraft and its occupant. He also denied that a drawing allegedly made by Alice Wells, and included in *Flying Saucers Have Landed*, could have been made at that distance. He maintained that he and Adamski's other companions did see the mother ship and some flashes of light, but no more.

Moseley was contacted by Jerrold Baker, who had worked at the hamburger stand between 12 November 1952 and 12 January 1953, and who was credited with taking the Kodak Brownie photograph of the Venusian scout ship on 13 December 1952. In a sworn statement, Baker denied having taken the photograph. It turned out that Adamski had taken the photograph, along with several others, on 12 December (not 13 December, as claimed in his book). Furthermore, Baker stated: 'I accidentally heard a tape-recorded account of what was to transpire on the desert, who was to go, etc., several days before the party left.'

Not only had the desert contact been pre-planned, but, according to Baker's wife, Irma, Adamski had changed the story since the first time she heard it. In a conversation with Adamski, Williamson had said that 'in order to get across to the public his teachings and philosophies, he couldn't be too "mystical", as he put it, and that he must present all the happenings on a very material basis because that is how people want them'. When Irma replied that this was tantamount to lying, he said, 'Sometimes to gain admittance, one had to go around by the back door,' (see Peebles, pages 118–19).

In reviewing the Adamski case, it is easy to see why ufologists, in the 1950s as well as today, have had so much trouble with the contactee scenario. And yet, as the skeptical researcher Curtis Peebles says, Adamski helped to define the mythology of alien encounters for the 1950s and 1960s.

Of course, he was not alone. Over the next few years, more and more people began to come forward with their own tales of thrilling adventures with the space people.

EMISSARIES FROM DUBIOUS REALMS

After Adamski's claims made headline news all over the world, it seemed that the space people decided to step up their programme of contact with humans. The result was a system of belief concerning life on other planets that captivated the public imagination, especially in the United States, where the majority of encounters seemed to occur. The defining characteristics of this belief system were that:

– advanced 'space brothers' were coming to Earth and contacting certain humans;

– the aliens were entirely benign and ethically advanced, invit-
ing people on numerous occasions to ride in their 'scout ships';
– the aliens' home worlds were entirely free from war, disease,
intolerance and all the other blights on our own civilization;
– the space brothers wanted to help us to progress spiritually
and ethically before issuing us with an invitation to join their
interplanetary commonwealth.

It has been noted by a number of writers that, during this period,
the aliens told the contactees that they came from planets within
this solar system, while in more recent years, they have claimed to
come from much further afield, from planets in distant star systems. For instance, it has become common knowledge among
those interested in the abduction scenario that the Greys have
given their own origin as the star system Zeta Reticuli. Even those
who fervently believe in the reality of alien visitation cannot
escape what this implies: the space brothers were said to come
from planets within our own solar system because the contactees
were not aware, in the 1950s and 1960s, that those planets are
utterly incapable of supporting humanoid life. In the years since
then, our deep-space probes have demonstrated the unlikelihood
of finding even bacteria on those planets. As this became public
knowledge, the aliens' origin changed, moving out into the
universe, to realms as yet unknown to science, where it could not
categorically be stated that life cannot exist.

While the skeptics have pointed to this as proof of hoax, claiming that the contactees alter the aliens' point of origin to make it
more believable, some ufologists have argued that the entities
themselves might be lying for their own reasons (see Janet and
Colin Bord, *Life Beyond Planet Earth?* page 76). Throughout the
ages, denizens of the supernatural world have been described as
liars and tricksters who are not to be trusted under any circumstances.

Since this is a history of alleged alien presence, the stories of the
contactees must not be ignored. They form an integral part of the
mythology we are creating with regard to our relationship with
the cosmos, and, because they constitute a direct connection
between the mythology of the distant past and the modern abduction scenarios (which have now virtually saturated public awareness), there is no logical justification for excluding them. They
also, at times, make extremely entertaining reading.

On 25 January 1958, a man from Venus paid a visit to the home of Mrs Mary King in North Devon. A few days previously, she had watched a UFO land near her cottage, so she was not entirely surprised by his appearance. They had a long talk, during which the Venusian (who was very similar in appearance to George Adamski's friend) told Mrs King that, although the Earth was given all knowledge, we discarded the good and kept the bad. But eventually, he reassured her, good would triumph, and then 'will come a period of love and fellowship and Space and Interspace travel will be easily possible and many, many more things will be possible, that you have not dreamed of. When this time comes,' the visitor told her, 'we shall be waiting to welcome you with outstretched arms, as true brothers and honourable children of One Creator-Father.' Mrs King's son, George King, founded the Aetherius Society in 1956. It claims to be in receipt of messages from 'Interplanetary Intelligences', and is still going strong.

A handful of contactees achieved a degree of fame comparable to that of George Adamski, publishing popular books and appearing regularly on radio talk shows, such as the famous *Long John Nebel Show*.

Howard Menger was ten years old when he experienced his first contact, near his home in New Jersey in 1932. An amazingly beautiful, golden-eyed woman in a shimmering one-piece garment came to him in a woodland glade and said: 'Howard, I have come a long way to see you, and to talk to you.' She described future plans being made for him, and told him that he would have further visits from her people, who came from Venus. Throughout the 1950s, Menger had regular contacts with the Venusians, and also with Martians and Saturnians. In fact, he claimed that he had known his second wife, Marla, in an earlier life, in which he was a Saturnian and she a Venusian.

Food seems to play a large part in the stories of the abductees, just as fairy food does in folklore. Menger wrote that alien food is far more nourishing than that of Earth. At one point, he and a fellow contactee had some processed potato which the aliens had given to them analysed. They found that it contained about five times more protein than Earth potato. According to Menger, the Venusians are about 2500 years ahead of us in terms of technology, and are keen to spread goodwill throughout the universe.

On 24 May 1952, Orfeo Angelucci was driving home after completing his night shift at the Lockheed Aircraft factory in Burbank, north of Los Angele, California, when he noticed a red light in the sky. He decided to follow the light, and eventually parked his car at an isolated spot. The red light departed rapidly, but before it did so, it released two smaller objects measuring just under a metre (3 feet) in diameter, which descended in front of the car. These fluorescent green globes seemed to be the source of a voice that instructed him to get out of the car. As he complied, the globes were transformed into a kind of video screen, displaying the heads and shoulders of a man and woman. These people said nothing, merely smiled at him, inspiring feelings he described as 'perfection', 'nobility' and 'radiance'.

As the figures faded from view, the voice began to speak again, giving a résumé of the now familiar philosophy of the space people (peace, love, understanding, no more nuclear tests, etc.). It then added that these beings were etheric in nature, and had no need of physical spacecraft, which were used only for the benefit of humans. (This in itself is rather interesting, since the alleged aliens were themselves confirming one of the more imaginative theories concerning their true nature, i.e. that they represent a non-human intelligence which utilizes spacecraft imagery merely to appear to humans in a form they can comprehend.)

Angelucci wondered to himself why the space people didn't land *en masse*, in order to demonstrate their presence to humanity. The voice immediately replied that to interfere with a planet's affairs would violate cosmic laws. 'Earth must work out its own destiny,' the voice said, before assuring Angelucci that they would meet again.

In July 1952, Angelucci had another contact, this time in a vacant lot beneath an elevated freeway, in which he happened to find a remote-controlled spacecraft. He promptly climbed aboard, and was taken on a roller-coaster ride 1600 km (1000 miles) straight up into space, while a hidden sound system on the spacecraft played his favourite song, 'Fools Rush In'. There followed another lesson in alien philosophy, this time in much greater detail, and delivered with the obvious intention of totally undermining Angelucci's sense of worth. 'Tears coursed down my cheeks,' he said. 'Under the spiritual scrutiny of that great, compassionate consciousness I felt like a crawling worm, unclean, filled with error and sin.'

He was then struck by a beam of intense light, to the accompaniment of the Lord's Prayer. Suddenly, he 'KNEW THE MYSTERY

OF LIFE!' Everyone was 'TRAPPED IN ETERNITY and ALLOTTED ONLY ONE BRIEF AWARENESS AT A TIME!'

Although any mention of his experiences attracted ridicule, even naked hostility, Angelucci felt compelled to publish them himself in an eight-page tabloid newspaper, *The Twentieth Century Times*. Eventually, however, he began to receive more favourable reactions, with many people reading his newspaper and attending meetings and conventions.

Another famous contactee, Truman Bethurum, worked in highway construction, and was engaged on a project in the Mormon Mesa, Nevada when he had his first contact. On the night of 27 July 1952, Bethurum took advantage of a lull in activity during the night shift and drove out into the desert to take a nap.

He awoke to see a flying saucer about 100 metres (300 feet) in diameter and 5.5 metres (18 feet) deep hovering silently a few feet above the ground. Ten small men were standing around his truck, watching him intently. They had dark hair and olive complexions, and were between 1.2 and 1.5 metres (4 and 5 feet) in height.

Bethurum asked them were they came from and, in a curious echo of folkloric imagery, they answered, 'Our homes are castles in a faraway land. You may speak to our captain in our scow.'

Bethurum found the captain to be a small but astonishingly attractive woman, who wore a black and red beret, a black velvet bodice and a red pleated skirt! Her name was Aura Rhanes, she said, and her people came from the planet Clarion, which was in our solar system, but invisible from the Earth, being on the far side of the Sun. She told Bethurum that all the planets in the solar system had an atmosphere similar to Earth, and many were inhabited.

Like Orfeo Angelucci, Truman Bethurum encountered much hostility when he told of his experiences; his wife and children even thought that all the time he had spent working in the desert had somehow unhinged him.

In the three months that followed, he met with Aura Rhanes 11 times, each time out in the desert. She described the conditions on Clarion: predictably, the inhabitants in peace and love and harmony with nature. Eventually, it seems, the space lady grew bored with her Earthling contact, in spite of promising to take him to Clarion one day. After their eleventh meeting, she did not return, leaving Truman Bethurum to wait forlornly, night after night, alone in the desert.

Frequently the UFO entities claimed to have come from places with nonsensical names, again prompting ufologists to choose between two possibilities: that the contactees were lying and betraying their poor knowledge of basic astronomy, or that the entities themselves were deliberately feeding humans erroneous information. For instance, on the night of 15 October 1979, Senhora Luli Oswald was abducted from a car while travelling along the Brazilian coast near Niteroi. Under hypnosis, Senhora Oswald described being medically examined. Also, she was told by one of the entities that some of them originate in Antarctica, and that there is a tunnel in Patagonia which leads, under the sea, to another world. (The alleged underground tunnel system is one of the most fascinating areas of ufology, and one we shall be looking at in greater detail in Chapter 6.) The entity then told Senhora Oswald where he came from: 'a small galaxy near Neptune'. This, of course, is utter nonsense: galaxies contain solar systems, not the other way around.

Later in the same year, Elaine Kaiser of Rhode Island, USA, was allegedly abducted from her bedroom and levitated up a beam of multi-coloured light. Hypnotic regression revealed that she had been taken into a spacecraft and examined by two alien beings. She asked one of them where he came from. He replied, 'Vector 4–2.4 million light years from here.' When asked who he was, the other entity replied, 'Kelb from Ceres star constellation.' Again, basic astronomy is found wanting here: Ceres is not a constellation but an asteroid orbiting the Sun in the asteroid belt between Mars and Jupiter, and 2.4 million light years would put Vector 4 well into intergalactic space, far from any potentially life-bearing worlds.

An additional feature of contactee claims, and another that ufologists believe undermines their authenticity, is the information imparted by the space people. No new scientific information is ever forthcoming, nothing that could be verified in a laboratory, of which scientists could say, 'We didn't know this before.' In fact, much of what the aliens have to say regarding their technology (when they condescend to give any information) tends towards the kind of gibberish found in bad science fiction.

Take, for instance, William Herrmann of South Carolina, who claims first to have been abducted in 1978 by humanoid beings. During one contact, the beings stated their origin as the stars Zeta 1 and Zeta 2 Reticuli. Much of the information they subsequently gave to him came via the medium of automatic writing. Here is an extract from one of these messages:

> Reticulan Technology
> Propulsion Evolutionary-Hypothesis:
>   A combination of gravity equilibrium manipulation by electromagnetic energy–mass conversion within a unified field of positive and negative particle beam fusions . . . using kinetic energy and harnessed static electricity a conversion takes place that increases the energy flow into the electromagnetic wave cohesive force chamber . . . thus resulting in action/reaction basis of fluctuation. The manipulation effect is maintained by continual increase and decrease of the electromagnetic wave MPS (manipulation per sequence). (Wendelle C. Stevens and William J. Herrmann, *UFO . . . Contact from Reticulum: A Report of the Investigation*, page 232.)

Although Wendelle Stevens stated that the contents of this message were totally out of character for Herrmann, the message does read rather like made-up nonsense. In his examination of the case in his book *Alien Identities: Ancient Insights into Modern UFO Phenomena*, Richard L. Thompson points out that if they had wanted to impart complex technical information, the aliens should have – indeed *would* have – included detailed definitions of all the terms used, so that the recipient(s) could make sense of it. It could be that the information was garbled somehow as it passed through Herrmann's mind in the process of automatic writing, but, as Thompson says, surely the aliens would have been aware of this difficulty, and would have taken steps to correct it.

Some of the information is easier to understand, and is rather striking. For example, in one communication we find a reference to 'ORBITAL ECCENTRICITY: 0.0167'. According to astronomy textbooks, the eccentricity of the Earth's orbit is 0.0167. The skeptics would argue that Herrmann simply picked up this information from a book and incorporated it into his 'communications'. Herrmann himself, however, seems too sincere cynically to have fabricated his story, and yet, it does seem unlikely that aliens would use this three-significant-digit notation in their description of the Earth's orbital eccentricity (see Thompson, page 193). Once again, we are left with a choice: either the human contact is pulling a fast one, or the aliens are.

Many people who grew up in the 1940s and 1950s lament the loss of the way of life of that time. While conceding that it was not a 'golden age' (every era has its problems), they will often say it had a sense of innocence that no longer exists. This is echoed by many writers, and more than once the blame of our loss of innocence has been placed firmly at the door of the nuclear sword of Damocles that has hung over our heads for the last five decades. (The American writer William S. Burroughs was in a restaurant, and the waiter asked him what he would like. He replied, 'A bass fished in Lake Huron in 1920.')

In looking at the tales of the contactees, one is struck by a similar sense of innocence or naivety in their descriptions of (in the vast majority of a cases) benevolent, even angelic, 'space brothers', gentle beings whose only message was one of peace, love, harmony and understanding. However, this was not to last. As we shall see in the following chapters, the attitudes of our mysterious visitors changed most disconcertingly over the next few years, leaving us apparently with fewer and fewer friends out there.

PART TWO

THE UNINVITED ARRIVE AT NIGHT

FOUR

The Descent into Malevolence

ENTER THE RETICULANS

DURING THE 1960S the aliens' *modus operandi* changed from the angelic to the demonic, almost as if they were echoing the Christian demonization of the pagan deities in previous centuries.

Perhaps the most famous case in the history of ufology, and the one usually credited with being the first modern abduction, as opposed to benign contact, is that of Barney and Betty Hill. The case has been described in numerous books, but I must include it because of its importance, and also because it illustrates so well the intermediate stage in the alleged aliens' treatment of humans.

Although the case did not come to public attention until October 1966, the encounter itself took place on the night of 19–20 September 1961. Barney and Betty Hill were driving home to Portsmouth, New Hampshire, from a holiday in Canada. Their route took them along US Highway 3 through the White Mountains. They expected to complete their journey by 2:30 to 3 am. They had decided to drive through the night because they had run low on money, their trip to Niagara and Montreal having been taken on the spur of the moment.

The night sky was clear, the Moon nearly full; below it and to the left shone a bright star. The couple were just south of Lancaster when Betty noticed the appearance of another star, much brighter than the first, between it and the Moon. The light seemed to be following the car, so Betty looked at it through a pair of binoculars, and saw what appeared to be a double row of windows.

Barney assumed the object was a plane, but stopped the car and went into a field with the binoculars to get a better look. What he saw filled him with panic. He ran back to the car, shouting hysterically that they were going to be captured. Through the binoculars, he had seen a group of beings at the windows of the craft; he had seen their eyes, staring back at him.

As the couple drove off, they heard a strange beeping sound that seemed to be coming from the rear of the car. Waves of drowsiness overcame them, and a while later they heard the beeping sound again. Betty turned to her husband and said, '*Now* do you believe in flying saucers?' 'Don't be ridiculous. Of course not,' he replied.

They arrived home in Portsmouth just after 5 am, approximately two and a half hours later than they should have done. Not long afterwards, they noticed a dozen shiny circles on the paint of the car's boot lid.

Ten days after the sighting, Betty began having bizarre nightmares about strange beings that had captured them and taken them into a flying saucer. A month after the sighting, the Hills were interviewed by Walter Webb of NICAP (National Investigations Committee on Aerial, Phenomena). On 25 November 1961 they were interviewed again. This time there were others present: C.D. Jackson and Robert E. Hohman of NICAP, and James McDonald, a retired Air Force major and friend of the Hills. During the interview, which lasted for 12 hours, Hohman asked, 'What took you so long to get home?'

As Curtis Peebles points out in *Watch the Skies!* (page 196), this question irrevocably changed the whole of ufology. Barney and Betty reacted to it with surprise and fear respectively.

On 14 December 1963, Barney and Betty began a series of hypnosis sessions with Dr Benjamin Simon, a highly respected Boston psychiatrist and neurologist who had a great deal of experience with hypnosis. According to Betty: 'We went to Dr Simon to get relief from the emotional trouble, and to determine what its cause was. In other words, we'd gone for medical help, not to find out about a UFO experience.'

It is essential to bear in mind that the sessions were designed to examine any connection that might have existed between the alleged UFO encounter and Barney's physical problems, which included stomach ulcers. Also, there were a number of psychological factors that could well have had some bearing on their states of mind at the time of the alleged encounter; these include the couple's interracial marriage, their previous marriages, and their involvement with social work and civil rights.

Barney and Betty were hypnotized separately, and it was only when Dr Simon was satisfied that his work was complete that he allowed the subjects to listen to the tapes of their testimony. The Hills independently told a story that closely matched the strange nightmares. Here are some extracts from the tapes:

BARNEY: I started to get out of my car, and put one foot on the ground. And two men were standing beside me, helping me out. I felt very relaxed, yet very frightened. They didn't say anything. I knew I was walking, or moving down the road from the position of where my car was parked. And I could see the ramp that I went up . . . I could hear a humming sound that they seemed to be making. I was afraid to open my eyes. I had been told not to open my eyes, and it would be over very quickly. And I could feel them examining me with their hands. They looked at my neck, and I could feel them touching my skin right down my back. As if they were counting my spinal column. And I felt something touch right at the base of my spine, like a finger pushing, a single finger.

BETTY: They led Barney right past the door where I'm standing. So I said: 'What are you doing with Barney? Bring him in here where I am.' And the man said: 'No, we only have equipment enough in one room to do one person at a time. And if we took you both in the same room, it would take too long. So Barney will be all right, they're going to take him into the next room. And then as soon as we get through testing the both of you, then you will go back to your car. You don't have to be afraid.' . . . And they rub – they have a machine, I don't know what it is. They bring the machine over and they put it – it's something like a microscope, only with a big lens. I had an idea they were taking a picture of my skin. And they both looked through this machine . . . Then they took something like a letter- opener and they scraped my arm here, and there was like little – you know how your skin gets dry and flaky sometimes, like little particles of skin? And they put something like a piece of cellophane or plastic, they scraped, and they put this that came off on this plastic [*sic*].

After the examinations had been completed, Betty was shown a three-dimensional star map by the entity she called 'the leader'. In one of the hypnosis sessions, she described their discussion about the map:

> I asked him where he was from. Because I said that I knew he wasn't from the Earth . . . and he asked if I knew anything about the universe. And I told him no. I knew practically nothing . . . . And he went across the room . . . there was an opening. And he pulled out a map . . . . It was an oblong map . . . . And there were all these dots on it . . . . Some were little, just pinpoints. And others were as big as a nickel . . . there were curved lines going from one dot to another. And there was one big circle, and it had a lot of lines coming out from it. A lot of lines going to another circle quite close but not as big . . . . And I asked him what they meant. And he said that the heavy lines were trade routes . . . . The solid lines were places they went occasionally. And he said the broken lines were expeditions . . . . So I asked him where was his home port, and he said, 'Where were you on the map?' I looked and laughed and said, 'I don't know.' So he said, 'If you don't know where you are, then there isn't any point in my telling where I am from.' And he put the map . . . back in the space in the wall.

In 1968, Marjorie Fish, a schoolteacher and amateur astronomer, made a three-dimensional model of Betty's drawing (which, since it did not include any star names, was meaningless), in an effort to make some sense of it. The model was constructed of beads and string, and it was Fish's intention to attempt to match up the map with the nearer stars to our solar system. The results of her endeavours drew as much attention as the Hill abduction itself. According to astronomer Terence Dickinson, the Fish map was a view from several light years beyond the stars Zeta 1 and Zeta 2 Reticuli, looking back towards the Sun and the star 82 Eridani.

In an article on the Fish interpretation, Dickinson said that the 15 stars on the map are all basically like the Sun, and could theoretically have planetary systems. However, skeptics pointed out that, with the large number of stars in the region, the Hill map is open to any number of alternative interpretations.

Notwithstanding the possible alternative interpretations of the map, the Zeta Reticuli star system has now entered UFO mythology, and is accepted without reservation by believers in the extra-terrestrial hypothesis as the home of the Greys. This is curious, in view of the fact that the beings described by the Hills looked nothing like Greys. Their eyes were a little larger than ours, with a wider lateral field of vision, but still contained irises and pupils, rather than being gigantic, black and featureless. Likewise, their cranium was a little larger than that of a human, but was nowhere near as expanded and melon-like as that of the Grey. In fact, we surely have the Fish interpretation to thank for ufology's current fascination with Zeta Reticuli, since this was the first time that verification of the aliens' point of origin was attempted in anything approaching a scientific manner.

As mentioned earlier, when Betty asked the entities' leader for some proof of their encounter, he picked up a book containing strange symbols and gave it to her. This provoked a heated discussion among the aliens, and the 'leader' was persuaded by his crewmates that it would be better if the Hills had no proof of what had happened to them. He took back the book from Betty.

Although he concluded that Barney and Betty were not lying about their encounter, Dr Simon believed that the experience had been entirely subjective – in short, it had been a particularly vivid dream. He discovered that the 'events' Betty described correspond closely with standard dream symbolism.

For instance, Betty seems to have had an unhappy childhood. She was a voracious reader as a child, which is often a means of defence against conflict and depression, implies and a wish to escape into fantasy. Betty's mother had been an extremely strong character; her father had been quite the opposite, a trait shared by Barney, who seemed to have been forced by Betty into accepting the reality of the 'abduction' (see Peebles, page 198). There is much parental symbolism in the abduction scenario:

> . . . being escorted to the saucer, the benevolent nature of the leader, the examiner's questions about food in a room with a table. (Food = mother = nurturing = somebody taking an interest in her.) The leader and examiner are also taller than the other aliens which is symbolic of authority figures. (Peebles, page 198)

A very striking symbol is the alien leader taking away the book (a vitally important piece of supporting evidence), which corresponds to Betty's mother limiting her reading.

There were also some contradictions in the story. For instance, according to Betty, the aliens were fascinated by human notions of time. When they discovered that Barney had false teeth, and were told by Betty that this was because he was getting older, they were astounded, and asked her to explain the concepts of 'old age', 'life span' and 'year'. Yet, at the end of the encounter, when Betty was about to leave the saucer, the leader said; 'Wait a minute.' Dr Simon pointed out that contradictions of this kind are common in dreams, which are not literal replays of events, but invariably represent material (conflicts and repressed desires, for example) disguised by means of symbols.

In the introduction to John G. Fuller's book about the encounter, *The Interrupted Journey*, Dr Simon wrote: 'Their existence (the UFOs) as concrete objects is of less concern to me than the experience of these two people showing the cumulative impact of past experiences and fantasies on their present experiences and responses.'

I said earlier that the Hill case is important because it illustrates the gradual (adverse) alteration in the relationship between human beings and alleged aliens. This can be further seen in the reaction of the UFO community to the case at the time. The National Investigations Committee on Aerial Phenomena (NICAP) and its then director, Donald E. Keyhoe, accepted the Hills' sighting of the UFO, but not their abduction by its crew. Frank Edwards, a journalist and prolific writer on the subject of UFOs, considered the Hill case to be on a par with Adamski's claims, i.e. 'interesting if true'.

The British journal *Flying Saucer Review*, on the other hand, defended the case, and even tried to link it with the Villas Boas case in Brazil. In this extremely well-known encounter, Antonio Villas Boas was out ploughing a field on his farm one night in October 1957, when he was abducted by strange entities, taken into their spaceship and forced to have sex (which he rather enjoyed) with a small woman, who told him through sign language that their issue would be taken to the stars with her.

The Hill case has elements in common with both the contactee and abduction scenarios. Betty had a long conversation with the alien leader, much as the contactees had done with their space friends (in subsequent years, Betty maintained that she considered the aliens to be her friends, and wished that they would return one day). On the other hand, she and Barney had not been invited into the saucer – they had been made to enter, and submitted to a medical examination which, if not traumatic, had nevertheless been rather demeaning. There was also the appearance of the aliens, which was a far cry from the beautiful, almost Christlike aspect of the 'space brothers'. Finally, and most importantly, there was the period of missing time, a concept that was, in later years, to occupy centre stage in the drama of human–non-human encounters.

DECLINE AND FALL

Not only has the nature of human–alien encounters become more traumatic in the years since the 1950s, it has also become more complex and multi-layered. Many writers on the subject have commented on how the technology of the aliens seems to be only one or two jumps ahead of our own. For example, the Great Airship sightings of the late 1890s (see Chapter 8) presaged the world-wide use of airships only a few years later. Likewise, the pregnancy test conducted on Betty Hill by means of a needle inserted into her navel only narrowly anticipated similar advances in our own medical technology. In the abduction scenario, however, the process seems to be working in reverse, with our own advances in genetic engineering influencing the accounts given by the percipients.

There are no prizes for guessing what the skeptics would say about this. Indeed, it could well be argued that the aliens' apparent desire to harvest the sperm and ova of humans in order to reinvigorate their dying species is a direct result of our own apprehension at the ongoing advances in genetic engineering, what might be called 'the Frankenstein syndrome'.

Dr David Jacobs, a historian at Temple University, Philadelphia, has documented a number of discrete elements in the abduction experience. Not every abductee will be subjected to all of them. These elements are as follows:

1. The initial appearance of the aliens and the taking of the percipient;
2. Medical probing with various instruments, bonding with the aliens and breeding experiments;

3. Machine examinations, mental testing and presentation of hybrid children;
4. Sexual activity and other procedures;
5. The returning of the percipient to his or her native environment.
(See David Jacobs, *Alien Encounters: First-hand Accounts of UFO Abductions.*)

In the following pages, I will give examples of each of these elements, together with some comments on both their credibility and their implications.

1. The initial appearance of the aliens and the taking of the percipient.

If we really are dealing with non-human species, the extent of their technological superiority is evident from the very outset of interaction with them. An abduction typically begins with the percipient in a relaxed situation, usually lying in bed, preparing to go to sleep, or even already asleep.

He or she will then become aware of a presence in the room that does not belong there; frequently, this will be accompanied by an awareness of an intense bluish light that has no immediately identifiable source. The percipient will later testify that they were startled by this unusual situation into full wakefulness, whereupon they become aware of a small humanoid figure moving towards them. Initial feelings of terror give way to a strange sense of recognition, as if they know who it is.

If the percipient happens to be with anyone at the time (a spouse or partner, for instance), the other person is rendered totally inert or 'switched off', so that no amount of shouting or shaking will awaken them.

At this point, the process known as 'floating' occurs: the percipient rises out of bed, apparently at the visitor's instigation, and is moved bodily out of their home. A frequently cited feature of this process is the ability of the visitor(s) to move the percipient through solid objects, such as a wall or a closed window.

The percipient may be floated up to an waiting UFO, or transported some distance away to a secluded area, where a UFO awaits them on the ground. In the majority of cases, the UFO has no obvious door or hatch: entry is most often effected through a lighted area on the surface of the craft, usually on the bottom.

An alternative starting-point for an abduction experience was discussed earlier. This involves the percipient driving alone along an isolated stretch of road, whereupon he or she will become aware of a strange, unidentified light in the sky. The engine of the vehicle fails, bringing it to a halt; conversely, the driver will feel an intense need to pull over and stop. The abduction will then proceed.

The concepts of floating and passing through solid objects have reminded more than one commentator on abductions of so-called 'out-of-body experiences' (OBEs). A typical OBE involves the sensation that the percipient has somehow left his or her body, and temporarily exists in a non-physical, 'astral' or 'spiritual' form. This raises the possibility that abductions, assuming that they do actually occur, may do so on a purely psychological level.

This idea is supported by at least one very striking case, which was documented by Keith Basterfield, the research officer for UFO Research Australia, and presented at the abduction conference held at MIT in 1992. The case involves Maureen Puddy, a 37-year-old housewife from Rye in Victoria, Australia.

At 9.15 pm on 3 July 1972, Mrs Puddy was driving home after visiting her son in hospital near Melbourne, when the road was suddenly bathed in blue light. Looking up, she saw a disc-shaped craft, and became aware of a humming noise, which she described as being similar to that of an elevator moving. In panic, Mrs Puddy drove away from the object as fast as she could. The object pursued her for about 13 km (8 miles), then there was a streak of light and it was gone.

On 25 July 1972, Mrs Puddy was again driving home, when the incident was repeated, at the same location and time. This time, her car's engine cut out and the vehicle came to a halt at the side of the road. She then heard a voice which seemed to come from inside her head. It said, 'All your tests will be negative.' After a short pause, the voice added, 'Tell the media, do not panic, we mean no harm.' After another pause, the voice concluded, 'You now have control.' Her car's engine immediately started, the blue light went out and the object disappeared.

She reported this incident (as she had the first one) to the RAAF, who sent her another form to complete. The following day, she telephoned three television stations, one of which interviewed her.

On about 22 February 1973, Mrs Puddy felt an 'eerie presence' in the house, and caught a message telling her, 'Go back to the same meeting-place.' She telephoned the Victorian UFO Research Society and two members, Judith Magee and Paul Norman, agreed to meet her at the location of her sightings.

While she was driving to the spot, Mrs Puddy was astounded to see an entity appear in the front passenger seat beside her. The entity had long blond hair and was wearing a white ski suit. As soon as it had appeared, the entity vanished.

When Mrs Puddy arrived at the spot, she and the two investigators sat in her car and waited. Presently, she became aware of the same 'man' standing outside the car and beckoning to her. She refused to get out of the car. Neither Judith Magee nor Paul Norman saw him.

Suddenly, Maureen Puddy fainted and, although apparently unconscious, began a verbal description of what she was experiencing. She said that she was in a round room, with a mushroom-shaped object covered with hieroglyphics rising from the floor. The entity was there, and he told her to describe what she was seeing. There were no doors or windows in the room – no visible means of escape – so Mrs Puddy began to be afraid, and started to cry. She then came to in the car, with no conscious memory of what had transpired.

About a week after these events, Mrs Puddy was driving with her son, who was sitting in the front passenger seat beside her. Suddenly, the entity appeared again, sitting between them on the bench seat. The weather was bad, with rain and poor visibility. However, while the 'man' was there, the weather conditions improved dramatically, with visibility increasing for miles. Then he disappeared, and the poor visibility resumed.

In a letter written to the novelist and journalist C.D.B. Bryan, Keith Basterfield says that there does not appear to be anything in mainstream psychology (i.e. lucid dreams, transient memory disorders, hypnagogic and hypnopompic imagery, fantasy-prone personality theory, etc.) that can fully account for abductions. However, he recommends that, before accepting the extra-terrestrial hypothesis (ETH), we must continue with research into altered states of consciousness, of which Mrs Puddy's experience seems to be a very fine example (see C.D.B. Bryan, *Close Encounters of the Fourth Kind: Alien Abduction and UFOs – Witnesses and Scientists Report*, pages 94–9; also, Jim Schnabel, *Dark White: Aliens, Abductions and the UFO Obsession*, pages 116–17).

2. Medical probing with various instruments, bonding with the aliens and breeding experiments.

Once inside the UFO, the percipient is utterly at the mercy of the aliens, who proceed to conduct various tests with apparently sophisticated mechanical instruments. Although the entities frequently assure the percipient that he or she will not be hurt or injured, these examinations are frequently very painful. Occasionally, one of the entities (sometimes referred to as 'the doctor' because of its apparent authority over the others) will perform some action, such as waving a hand in front of the percipient's forehead, that instantly eases the pain or discomfort.

The percipient, having been placed on a table, is comprehensively examined by several entities, who seem to pay close attention to bone structure and joints, manipulating ankles, knees and elbows as if curious about their construction. (Although, if we take a literalist stance, this might be explained by the entities' reported lack of jointing in the limbs, it still seems strange that they should be fascinated by human jointing on so many occasions; they should surely familiar with the human skeletal structure by now.) In the case of female percipients, the entities conduct a gynaecological examination, taking samples of the lining of the vagina or uterus; with male percipients, the sexual organs are examined and palpated (Jacobs, page 91).

If the percipient has had previous abduction experiences, the entities look for physical changes. If they find any, they are immediately concerned, and sometimes ask the percipient what has occurred. For instance, one abductee had a streak of her hair dyed blonde, leading the entities to conclude that she had been unwell (Jacobs, page 93).

Of all the procedures carried out by the entities, that of implanting artificial objects into the bodies of abductees is the best known, and has received considerable attention in the media. The objects implanted are usually small, spherical and metallic, and are inserted in the abductee's ear, nose or sinus cavity by means of a long, needlelike device. Some researchers have speculated that these implants might be tracking devices, enabling the entities to home in instantly on any person they wish to abduct. Others suggest that they might monitor the physiology of the abductees while separated from the entities. A slightly more paranoid theory is that the implants are actually receivers, through which the abductee's mind can be controlled by the aliens, implying that abductees could unwillingly be used for nefarious purposes.

Ufologists are principally interested in the implants because they might at last provide physical proof of the reality of alien visitation and interaction with humans. A former CIA agent, Derrel Sims, has recently risen to prominence in the field by virtue of his radical approach to both the phenomenon of implants and that of UFO abductions in general.

Sims is the Chief of Abduction Investigations and Director of Physical Investigations for the Houston UFO Network (HUFON). An abductee himself, he has been investigating UFOs for 25 years, and places a high priority not only on obtaining hard physical evidence in the form of retrieved implants, but also on confronting the entities whenever they attempt to stage an abduction. Sims's ultimate objective in so doing is to establish direct contact with the entities, and he has achieved some remarkable results.

In December 1992, HUFON arranged a meeting, called 'Alien Abductions: Working with Abductees', to identify victims of multiple abductions (where the entities return to percipients throughout their lives), and introduce hypnotic suggestions that would enable percipient to recall more of what occurred during their experiences and to play a more active role in them. On the evening of the HUFON meeting, several abductees had encounters in which the entities hastily retrieved implants inserted earlier. Sims believes this was a direct result of his new approach to interaction with the entities.

One of his most striking successes involves a woman named Laura, who was allegedly close to breakdown as a result of frequent abduction experiences. Sims carried out a procedure called 'reprogramming' in which Laura was told, under hypnosis, to react with hostility to any future abduction.

On 5 April 1993, Laura was again visited by the entities, who came through the wall. She mentally beckoned them closer, and when one of them complied, she grabbed its black eye-shield, which tore in half. This caused the entities to retreat. When they returned two weeks later, Laura grabbed one of them round the waist and pulled out its whole eye-shield, revealing an orb which seemed to be constructed of five separate pieces, behind which small white dots moved back and forth, leaving traces on the surface. This event threw the entities into confusion, and they left through the wall, taking their injured colleague with them.

Sims is extremely cautious with regard to the physical evidence in the form of implants that he has retrieved from abductees. He always sends them for analysis by members of the scientific and medical communities. However, the devices so far examined have proved to be composed of materials common on Earth. While there may be a very good reason for this within the context of genuine alien activity, it nevertheless means that categorical proof (i.e. scientifically documented evidence of materials that could not have been manufactured on this planet) has not yet been obtained.

After the physical examination and the insertion or retrieval of implants, a process Dr Jacobs calls 'Mindscan' takes place. In this process, one of the entities, usually the 'Doctor', approaches the percipient and stares deeply into his or her eyes. It seems that this process can either instill fear (a feeling that the entity is somehow entering the percipient's mind and 'stealing memories'), or a calming and soothing effect (Jacobs, page 99).

The process of 'Bonding' is intimately related to Mindscan. During Bonding, the doctor will induce powerful pleasurable emotions in the percipient, which leads to a feeling that the entities are benign and have our best interests at heart.

After these processes comes another element that has received a great deal of media attention: the harvesting of female ova and male sperm. The ova are apparently taken from the body via either the vagina or the abdomen. In the case of sperm collection, a tube like a vacuum-cleaner hose is placed over the penis, inducing ejaculation. Material taken from the human body is then placed in some form of container and taken from the room.

At this stage, some female abductees are apparently implanted with a fertilized ovum, and immediately sense that they are now pregnant (Jacobs, page 108). In others, the opposite will occur: what appears to be a foetus is extracted from the uterus of a pregnant abductee. Later on, in normal life, the abductee (unaware of what has been happening to her) will be at a loss to explain the fact that she is no longer pregnant, that her baby has vanished.

In an article written for *Fortean Times*, Peter Brookesmith interviewed Dr Barbara Skew, formerly of the Royal United Hospital, Bath, England, and currently staff gynaecologist at Southmead Hospital, Bristol. Dr Skew gave her opinion on the material presented by Dr Jacobs (and Dr John Mack of Harvard Medical School and Budd Hopkins) as strong supporting evidence for the idea of alien abductions:

This is clearly a failure of proper diagnosis. It is perfectly possible for false-positive pregnancy tests on urine to occur. Bimanual palpitation [vaginal examination] of the uterus is unreliable even in experienced hands, especially for pregnancies of fewer than eight weeks. The only truly reliable method of diagnosis is ultrasound scanning, in which (if pregnancy exists) an intra-uterine sac can be seen and photographed. Ultrasound has been freely available for 20 years at least, is cheap, non-invasive and absolutely diagnostic. Without [such] photographic evidence . . . I would be very sceptical that a pregnancy was there in the first place.

Amenorrhea [lack of periods] may be confused with pregnancy. Most gynaecologists have seen at least one woman who maintained she was pregnant and was proved not to have been. The more suggestible the patient, the more easily she will convince herself she is pregnant.

One of the more common causes of amenorrhea is polycystic ovary syndrome, a condition in which the ovaries do not function normally and the normal cyclic release of an egg is disordered. Normal ovaries may sometimes develop small cysts when a follicle containing an egg fails to pop and goes on secreting hormones that maintain the endometrium [lining of the womb] – this is the so-called 'functional follicular cyst'. Most of the endocrine (e.g. thyroid, adrenal, pituitary) disorders cause period disorders. Severe weight loss or gain has a profound effect on menstrual cycles as well. This list is by no means exhaustive, but you can already see that it could be quite easy to misdiagnose pregnancy especially if [one is] led by the patient to believe she is pregnant. (*Fortean Times*, Number 85, February/March 1996, page 23)

Dr Skew adds that descriptions of egg harvesting, embryo implantation and needles in abdomens sounded to her like 'the rather sketchy ideas that lay people imagine about such procedures', and that the material on abductions shown to her by Peter Brookesmith 'shows a lamentable lack of any sort of scientific content. It would appear to resemble much more closely the well-known psychiatric condition of *folie à deux*, in which the deluded person draws in the sane one and involves them in the madness by convincing them of its truth!' (ibid., page 23).

In view of orthodox medical opinion, we must bear in mind that, while the implanting and extraction of foetuses (like implanted devices) may be taking place, the evidence as it stands does not prove beyond any doubt that they are.

3. Machine examinations, mental testing and presentation of hybrid children

At this point, the abductee either remains on the examination table or is led to another room. A complex machine is then lowered from the ceiling, and sweeps over the body, possibly taking physiological measurements. In the 'Imaging' process, the abductee is placed in front of a viewing screen and shown various images, usually of a very disturbing nature, including apocalyptic destruction. In his books *Communion* and *Transformation*, Whitley Strieber has described scenes in which enormous boulders fly off the surface of the Moon and plough into the Earth, utterly destroying it.

Alternatively, the scenes may be of a highly agreeable, even romantic, nature, instilling feelings of joy or contentment (Jacobs, page 136). It has been speculated that the entities wish to study the emotional processes of humans, possibly because their own emotions have somehow become atrophied, and they find our enormous capacity to feel emotion interesting. It has even been mooted that the entities actually feed on emotion, finding terror particularly toothsome!

The presentation of so-called hybrid children to the abductee is one of the most profound and disturbing of the events that occur during an encounter. After passing through a room lined with glass cases containing tiny humanoid forms floating in some sort of liquid, the abductee is taken to another location, which has been described as a 'nursery' by Dr Jacobs and others. Here, the abductee is shown children who are the result of the combination of human and alien genetic material. The children are usually described as being frail, listless and sickly-looking, with sparse hair on their disproportionately large heads.

Frequently, the abductee will be told that one or more of the children are hers, and that she should feel proud of having contributed to such a wonderful event. The entities will often try to persuade the abductee to hold the children, apparently because human contact is essential to their development, perhaps even to their survival.

4. Sexual activity and other procedures

As if all that has gone before were not traumatic enough, some abductees are forced to engage in sexual activity with other human beings who have been taken aboard the same craft. During these procedures, the other person appears to be desensitized, as if only semi-conscious. Needless to say, the abductees are extremely distressed by what the entities force them to do, not least because they are also compelled to look into the aliens' eyes throughout.

Once again, it appears that the entities are extremely interested in emotional responses to certain stimuli. Occasionally, a couple will be making love in their home, when one of them will become aware that they are being watched by aliens in the room, yet be unable to stop (Jacobs, page 198).

5. The returning of the percipient to his or her native environment

The departure of the abductee from the alien environment is as sudden and unceremonious as their arrival. Once the aliens have completed their various procedures, they tell their victim that it is now time to go, and take him or her to what is apparently the lowest deck in the UFO. Usually they are placed on a circular area on the floor, and their next sensation is one of floating down out of the craft and back to their home.

Frequently, one or more aliens will accompany the abductee and make certain they have returned safely to the location from which they were initially taken. However, mistakes are occasionally made. A female abductee may awake in the morning to discover that her night-dress is inside out. Alternatively, she may wake up standing in her bedroom, outside her house, or even several kilometres from home. The reason for this is not known; it may imply an uncaring attitude on the part of the aliens: as far as they are concerned, it is enough that the abductee has been returned to Earth; they are not particularly bothered *where*.

Abductees often discover anomalous marks on their bodies following an encounter, such as bruises, rashes or indentations (the so-called 'scoop marks'), implying that tissue has been excised. Occasionally, a sticky, clear substance will be found around the genitals, and strange stains will be discovered on the bedsheets (Jacobs, page 218).

Amnesia sets in almost immediately, with the abductee

retaining only a vague feeling that something unusual has happened. They usually wake up feeling tired, as if they have not had a good night's sleep.

What are we to make of reports such as these? Obviously, *something* very interesting is occurring. With the exception of a few highly publicized (and dubious) cases, the vast majority of abductees are extremely reluctant to have their identities divulged – some insist on anonymity – and will agree only after a high degree of trust has been established between them and the researcher examining their case.

There are a number of possible alternative explanations for UFO abductions. The one favoured by many researchers is that we really are dealing with scientific expeditions from another planet. Believers in the extra-terrestrial hypothesis for abductions tend to throw up their hands in despair whenever the word 'hallucination' is mentioned. However, if we look closely at this explanation, we find that it does not dismiss the abduction experience as an insignificant by-product of feeble minds, as indeed it should not: a glance at the professions of many abductees (writers, doctors, lawyers, police officers, pilots, etc.) exposes the facileness of such an assertion.

The phenomenon of sleep paralysis is medically documented and affects a significant number of people. Typically, the percipient will wake suddenly in bed, but be utterly unable to move. He or she will be aware of a presence in the room; sometimes this presence will remain unseen, but sometimes it will take the form of one or more entities standing around the bed. Terrifying as this experience may be, it is short-lived, with the entities disappearing as the percipient returns to full wakefulness. Such experiences are caused by the mind waking up while the body in effect remains asleep. The perceived presence or entities are the remnants of dream imagery that has been carried over into the semi-waking state. The conscious perception of this imagery is also known as a 'hypnagogic' or 'hypnopompic' vision. (Hypnagogic refers to the intermediate state between waking and sleeping; hypnopompic refers to the opposite state, intermediate between sleeping and waking.)

I myself have experienced a hypnopompic vision, and can certainly vouch for its strangeness. I awoke one morning a few years ago, looked up at the ceiling and saw my cat (which had died not long before) floating over the bed. Fortunately, I had read of such things, and knew what was happening, otherwise I might have screamed the house down!

Someone who, unaware of the truth behind such visions, awoke to see what they assumed to be a group of entities departing from the room might well suspect that something extremely unusual was afoot. If, in their anxiety, they then sought hypnotic regression at the hands of a researcher who believed in the reality of alien abductions, there would be a risk that the researcher would unintentionally ask leading questions, resulting in the confabulation of an abduction scenario. Under hypnosis, the human mind tends to behave as it thinks is required.

An extension of this idea is the so-called 'old hag' phenomenon, in which supernatural entity attacks and nearly suffocates the victim in bed. In his report on the 1992 Abduction Study Conference at MIT, C.D.B. Bryan refers to a book entitled *Fire in the Brain* by Ronald K. Siegel, an associate research professor in the UCLA School of Medicine's Department of Psychiatry and Behavioral Sciences. In his book, Siegel describes his own blood-chilling encounter with a cigarette-smoking old hag, followed by his ingenious explanation for the phenomenon.

At 4:20 am, he heard footsteps approaching his bed, and then heavy breathing. Siegel sensed a 'murky presence' in the room; when he tried to throw off the bedclothes and get up, he felt himself pinned to the bed by an unseen weight on his chest. He also noticed a musty 'old' smell. When he saw a shadow fall across his bedside clock, he became genuinely frightened. At that point, a voice began to whisper in his ear, accompanied by a thick stench of tobacco. The words made no sense, sounding like English spoken backwards: Siegel's mind was suddenly filled with images of rotting swamps, toadstools and bizarre reptiles. A hand grasped his arm and held it tightly, and part of the mattress next to him depressed as something apparently climbed on to the bed. As the thing straddled his body, Siegel sensed a 'texture of sexual intoxication and terror in the room'.

Only when he had started to lose consciousness did the voice stop and the presence slowly retreat from the room. His torment at an end, Siegel jumped from his bed, grabbed a flashlight and searched his home, certain that an intruder had threatened him and was still somewhere nearby. Of course, there was no such intruder.

Siegel's explanation for this terrifying experience, which at the time felt utterly real, is as follows: he was, in fact, suffering simultaneously from sleep paralysis *and* a hypnopompic hallucination. The swamp imagery was indicative that some REM activity had been carried over from the sleeping state to the hypnopompic state. Siegel explains that the succubus imagery may be, as Jung postulated, a racial memory implanted in our genes in the distant past, when our ancestors feared the night and the many predators it brought. On the other hand, it may be a powerful echo of the colossal, looming shapes of the infant's perceptual world.

However, explanation is still required for the actual physical sensations associated with the experience, such as the pressure on the chest, the musty smell and, in Siegel's case, the suffocating stench of tobacco. As the body struggles against sleep paralysis, it becomes highly sensitized, becoming acutely aware not only of its own rigid muscles, but also of the bed-covers, which are translated by the hypnopompic brain into pressure from an unseen body. Perspiration can contribute to this feeling of something folding its slimy body over the victim's, and can be misinterpreted as the smell of another person. The movement of the mattress was, Siegel believes, due to his own frantic struggles.

In this terror-induced state of hypersensitivity, Siegel's brain seized on every stimulus, no matter how insignificant, and magnified it. Thus a familiar shadow cast by a streetlight through the window took on a far more sinister aspect. The smell of tobacco came from the cigarette smoke that occasionally wafted up through Siegel's windows from the apartment below; once again, this was magnified by its passage through Siegel's frenzied nervous system.

The human mind invariably tries to process incoming sensory data in the most familiar terms available to its view of experiential reality. Thus, the physical sensations described above resulted in the best 'fit' available to the brain in its terrorized and sensitized state. Siegel added:

> I was not the first to be terrorized by such an experience. Throughout history many people have reported attacks by the *same* intruder. I was right when I said she smelled old. The Babylonians called her Lilitu, demoness of the wind, who seduced men by night. The Jews called her Lilith, the hairy night creature. She was the succubus of ancient Rome who

leaped upon the sleeper and rode him to love or death.
Then, in the Middle Ages, she became the witch Lamia.
Finally, in Old Germany, she was known as the *mare*, the old,
ugly woman who sat on the chest of the sleeper and produced
the evil dreams we now call night*mares*. (Ronald K. Siegel, *Fire
in the Brain: Clinical Tales of Hallucination*, pages 83–85, quoted
in Bryan, page 184)

In the 1980s psychologists concluded that some people possess
what is known as a 'fantasy-prone personality' (FPP). Among their
not unenviable attributes are above-average intelligence, a high
degree of creativity and an active fantasy life. They have other
talents that some might consider to be paranormal, such as the
ability to know what another person is thinking; their dreams
often foretell the future with unsettling accuracy. They are also
prone to out-of-body experiences.

At its most extreme, the fantasy-prone personality can fall victim to dissociative disorders. According to Jung, 'For the sake of
mental stability and even physiological health, the unconscious
and the conscious must be integrally connected and thus move on
parallel lines. If they are split apart or "dissociated", psychological
disturbance follows.' (See C.G. Jung, *Man and his Symbols*, page
52.) When one or more mental processes are split off from the rest,
the results can be startling and unsettling, including hallucinations
and hysterical illnesses. The latter could be considered a possible
cause of the mysterious bruises and scars reported by abductees,
together with our perfectly normal capacity for causing ourselves
minor injuries, unnoticed at the time, in the course of a normal
day's activities. More serious dissociative episodes might include
chronic self-hypnosis and amnesic somnambulatory fugues
(Schnabel, page 122).

A variation on the hallucination theme comes from Michael A.
Persinger, a psychology professor at Laurentian University in
Ontario, who suggests that UFOs are geologically produced light-
forms. In the event of a low-intensity earth tremor or an earth-
quake, piezoelectricity (or 'seismoelectricity') creates an ionization
effect in the atmosphere close to the fault line. In his 1977 book,
Space – Time Transients, written with Ghislaine F. Lafrenière,
Persinger adds that these electromagnetic effects could also have a
'scrambling' effect on human brain rhythms, triggering hallucinations. (See *The Age of the UFO*, ed. Peter Brookesmith, page 73.)

HIGH-TECH MYSTICISM

If we accept neither the extra-terrestrial hypothesis nor hallu-cinations as a possible cause for alleged alien encounters, we find ourselves drifting into a realm that is even more bizarre, and certainly more aesthetically satisfying, than that of the galactic goon squad which features in much of the UFO literature.

The journalist Keith Thompson makes a very interesting point in his book *Angels and Aliens: UFOs and the Mythic Imagination*. He states that the continuity of what he terms 'the overall UFO mythology' is maintained through a dialectic between two mutu-ally exclusive interpretations:

> . . . because the events of UFO encounters are typically
> surrealistic – dreamlike, fantastical, at once less than and
> more than real – the psyche reaches for interpretations in
> order to bridge the gaps. Some UFO researchers seek
> exhaustive answers by focusing entirely on the surface
> events, trying to prove that it's all happening just as it appears
> to be happening. These are ufology's 'surface literalists'.
> Others look beneath the surfaces for the exhaustive truth,
> trying to prove that nothing is as it seems in UFO encounters,
> that truth lies never in the events themselves but only
> 'elsewhere'. These are ufology's 'depth literalists'. (Thompson,
> page 39)

He goes on to remind us that the phenomenon itself does not seem to want either of these viewpoints to prevail, since contradictory evidence is provided whenever one appears to be gaining the upper hand.

This dichotomy between events occurring in what we call 'con-sensus reality' and their underlying symbolic/mythopoeic antecedents also characterizes the relationship between humanity and the supernatural world in traditional cultures.

It is entirely natural that the human imagination, when faced with the mysteries of time, mind, life and death, should do every-thing in its power to solve those mysteries, to search for answers or, at least, to ask questions. Even today, we can observe the ele-gant solution to this problem in societies such as the Innuit of northern Canada, a culture that relies on the knowledge and wis-dom of very special people: the shamans.

A shaman is a highly respected member of his society, and yet, due to the nature of his work, he remains subtly apart from it. His work involves interacting with the unseen, the spirit world that surrounds and influences the world that can be apprehended by the normal senses, and in which ordinary people are imprisoned for the duration of their lives.

The process of becoming a shaman is not an easy one: the altered state of consciousness that is required is not accessible to all, and many shamans achieve it only at a moment of great trauma, due to severe illness or injury, for example. At the point where death is almost upon him, the prospective shaman may make contact with the gods and spirits of the natural world, and, if he is fortunate enough to survive the experience and return to health, he will find that he has attained a highly privileged position among his fellows.

From then on, it is the responsibility of the shaman to maintain contact with the spirits of nature, believed by the society in which he lives to influence the lives and fortunes of the people. For instance, on the eve of a hunt, the shaman must re-enter the altered state of consciousness in order to contact the relevant gods and ask their permission and blessing, so that the hunt will be successful. Likewise, when a person falls ill, it will be left to the shaman to consult the spirits as to the best course of action to take, in order to ensure the recovery of the patient.

However, the call to shamanism does not always entail suffering serious injury or illness. An example of the alternative route can be found in the life of the Oglala Sioux holy man Black Elk, who was born in 1863 at Little Powder River, and was the second cousin of Crazy Horse.

For Black Elk, contact with the world of spirits occurred spontaneously when he was five years old. Looking up at the sky, he saw two human figures descending from the clouds, accompanied by sounds of thunder. As they approached, they sang a song: 'Behold, a sacred voice is calling you; All over the sky a sacred voice is calling.' Black Elk related his encounter to his biographer, John G. Neihardt, whom he met in 1930:

> I sat there gazing at them, and they were coming from the
> place where the giant lives [north]. But when they were very
> close to me, they wheeled about toward where the sun goes
> down, and suddenly they were geese. Then they were gone,

and the rain came with a big wind and a roaring. I did not tell
this vision to anyone. I liked to think about it, but I was afraid
to tell it. (J.G. Neihardt, *Black Elk Speaks*, page 16)

However, when he was nine, Black Elk had a long and very complex series of visions, in which he met his 'Grandfathers', who
were actually 'the Powers of the World'. While he was undergoing
this alteration in consciousness, he was treated by a medicine-man
named Black Road. When he told Black Road what had happened
to him, the old medicine-man told him he would have to perform
his vision for all to see. The mythic encounter would have to be
'grounded'.

When he was 17, Black Elk performed a 'horse dance', in
which he repeated the songs he had been given in his visions. As
Nevill Drury writes in *The Elements of Shamanism*, at one point
during the dance, all the horses in the village seemed to neigh in
unison; and Black Elk, on looking up to the skies, saw his vision
again. The Six Grandfathers were looking down upon him once
more.

It was as if the mythic world and the physical world had
become one. . . . Here was dramatic confirmation of Black
Elk's ceremonial undertaking to share his visions with his
people. Clearly the Grandfathers had observed the ritual
re-enactment and were well pleased. (Drury, page 69)

When the horse dance was over, Black Elk felt as if he were walking above the ground, rather than upon it. All the people in the
village were very happy, some saying that they or their relatives
who had been feeling ill were now well again. 'Even the horses
seemed to be healthier and happier after the dance,' adds Drury.

Shamans like Black Elk performed (and still perform) a vitally
important function within their cultures, in which ongoing interaction with the subtle but immensely powerful world of nature
and its spiritual denizens is of great significance in everyday life.
It would be a grave mistake to look with amusement or conde-
scension upon a shaman asking permission of spirits to hunt their
animals. For interaction with the spiritual aspects of existence,
through the offices of one qualified to do so, is as familiar a
concept in our own culture as in those in North America or
Siberia.

Since prayer is the act of communing with the Divine or the supernatural, our own religious consciousness also depends on a group of people who act as intermediaries between the average member of our society and the supernatural (whether qualified as God, the Creator, or the First Cause, etc.). As Rosemary Ellen Guiley states in her *Harper's Encyclopedia of Mystical & Paranormal Experience*, prayers may 'acknowledge a supreme deity; a pantheon of deities, saints, and divine personages; ancestral spirits; or the spirits and forces of nature'. However, while the act of prayer can be and is performed by millions of private individuals every day, there are many occasions when matters of a spiritual, ethical or social nature require consultation between the individual and a representative of the religion to which the individual belongs.

This may seem obvious, but it is important to emphasize the reliance that the human species, throughout its history, has placed upon the teachings and advice of these intermediaries, be they priests or shamans, gurus or cult leaders. We hunger, as did our ancestors, to approach the divine, the non-material; we have a powerful and firmly entrenched need to become aware of the meaning of our existence in this apparently empty universe. And for that awareness, we look to the priests and the shamans and others to help us. Who among us would not like to undergo an experience similar to Black Elk's, in which the machinery of reality is revealed; in which nature is apprehended as the just and magnificent and *meaningful* thing that it is?

Of course, such revelations are not experienced by everyone; and so, throughout the world, human beings trust in the guidance and teachings of those who are better qualified to speak with authority on matters divine or supernatural . . .

It seems clear enough that the so-called 'developed world' is becoming more and more secularized: in the United Kingdom, for instance, only about 4 per cent of the population attend church on a regular basis. I would argue that this decline in religious sensibility is due not so much to a turning away from the spiritual *per se*, but rather is a result of a world-view that is subtly shifting away from notions of a single, supreme deity towards a less well-defined, more nebulous awareness of an 'alternative' reality, one that can intersect with and influence our own.

With the continued and accelerating advancement of science, it seems natural that some should echo Laplace's sentiments, and feel no need to include the 'God-hypothesis' in their world-view.

That these sentiments should begin to spread among the rest of us, as knowledge about our world and the surrounding universe increases, seems natural also. However, when the concept of God is eroded and ultimately dispensed with, it leaves a void which the human mythic imagination refuses to tolerate.

Even a cursory examination of the relevant literature shows that alleged encounters with the paranormal and supernatural are as common today as they ever were; moreover, they generate just as much interest. One has only to look at the number of television programmes that are based, in one way or another, on 'the unexplained' (particularly in the United States), to see that interest in such subjects is deep and wide-ranging.

The huge numbers of books that are published and sold, the television programmes that are watched by millions, prove that we still need to wonder at the vast and shadowy world of the supernatural, to ask whether those enchanting shadows can ever be dispelled by the cold glare of science. The mythic imagination, the essential faculty that has guided and overseen our cultural development since the first appearance of consciousness itself, must be nourished and sustained, even in the face of an increasingly scientific and empirical world view.

With the continued development of ufology over the past five decades, in which the flying saucer has become one of the century's most powerful icons, it seems that we have found a new set of core beliefs with which to apprehend the universe and our likely place in it.

As with the shaman, who is called to mediate between physical reality and the deeper reality of the supernatural realm, those who encounter non-humans seem to be influenced by similar (if not identical) processes. These processes serve to deconstruct the rigid and narrow Aristotelian world-view which prevails in twentieth-century Western culture. This either/or dichotomy is gradually being eroded to make way for a 'more fluid and semantically fruitful' mode of experiential existence (Thompson, page 186).

It remains frustratingly unclear where the origin of these processes lies. Perhaps this lack of clarity is a function intrinsic to them. The origin may lie somewhere within the human mind; or it may lie with an intelligence that is separate from humanity. Whitley Strieber has speculated that non-human encounters might well be what evolution looks like when applied to a conscious species.

PART THREE

CONSPIRACY CENTRAL

FIVE

Fallen Angels

A T THIS POINT, we must turn our attention to an area of the alleged alien presence that has grown over recent years into a vast and sinister network of truths, half-truths and rumours, including everything from crashed alien spacecraft to experiments in teleportation, from shadowy secret societies to slave labour on other planets. I doubt that anyone could have foreseen the direction the subject of ufology has taken, especially in view of the benign and spiritually uplifting nature of the initial non-human contacts of the 1950s, and yet the antecedents to these developments have been present throughout the last hundred years or so.

In keeping with the established paradoxical nature of the UFO phenomenon, highly impressive and well-documented cases are frequently presented in the literature alongside lurid and unsubstantiated tales that read like the contents of a science fiction writer's waste-basket. In fact, these cases are valuable, not so much for what they tell us about UFOs, but for what they tell us about the mythopoeic capacity of the human mind in the late twentieth century. I therefore present a broad range of material, traversing the full spectrum of credibility, and attempt to examine the possible reasons for the rise to prominence of the more outrageous reports and theories.

I will begin in this chapter with what is probably the best documented and most intriguing UFO event ever reported.

THE ROSWELL UFO CRASH-RETRIEVAL

Although the large number of books and articles that have been written about this event might have justified giving it merely a cursory mention, much new information has recently come to light, thanks to the tireless efforts of Kevin D. Randle and Donald R. Schmitt. Their 1991 book *UFO Crash at Roswell* had already provided what is perhaps the definite account of what happened on that far-off summer night in New Mexico in 1947. However, in 1994 they published *The Truth About the UFO Crash at Roswell*, which contains much new and surprising material, including testimony from yet more firsthand witnesses.

On a recent trip to Roswell, I visited the International UFO Museum and Research Centre at 400 North Main Street. I watched a fascinating video presentation of the testimony of Jim Ragsdale, who saw the object come down on the evening of 4 July 1947. I also met Glenn Dennis, who worked at Ballard's Funeral Home at the time, and is one of the key witnesses to the event.

As might be expected of an investigation that has been conducted by numerous people over nearly two decades, the mass of information accumulated is daunting, to say the least, especially since some of it is contradictory. However, the diligent work of Randle and Schmitt represents the latest conclusions of the ongoing Roswell investigation; for this reason, and because of the additional testimony they have secured, I will follow their description of what happened.

The event that has come to be popularly known as 'The Roswell Incident' actually began on 1 July 1947, with the arrival of unidentified targets on the radar screens of the military facilities in Roswell, the White Sands Proving Ground and Alamogordo. The behaviour of these targets defied explanation in terms of conventional aviation.

The following evening, Mr and Mrs Dan Wilmot were sitting on the porch of their home in Roswell, when they saw a bright object flying overhead and heading in a northwesterly direction.

On 4 July a number of military observers from Washington DC arrived at White Sands in order to observe the radar traces that were still occurring over the Proving Ground. On the same evening, during a violent thunderstorm near Corona, New Mexico, rancher W.W. 'Mac' Brazel heard a loud explosion that seemed different from the accompanying thunderclaps.

Shortly before 11:30 pm, an object on the radar screens at the military facilities disintegrated in a 'starburst', leading the observers to conclude that it had crashed.

Jim Ragsdale and his companion, Trudy Truelove, had decided to go camping for the Fourth of July holiday weekend, and had driven north from Roswell on Highway 48 (now Pine Lodge Road). At about 11:30 pm, they were startled by the roaring passage overhead of a bright, glowing object, which ploughed into the ground about 1.5 km (1 mile) from their campsite.

Ragsdale convinced Truelove that they should search for whatever had crashed. Taking a torch, they drove across the rough terrain until they came to the edge of a low cliff. From this vantage point, they could see the wreckage of a strange object that had collided with the side of the cliff. Then the torch started to fail, so they decided to return to the campsite.

The following day, Saturday 5 July, a group of archaeologists working near Roswell discovered the crash site. One of them went back to town to inform the sheriff, George Wilcox. Wilcox then contacted the fire department, which despatched a truck to the site, about 56 km (35 miles) north of Roswell. The police were also notified, and accompanied the fire truck to the site.

The military also went to the scene, since their radar tracking of the object had told them its location. Finding the civilians there, they escorted them away from the area, and cleaned and secured it within six hours. Five bodies were discovered and removed.

Jim Ragsdale and Trudy Truelove had already driven back to the cliff edge and had got close enough to the wreckage to retrieve a few of the pieces. According to Ragsdale, 'You could take that stuff and wad it up and it would straighten itself out.' There was other wreckage that had the opposite properties: 'You could take it and put it into any form you wanted, and it would stay there. You could bend it in any form, and it would stay. It wouldn't straighten out,' (see Randle and Schmitt, *The Truth About the UFO Crash at Roswell*, page 9).

Ragsdale and Truelove also saw some bodies, which the former described as being like midgets, 1.3 to 1.5 metres (4 or 5 feet) tall. At this point, Trudy Truelove became very frightened, and insisted they leave. Ragsdale agreed, not least because they could now hear the approach of heavy vehicles.

Retreating to a safe distance, they watched as the military conducted their operations at the crash site. Before returning to their campsite, they discarded the pieces of wreckage they had collected, fearful that they would be arrested if they were discovered with it.

Meanwhile, Mac Brazel was out inspecting his pastures after the heavy rains of the night before, when he discovered a field of debris containing the now famous metal foil and I-beams. Brazel took a few pieces of the metal and went to his nearest neighbours, Floyd and Loretta Proctor, who suggested he take it into Roswell to show Sheriff Wilcox.

At 1:30 pm the phone rang at the Ballard Funeral Home in Roswell. Glenn Dennis picked it up and spoke to the Mortuary Officer at the Roswell Army Air Field.

'This is just a hypothetical situation,' he said, 'but do you have any 3-feet or 4-feet long hermetically sealed caskets?'

Dennis answered, 'Yes, we have 4 feet.'

'How many you got?'

'One.'

'How soon before you could get more?'

'If we called the warehouse in Amarillo, Texas, before 3 pm today, they can have them here tomorrow morning. Is there some kind of crash?' Glenn was curious, since the Ballard Funeral Home was contracted by the base to handle casualties from air crashes.

'No,' replied the base Mortuary Officer, 'this is just for our information.'

About an hour later, the officer called back, and again spoke to Glenn. Assuring him that there had been no crash, the officer asked, 'How do you handle bodies that have been exposed out in the desert?' (See John H. Sime, 'Funerals of Extraterrestrials: A Funeral Director Crosses Paths with a UFO in 1947' a pamphlet available from Roswell UFO Museum and Research Centre.)

Glenn went through the steps he would take to deal with bodies that had been burned or subjected to severe trauma. He recalls:

The next question was, what would you do where you wouldn't change any of the chemical contents, you wouldn't destroy any blood, you wouldn't destroy anything that might be very important down the road. What would your process, the chemicals you use, [do that] would change the chemical contents [of the blood]. (Randle and Schmitt, *The Truth About the UFO Crash at Roswell*, page 14)

The funeral home also handled ambulance facilities for the base, and later that day, Dennis was required to pick up an injured airman and take him back to the airfield. As he drove to the rear of the hospital, he saw three old field ambulances. On his way into the emergency room with the airman, he glanced into the backs of the ambulances, and saw some wreckage, part of which he described as being like the front part of a canoe.

Once inside, Dennis decided to go to the lounge for a Coke. One of the nurses spotted him and suggested he leave at once, otherwise he would get into trouble. She was too late, however: Dennis was spotted by an officer, who asked him what he was doing there. When he explained the situation, the officer told two MPs to get him out as fast as possible.

It was then that Dennis heard a voice say: 'I'm not through with that SOB yet. Bring him back.' The speaker was a red-haired captain, who told Dennis that there had been no crash and that 'he hadn't seen anything.'

Somewhat displeased at being called an SOB, Dennis informed the captain that he couldn't intimidate a civilian, and told him to go to hell. The captain replied, 'Don't kid yourself, young man. Somebody'll be picking your bones out of the sand.' Dennis was then escorted from the base and back to the funeral home.

On 7 July, Dennis contacted one of the nurses and asked to meet her. She agreed to meet him at the officers' club. Over lunch (which she could not bring herself to touch) she described how she had been asked by two doctors to take notes while they performed a preliminary autopsy on three small bodies. She said that it was the most horrible thing she had ever seen; she was still extremely distressed as she described to Dennis the awful stench that issued from the corpses, an odour that eventually drove even the doctors from the room.

According to the nurse, whose name has recently been established as Naomi Maria Seiff (see Timothy Good, *Beyond Top Secret: The Worldwide UFO Security Threat*, page 478), the beings had disproportionately large heads, with flexible skulls, like a baby's. The eyes were large and deep set; the noses were concave rather than convex; the mouths were just slits, with a hard, cartilaginous plate instead of teeth.

The nurse was so disturbed by what she had seen that Dennis suspected she was going into deep shock. After giving him a sketch of the dead beings, she excused herself and returned to the barracks. Dennis never saw her again. Subsequent enquiries revealed that Seiff was later transferred to England, where she died in a plane crash during a training mission. According to Timothy Good, no evidence for such a crash has ever been found (Good, page 478).

The previous day (Sunday, 6 July), Mac Brazel had taken some of the debris to Sheriff Wilcox, who was intrigued and suggested he contact Roswell Army Air Field.

Colonel William Blanchard, commanding officer of the 509th, Bomb Group, ordered Major Jesse A. Marcel, air intelligence officer, to interview Brazel at the sheriff's office and examine the material. A look at the material convinced Marcel that it would be worth examining the crash site. After returning to Roswell Army Air Field to brief Blanchard, Marcel escorted Brazel back to his ranch. Captain Sheridan Cavitt, the senior counter-intelligence agent assigned to the base, accompanied them.

Meanwhile, Colonel Blanchard obtained some of the debris from the sheriff's office. The debris was sealed in a courier pouch and flown to Washington DC via Fort Worth Army Air Field.

On Monday, 7 July, Brazel took Marcel and Cavitt to the crash site, which was 1280 metres (three quarters of a mile) long and 60 to 90 metres (200 to 300 feet) wide. They loaded Marcel's car and Cavitt's Jeep with pieces of the light but incredibly tough debris, and drove back to Roswell.

Additional firsthand testimony came from Jesse Marcel Jr, who says that at 2 am on 8 July, Major Marcel arrived at his house and woke his family, so that they might take a look at the extraordinary material he had collected.

By 11 am, first Lieutenant Walter Haut had finished the press release he had been ordered to write. He took it into Roswell and gave it to two radio stations and the two daily newspapers. By around 2:30 pm, the story had been picked up by the AP wire, and the world was about to know that a 'flying disc' had been discovered.

Marcel was ordered to fly the debris to Wright Field (now Wright-Patterson Air Force Base) at Dayton, Ohio, for analysis. The B-29 made a stopover at Fort Worth Army Air Field, where General Roger Ramey took charge and ordered a press release stating that the debris was nothing more unusual than the wreckage from a weather balloon. Parts of a weather balloon and its attached tin foil radar target were promptly displayed at a press conference.

While this deception was being carried out, the genuine Roswell wreckage arrived at Wright Field. Marcel was sent back to Roswell AAF, while Mac Brazel was interrogated by the military for nearly a week. This resulted in Brazel changing his story concerning the wreckage, and ensured his virtually total silence on the subject for the rest of his life.

According to Colonel Thomas DuBose, Chief of Staff to Major-General Roger Ramey at Fort Worth Army Air Field, in an interview with Kevin Randle and Donald Schmitt, 'We had orders from on high to ship the material directly to Wright Field by special plane . . . The weather balloon story was a complete fabrication designed to get the reporters present off Ramey's back in a hurry.'

That the genuine Roswell wreckage was flown in secret to Wright Field, was confirmed to Kevin Randle and Donald Schmitt by Brigadier-General Arthur Exon (retired), who became commander of the base in 1964. Exon also claims to have handled some of the material, which was subjected to numerous scientific tests (Good, page 465).

The most recent US Air Force explanation for the Roswell Incident concerns the testing of equipment under Project Mogul, a top secret project aimed at detecting Soviet nuclear tests. As Timothy Good makes clear, the witnesses' description of the wreckage does tie in, to a certain extent, with materials used in the Mogul equipment, implying that a Mogul balloon may well have come down near Roswell. However, this explanation does not explain all the facts; furthermore, Major Marcel was familiar with balloon wreckage, and was adamant that the material he handled had not come from a terrestrial device.

It has been mooted that the military came up with the crashed disc story in a misguided attempt to divert attention away from the top secret nature of the debris, and then discovered that this story only compounded their problems. This does not sound very plausible, since it would have been simplicity itself to state at the outset that the wreckage came from an ordinary weather balloon, without concocting a bizarre cover story involving crashed alien spaceships.

FROM THE SUBLIME TO THE RIDICULOUS?

The concept of crashed UFOs first gained widespread exposure through the writings of *Variety* columnist Frank Scully, whose 1950 book *Behind the Flying Saucers* became a bestseller in the USA. Scully's work is very well known in ufological circles, but widely regarded as being of little value. I will, however, provide an overview of Scully's claims, since they offer a valuable lesson about the dangerous ease with which unsubstantiated information (and outright hoaxes) can be accepted at face value, if only temporarily.

Scully's chief source of information was one Silas Newton, a wealthy businessman who worked in the oil industry. Newton had given a lecture to 350 students at the University of Denver on 8 March 1950. According to Newton, three alien spacecraft crashed in North America in 1948. One of the craft allegedly came down near the town of Aztec, New Mexico. The object was said to be 99.99 feet (30.5 metres) in diameter, a measurement that sounds mysterious and intriguing until one realizes that alien calibrations would surely have nothing to do with feet and inches. It was made of a light metal similar to aluminium, but which was able to withstand temperatures up to 10,000° F. Entry into the disc was eventually effected by means of a small lever that was manipulated through a crack in one of the portholes, revealing a hidden door.

A crew of 16 was discovered – all of them dead – inside the disc. The investigators were able to dismantle the machine, and found that it was made up of segments which fitted in grooves and were pinned together around the base.

According to Scully, Silas Newton had been given this information by one of the scientists who had examined the disc and its crew. The scientist was given the pseudonym 'Dr Gee' by Newton, who claimed that he was actually a composite character based on several scientists involved with the retrieval.

Although *Behind the Flying Saucers* enjoyed tremendous success, selling 60,000 hardback copies in its first two years, that success was not to last. The book was utterly discredited by J.P. Cahn, a journalist with the *San Francisco Chronicle*, who had set up a meeting with Scully and Silas Newton.

The meeting took place at the Palace Hotel in San Francisco. Cahn had brought along Scott Newhall, also of the *Chronicle*. During the meeting, Newton produced a handkerchief containing two metallic discs about the size of a five-cent coin, and two fine-toothed gears a little over twice that size. Later, Newton produced several photographs, which he placed on his lap face down. This dramatic effect was not lost on Cahn. When Newton revealed the photographs, Cahn saw that they showed desert scenes. 'That's where the first saucer landed,' said Newton.

At one point, Cahn caught a brief glimpse of one photograph that Newton hadn't shown them. It appeared to show a disc-shaped object lying on its side. This was another piece of Newton theatrics obviously staged for Cahn's benefit.

In order to get to the bottom of the mystery, Cahn decided to pull an audacious stunt. His intention was to procure one of the small discs Newton had shown him, without the latter's knowledge, and then to have it analysed.

Scott Newhall produced several fake discs of similar appearance to Newton's, so that a switch might be effected. While trying to set up another meeting with Newton, Cahn investigated the man's background, and discovered that he had been arrested twice in the 1930s for grand larceny and false securities statements, although these charges were dismissed.

Cahn then decided to take a look at Newton's telephone records, and noticed that he was making a lot of calls to one Leo A. GeBauer in Phoenix, Arizona. According to Newton, the mysterious Dr Gee lived in Phoenix.

It was then that Newton finally agreed to a meeting. He showed Cahn the discs again and, with admirable sleight of hand, Cahn managed to substitute one of his fakes for one of Newton's discs. He then took the disc to the Stanford Research Institute, where a comprehensive analysis was conducted. Newton's 'alien' disc was revealed to consist of aluminium, of the type used in pots and pans.

When Frank Scully was confronted with this information, he identified Dr Gee as Leo GeBauer and agreed to help Cahn expose the hoax. GeBauer claimed to hold degrees from the Armour Institute, Creighton University and the University of Berlin, but subsequently admitted that his only qualification was a degree in engineering from the Louis Institute of Technology. Scully had claimed that GeBauer had led 1,700 scientists doing 35,000 experiments with a budget of $1 billion in top-secret magnetic research. In fact, GeBauer had only been a maintenance man at the AiResearch Company. He also denied being Dr Gee.

Cahn took this evidence to Scully. The writer's response was an angry letter and even angrier phone call.

When Cahn's article was published in *True* magazine, the publication began to receive letters from people who had been conned over the years by Newton and GeBauer. The duo had sold worthless stocks and fake machines, but had escaped justice by virtue of the three-year statute of limitations.

However, a chance to bring Newton and GeBauer to book at last came in the person of a Denver millionaire named Herman Flader. He had lost a total of $231,452 in various scams involving bogus oil-detecting equipment which, according to Newton and GeBauer, worked on the same principles as flying saucers, but were actually surplus US Army radio-transmitter tuning units. Flader was able to provide proof in the form of cancelled cheques which had been signed by Newton and GeBauer; some of them were dated within the three-year statute of limitations. Flader agreed to press charges, along with Herman Corsun, a Phoenix delicatessen owner who had been conned out of $3350 by GeBauer.

Charges of conducting a confidence game were filed against Newton and GeBauer on 10 October 1952. The trial began on 10 November 1953. Both men were found guilty.

For Scully's part, he wrote to Cahn:

> My chief witnesses as you describe them have not repudiated
> one sentence of *Behind the Flying Saucers*. Dr Gee was a
> composite of 8 different scientists, whose stories were tape
> recorded and then synthesized by me where they were in
> substantial agreement. (Peebles, pages 80–84)

A HYPOTHETICAL LANDING?

If some reports of landed alien spacecraft can be clearly shown to be hoaxes, others are less amenable to such mundane explanations. Of course, this may be because of the lack of documented information, which in turn could be due to a number of reasons. There may be no documented information available because there *is* none outside the fertile imagination of whoever is presenting the report; on the other hand, it may be that documentary evidence has been suppressed by the authorities, who are eager to hide their knowledge (or their ignorance) of what has happened.

One of the most curious cases of alleged alien contact was presented by Robert Emenegger in his 1974 book *UFOs Past, Present and Future*, which was published in conjunction with a documentary film of the same title. In a chapter entitled 'On Being Contacted', Emenegger presents an incident which, as he coyly puts it, 'might happen in the future – or perhaps could have happened already'. According to Emenegger, the incident happened (or will happen) at Holloman Air Force Base in New Mexico. At 5:30 am, an unidentified flying object approaches the base from the southwest. It does not respond to requests for identification, prompting a red alert. By chance, cameramen and technical personnel from the base photographic team are aboard a helicopter on a routine photographic assignment at the time, and they manage to film a trio of objects hovering in the sky above the base. A second camera crew, which has been filming a test launch, also film the objects as one of them breaks formation and descends towards the ground. The events are captured on approximately 180 metres (600 feet) of 16 mm colour film.

The UFO hovers about 3 metres (10 feet) above the ground for nearly a minute, and then lands on its tripod undercarriage. The base commander, along with two officers and two scientists, arrives at the scene and waits in trepidation for the next development. A panel in the UFO's hull slides open and three beings disembark from the craft. Dressed in tight-fitting jumpsuits, the visitors are short, with blue-grey complexions, wide-set eyes and prominent noses. They wear strange, rope-like headpieces.

The base commander, officers and scientists greet the beings and arrange, through 'some inaudible sort of communication', to take them to 'the end of Mars Street to the west area building number 930' (see Emenegger, *UFOs Past, Present and Future*, pages 127–9).

The putative year of this occurrence is 1964, although this is open to debate. Emenegger presented 'the Holloman scenario' to five leading American social psychologists, who were asked to draw up a report on the likely reaction of the public, should incontrovertible evidence ever be released.

As might be expected, their opinions differed somewhat. Dr Elliot Aronson of the University of Texas declared that very few people would react in an extreme way; there would be very little panic of the kind that greeted Orson Welles' infamous radio adaption of *The War of the Worlds*, mainly because the social and political situation in 1974 was markedly different from what it had been in 1938. In 1974, there was no 'clear and present danger' to which the concept of alien visitation could be attached in the public mind; hence, the arrival of aliens would, according to Aronson, 'not be terribly startling to most people', especially since the Holloman scenario describes friendly communication between the government and the visitors (Emenegger, page 131).

Aronson concluded that the public could basically be broken down into two types of individual: the person who had always been committed to a belief in intelligent alien life and thought that UFOs represent a real phenomenon; and the person who had always dismissed the notion of UFOs and intelligent humanoid life in outer space as nonsense. The former would calmly accept the evidence presented as confirming previously held beliefs; the latter would suspect a hoax of some kind, regardless of whether or not the government was involved. Ironically, this would, in effect, be the very opposite of the situation that gave rise to the panic inspired by the radio adaption of *The War of the Worlds*. Instead of the 'clear and present danger' of the approach of World War Two resulting in an unquestioning belief that a powerful enemy (the Martians) had arrived to enslave the planet, the skeptic would assume, even in the face of apparently incontrovertible evidence to the contrary, that the government had faked the alien contact for their own nefarious purposes, possibly to divert attention from the Watergate scandal or the energy crisis, for example.

It is clear that with the Holloman landing we have entered the most intriguing – and frustrating – area of the field of alleged alien contact: the shadowy realm of rumour that can be neither proved or refuted beyond reasonable doubt. At first glance, it might seem that the Holloman scenario is nothing more than that: a hypothetical situation acting as a jumping-off point for psychological speculations on the public reaction to proof of extra-terrestrial intelligence, should it ever appear.

And yet, in her 1995 book *UFO Retrievals: The Recovery of Alien Spacecraft*, Jenny Randles tells us that she asked Robert Emenegger for his opinion on the evidence for alien contact. He replied, 'from my information it [an alien landing] has happened in May of 1971 . . . other reports put it also on 30 December 1980 in England, both at military bases' (*UFO Retrievals*, pages 97–8).

As Randles states, the 1980 event is the famous Rendlesham Forest incident, in which the arrival of an anomalous object was witnessed by military personnel from the joint RAF/USAF Woodbridge base. Could the 1971 event have been the Holloman landing?

The strange and frightening realms of rumour (hard to sub-stantiate, yet hard to dismiss) permeate the entire field of ufology, and we shall be plunging headlong into them in Chapter 9. Constant vigilance is essential when studying the subject of ufolo-gy. It is easy to be seduced by rumour, which erodes impartiality and replaces it with a self-feeding paranoia. In a memorable scene from the popular television series *The X Files*, FBI agent Dana Scully warns her colleague Fox Mulder; 'The truth *is* out there, but so are lies.' However, we should not forget that the truth consists of the mundane as well as the unusual. An example of this is another famous UFO event, the Kecksburg incident, which, in spite of its apparent strangeness, seems more amenable to a non-alien explanation than a genuine UFO incident.

WHAT CRASHED AT KECKSBURG?

Although not quite as well known as Roswell, the Kecksburg inci-dent is still one of the more intriguing and better documented of the so-called 'crash-retrievals'. However, the question remains: did an alien spacecraft really land there? And if not, what did?

Kecksburg is a small rural community in Westmoreland Country, Western Pennsylvania, USA. Just over 30 year ago, on 9 December 1965, an object allegedly crashed to Earth in a wooded area near the town, causing local witnesses to fear that an aircraft had met with disaster.

In fact, earlier that afternoon there had been reports of a large fire-ball hurtling through the sky over Canada, as well as parts of Michigan, Indiana, Ohio and Pennsylvania. According to Stan Gordon of the Pennsylvania Association for the Study of the Unexplained (PASU), who has been investigating this case for many years, the fire-ball was seen by a large number of people and caused much excitement as it passed over the Pittsburgh and Greensburg areas.

At about 4:47 pm, the object apparently touched down in a wooded ravine near Kecksburg, its bright glow giving rise to the fears of a downed aircraft. Local authorities later verified that no aircraft were missing. Nevertheless, debris reported to have fallen from the object started fires near Elyria, Ohio.

John Murphy, the news director at radio station WHJB in Greensburg, Pennsylvania, was contacted some time after 6:30 pm by Frances Kalp, who told him that the object had crashed into the woods near her home. Murphy decided to alert Troop A of the Pennsylvania State Police, who in turn arranged to meet Francis Kalp at the crash site. It was at about this time that volunteer fire-fighters began to search the woods for signs of crashed aircraft.

John Murphy left for the scene as soon as Kalp had informed him of what had happened. There he saw the state police fire marshal, Carl Metz, and a state investigator, Paul Shipco, enter the woods with a yellow Geiger counter and flashlights. While the search was going on, Murphy took the opportunity to interview Frances Kalp and her children.

About 15 minutes later, Metz and Shipco returned from the woods. They were curiously reticent about whatever they had discovered there. When Murphy asked Metz if he had found anything, the latter replied, 'I'm not sure.' Noting his puzzled expression, Murphy rephrased the question. 'After you make your report to the [state police] captain, do you think that you or the captain may have something to tell me?'

Metz replied, 'You'd better get your information from the army.'

This mention of the army was surprising, given the apparent nature of the event (a fire of uncertain origin). Murphy called Captain Joseph Dussia of the Pennsylvania State Police, who advised him to go to the Troop A state police barracks in Greensburg, where a joint statement would probably be made by the police and the US Army.

Although Captain Dussia told Murphy that a search of the woods had revealed absolutely nothing, Metz declared that he was going back out with members of the military to continue searching. At that point, a state police trooper arrived, and reported that he had witnessed a pulsating blue light in the woods. When Murphy suggested he accompany Metz and the military personnel, he was very firmly told that that would not be possible.

Access to the crash site within the woods was poor, and the few dirt roads leading to it were soon clogged with the cars of radio and television reporters and crews. Some of them managed to get fairly close to the site, and reported that the state police had cordoned off a section of the woods.

However, Stan Gordon managed to interview a volunteer fire-fighter named Jim Romansky, who claimed to have got to the crash site before the area had been sealed off. Romansky stated that the object that had impacted into a stream bed was not a meteorite. Rather, according to Romansky, it was a manufactured object, shaped like an acorn and 3 to 4 metres (9 to 12 feet) in diameter. Close to the bottom of the object, Romansky saw a gold-coloured, bumper-like protrusion, covered with curious writing. 'There were no wings, motors, or a fuselage, as we know them,' he said. He described the writing as resembling 'ancient Egyptian hieroglyphics'.

Romansky's story was corroborated by another witness whom Gordon and other members of PASU managed to interview. Bill Bulebush saw the object's final approach to Earth while he was working on his car. The object described a number of S-turns in the sky before vanishing among the trees. Bulebush immediately set off to investigate, and discovered an area in the woods that was illuminated by 'arc-welding flames and bluish sparklers'.

Using a torch (it had since become dark), he examined the object from a distance of about 4.5 metres (15 feet). He also described it as acorn-shaped, with a gold band around the bottom, and roughly 3.5 metres (12 feet) long and about 2 metres (6 or 7 feet) in diameter.

Romansky described the arrival of men in 'business suits' whom he assumed were the military, and who ordered the fire-fighters to leave the area. Then a military flatbed truck arrived. Several hours later, the truck left the area, carrying a large, bell-shaped object covered with a tarpaulin.

A small farmhouse near the impact site was commandeered by the military as a command centre for the duration of the event. Recent information suggests that the object was transported that night to Lockborne Air Force Base in Columbus, Ohio, for a short time. The object was then transported to Wright-Patterson Air Force Base in Dayton, Ohio. According to informants, the object was sealed up under special conditions inside a building. Its present location is unknown.

That *something* fell to Earth at Kecksburg is undeniable. The question is, what was it? It has been confirmed that a malfunctioning Soviet Venus probe, KOSMOS 96, re-entered the Earth's atmosphere above Canada at 3:18 am on the day of the discovery at Kecksburg, which led to speculation that this was actually what was recovered. However, there are problems with this explanation. The US Air Force Foreign Technology Division at Wright-Patterson Air Force Base denied that they had retrieved a Soviet spacecraft. Apparently, the Soviet Embassy also denied that the crash was part of the KOSMOS 96. According to Stan Gordon, the US Space Command reported that KOSMOS 96 re-entered the atmosphere *and* crashed in Canada at 3:18 am – 13 hours before the events reported at Kecksburg.

Apparently associated discoveries were made in Lapeer (Michigan) County, which tied in with observations of a fire-ball travelling across the sky before the crash at Kecksburg. A deputy in the sheriff's department, Lanny Tolly, found several handfuls of a substance similar to foil in the area where witnesses had reported seeing something come down. It was later revealed by analysis to be common household aluminium foil.

According to Eric T. Jonchkhiere, the Air Force deputy for technology and subsystems at Wright-Patterson Air Force Base, who wrote to Lapeer sheriff Kenneth A. Parks on 28 December 1965, the material that had been submitted for analysis was actually radar chaff. The letter states: 'This material is dropped by aircraft to confuse radar complexes when participating in interdiction exercises. "Chaff" can travel for many miles, depending on wind currents and wind velocities.'

Another possible explanation is that the fire-ball and associated material resulted from a meteorite entering the atmosphere. The fire-ball was described as having a 'train', which could have been caused by ionized air. According to Kevin D. Randle, who examines the Kecksburg incident in his book *A History of UFO Crashes*, this could account for the descriptions of the object as 'hovering or landing'.

However, as Randle also states, one of the most interesting aspects of the incident is the presence at the scene of a team of operatives from Project Moon Dust. Documents recovered by Clifford Stone of Roswell and Robert Todd of Pennsylvania, through the Freedom of Information Act, describe an official government project that operated from the mid-1960s through to the 1980s. The project was 'used in cases involving the examination of non-US space objects or objects of unknown origin'.

One such document, from the Department of the Air Force, dated 3 November 1961, says that the Project Moon Dust teams 'are comprised of three men each, to include a linguist, a tech man, and an ops man. All are airborne qualified.' The document continues:

Peacetime employment of AFCIN intelligence team capability is provided for in UFO investigation (AFR 200-2) and in

support of Air Force Systems Command (AFSC) Foreign
Technology Division (FTD) Projects Moon Dust and Blue Fly.
These three peacetime projects all involve a potential for
employment of qualified field intelligence personnel on a
quick reaction basis to recover or perform field exploitation of
unidentified flying objects, or known Soviet/Bloc aerospace
vehicles, weapons systems, and/or residual components of
such equipment.

The documents retrieved by Stone and Todd go on to describe in
greater detail the definitions applied to the members of each three-
man team:

a. Linguist: Personnel who can develop intelligence
information through interrogation and translation from Russia
and/or Bloc country languages in English.
b. Tech Man: Personnel qualified to develop intelligence
information through field examination and analysis of foreign
material, with emphasis on the Markings Program and
technical photography.
c. Ops Man: Intelligence team chief. Qualified to direct
intelligence teams in gaining access to target, in exploitation
of enemy personnel and material, and in use of field
communications equipment for rapid reporting of intelligence
information.
d. Airborne Personnel: Military trained and rated parachutists.
e. Unidentified Flying Objects (UFO): Headquarters USAF has
established a program for investigation of reliably reported
unidentified flying objects within the United States. AFR 200-2
delineates 1127th collection responsibilities.
f. Blue Fly: Operation Blue Fly has been established to
facilitate expeditious delivery to FTD [Foreign Technology
Division] of Moon Dust or other items of great technical
intelligence interest. AFCIN SOP for Blue Fly operations,
February 1960, provides for 1127th participation.
g. Moon Dust: As a specialized aspect of its over-all material
exploitation program, Headquarters USAF has established
Project Moon Dust to locate, recover and deliver descended
foreign space vehicles. ICGL #ns4, 25 April 1961, delineates
collection responsibilities.

Randle comments:

> What this means is that the government, more specifically the
> air force, has a contingency plan to deal with the retrieval of
> material from space. It is clearly outlined, and part of that
> responsibility surrounds UFO material, which means anything
> that is unidentified and could therefore be of extra-terrestrial
> manufacture. (Randle, page 161)

A three-man team (possibly Project Moon Dust) *was* dispatched to
the Kecksburg woods to investigate the landing, according to the
Project Blue Book files, thus vindicating the claims of various witnesses who said that they saw a number of military men, some of
whom were wearing white 'moon suits'.

The Project Blue Book files prove that the Air Force and other
government agencies took a great deal of interest in what happened at Kecksburg. A three-man team from the 662nd Radar
Squadron, which was then based in Pittsburgh, was involved with
the search. As Stan Gordon notes, even though the presence of
these personnel was verified by the newspaper accounts and Air
Force report, there is no mention of this activity in their records.
The implication is that this mission was classified.

Gordon has received information stating that a search was conducted by combined intelligence centre officials of the US Space
Command/NORAD intelligence data centre, but that this search
'revealed no unusual re-entry phenomena which would have triggered a special recovery or search activity in the designated region
during the period of Dec. 1–15, 1965'. He adds, however, that the
official contacted indicated 'that the records from 30 years ago may
not be reliable'.

Gordon describes the US Government's position on the
Kecksburg event thus: 'Officially the military has completely
denied any involvement directly or indirectly with any events surrounding the Kecksburg area on the evening of Dec. 9, 1965.' In
view of the Air Force's own records, not to mention the eyewitness
reports of military personnel being present, this doesn't quite ring
true.

That something crashed in Western Pennsylvania in 1965 can
scarcely be denied. However, in the absence of any further information, we will have to err on the side of caution and chalk this
one up to a spacecraft of Earthly origin.

LAS VEGAS, 1962

The Las Vegas crash of 18 April 1962 is one of the lesser-known cases in the annals of ufology, and yet it is one of the most impressive. In fact, in *A History of UFO Crashes*, Kevin D. Randle cites it as one of only two cases he has examined that can be said to be definitely authentic based on the research thus far conducted, the other being Roswell, (discussed above).

The Las Vegas incident began with the sighting of an object over Oneida, New York. It was flying in a westerly direction, and was soon seen over Kansas and Colorado. It brightly illuminated the streets of Reno, Nevada, and then turned towards Las Vegas, where it was tracked on the radar screens of Nellis Air Force Base. After flaring brightly, the object vanished from the screens at an altitude of 3000 metres (10,000 feet) (This is reminiscent of descriptions of the Roswell object disappearing from the radar screens after exploding in a 'sunburst'.)

The object was seen by thousands of witnesses as it crossed virtually the entire United States, but the Air Force dismissed the sighting as being the result of a bolide (a meteoric fire-ball). If the object *was* a bolide, it had the authorities as spooked as the civilians who had seen it streaking across the night sky. The North American Air Defense Command in Colorado Springs, Colorado, picked up the object on radar as it flew over Oneida and headed into the Midwest. A number of Air Force bases were alerted, and Luke AFB (near Phoenix, Arizona) went so far as to scramble fighters to intercept the intruder.

According to reports, the object touched down briefly near Eureka, Utah, disrupting an electrical power plant nearby, before returning to the sky and continuing west. It seems that the 'explosion' seen on the radar screens represented an actual explosion, which was witnessed by a large number of people in the region of Mesquite, Nevada. A search and rescue team was despatched from the Clark County Sheriff's Office, but found nothing to indicate that any kind of aircraft had crashed.

Researcher Kevin Randle, (who is probably the leading authority on UFO crash-retrievals) checked the files of Project Blue Book, now held in the National Archives in Washington, DC. He discovered that on 18 April 1962, there had indeed been a radar sighting at Nellis Air Force Base, and that although the sighting had, at first, been labelled as unidentified, that designation had later been changed to 'Insufficient Data for a Scientific Analysis' (Randle, page 81).

However, after a further search through the files, Randle discovered that a number of military officers had made reports on the object after the incident, one of whom, Captain Herman Gordon Shields, had been flying a C-119 aircraft over Utah. Shields reported that the cockpit of the aircraft had been lit from a source above the plane. Although the illumination was at first of a low intensity (leading the flight crew to assume it was from the landing lights of another aircraft), it gradually grew in brightness until it illuminated the ground 8 to 16 km (5 to 10 miles) around the plane. (Shields' craft was at an altitude of 2600 metres (8,500 feet).

Presently, the illumination decreased in intensity, revealing a cigar-shaped object flying to the left of Shields' plane. He said that the front part of the UFO was glowing very brightly, like a magnesium fire, while the aft section was of a yellowish colour, (Randle, page 83).

According to Air Force investigations, when the UFO came down near Eureka, Utah, it was bright enough to trip the photoelectric cells in the streetlights in the area.

On 8 May 1962, Dr J. Allen Hynek and Lieutenant-Colonel Robert Friend were sent to Utah to investigate the incident. After interviewing a number of witnesses, they came to the conclusion that a bolide had been responsible for the sightings.

However, Kevin Randle conducted a number of interviews with the principal witnesses, and their conflicting testimony regarding the UFO's direction of flight seems to imply that it changed course, which meteors do not do. In addition to this, the UFO disrupted the power supply as it flew over the town of Nephi, Utah.

That the military were extremely interested in the object's whereabouts is supported by Dan Johnson, who was working on his farm when the UFO flew over. Later, several men interviewed him and another witness, Maurice Memmott, who had been with him during the sighting, and asked him to show them where he thought the object had come to earth.

A number of residents of Nephi reported hearing loud explosions on the night of the UFO's arrival, perhaps 20 or 30 of them, strung together. After passing Nephi, the UFO changed course to the northwest and headed for Eureka, attracting the attention of yet more people as it did so.

Captain Shields' air crew was not the only one to spot the UFO during its flight. A Bonanza Air Lines pilot saw the object pass beneath his plane, which was flying at 3350 metres (11,000 feet). Several witnesses on the ground said that the object was flying at about 150 metres (500 feet) above them. According to Randle, this undermines the bolide theory, since the meteor would have been travelling at a low altitude for too long (Randle, page 89). The bolide theory is dealt a further blow by the fact that meteors are not normally tracked by radar: their ionized trails are sometimes detected, but they are represented on the radar screen as a streak, and not as a single moving point as described by the operators who tracked the Las Vegas object (Randle, page 90).

Responding to a letter from a New York resident, Major C.R. Hart of the Air Force public information office wrote:

> The official records of the Air Force list the 18 April 1962 Nevada sighting to which you refer as 'unidentified, insufficient data.' There is an additional note to the effect that 'the reported track is characteristic of that registered by a U-2 or a high balloon but there is insufficient data reported to fully support such an evaluation.' The phenomena reported was not intercepted or fired upon. (Project Blue Book Files, letter from Major Hart, SAFOI-3b, quoted in Randle, page 91)

As Randle states, the radar operator should have been able to tell the difference between a high-altitude balloon, with its erratic flight pattern in accordance with wind direction, and a jet aircraft under intelligent control. In addition to this, there are no records of a balloon launch or U-2 spy plane flight in that area at that time; even if there were, such mundane craft could not have accounted for the power disruption in Nephi, or that of several witnesses' cars.

Randle also quotes an unidentified Air Force officer, who entered the following in the Blue Book files:

> On April 18, 1962, the Air Force Defense Command was puzzled by an aerial object that exploded and seemed to be a meteor, but had the unique distinction of being tracked by radar 70 miles northwest of Las Vegas, Nevada in a blinding flash. An Air Force Defense Command alert reported the object was tracked and traced over New York, Kansas, Utah, Idaho, Montana, New Mexico, Wyoming, Arizona and

California, so that its light covered almost as much area as that created by the big hydrogen space bomb test held later in the Pacific hundreds of miles high. (Project Blue Book Files, quoted in Randle, pages 93–94)

What this strongly suggests is that the UFO was tracked by radar installations right across the United States, from New York to California. The Las Vegas sighting report tells us that the flight time of the UFO was 32 minutes, much longer than a meteor would take either to burn up in the atmosphere or hit the Earth. In other words, the UFO was travelling much too slowly to be a meteor. When we add this to the information we already have concerning the power cuts beneath the UFO's flight path, and the eyewitness reports from two independent air crews (not to mention the observers on the ground) regarding its altitude, we are left with the certainty that the UFO was not a natural phenomenon, but was almost certainly interplanetary in nature.

PHOTOGRAPHIC EVIDENCE

One of the most frustrating aspects of the entire field of ufology, and its associated field of alleged alien contact, is the lack of physical evidence to support the contention that the Earth is being visited by intelligent non-human beings, whatever their origin. For instance, with regard to photographic evidence, it is a sad fact that the more convincing a photograph appears, the greater is the danger of it being a hoax; conversely, the more hazy and insubstantial an object captured on film, the more likely it is to be a mundane object such as a bird or aircraft caught at a peculiar angle.

This may sound like a narrowly skeptical statement, but a truly open-minded attitude requires a willingness to accept that there have been a lot of photographic hoaxes in the past, and the vast majority have involved crystal-clear objects in close proximity to the camera. For a good example, we can look to the famous photographs taken by Paul Villa, photographs that still find their way into numerous UFO publications even today, and only occasionally as examples of fakery.

Villa took his pictures on 16 June 1963 and 18 April 1965 in Albuquerque, New Mexico. Undoubtedly, these photographs are among the most beautiful and striking of their kind on record, and show metallic, disc-shaped craft hovering in the air. According to

Villa, who claimed to be in telepathic contact with the crews of the ships, they came from the star group known as Coma Berenices.

I remember seeing these pictures for the first time when I was a young boy, looking through the illustrations in my uncle's UFO books in Genoa, Italy. My uncle has always been fascinated with this subject, and I can trace the genesis of my own interest in such matters to the warm afternoons I would spend each summer, poring over his extensive collection of UFO books. When I first saw Villa's photographs, I was astounded and delighted; they galvanized my young mind and instilled an intense curiosity about the mysteries of the universe that continues to this day.

It was therefore a bit of a disappointment when, years later, I read that Ground Saucer Watch, an organization based in Phoenix, Arizona that specializes in the scientific analysis of UFO photographs, had pronounced the Villa pictures fakes. The GSW computers proved that the spectacularly beautiful spacecraft from Coma Berenices were actually small models suspended close to the camera.

While still photographs of UFOs have always come under attack from skeptics (in some cases rightly so, as we have seen), there is reason to be optimistic that one day, incontrovertible proof will come in the form of camcorder footage. As technology continues to improve and prices continue to come down, more and more people are investing in hand-held video recorders. Switch on the television news any evening, and chances are that some of the footage shown in news reports will be credited to an amateur. In terms of ufology, this is a promising, development, not least because images on videotape are very much more difficult to fake than those on photographic stills.

One of the most impressive sightings captured on videotape was made by Tim Edwards, a restaurant owner in Salida, Colorado. Edwards took video footage of unidentified objects over a period of several months between 1995 and 1996. Edwards commented:

> The first experience was truly awesome. I felt deeply at the time that I was witnessing something of great scientific and historic importance for the world. I believe that the August 27th craft was sending a message to the world and wanted to be photographed, that its appearance was somehow just the beginning of more to come and that I was really fortunate to be part of it.

The object captured on video by Edwards is indeed very striking, appearing as a colossal cylinder hanging horizontally in the sky. The footage was analysed by Village Labs, a video and film laboratory in Glendale, Arizona. Village Labs subsequently issued a press release in which it said that the results of its analysis of the Edwards tapes were astounding. The release went on to state that the daylight taping of a very large UFO hovering at approximately 18,300 metres (60,000 feet) and travelling at approximately 16,000 kph (10,000 mph) displayed unprecedented movements and light activity, even for a UFO. The skeptics' initial response to the footage – that it merely showed an airship or blimp – was dismissed by Village Labs, which insisted that the object was a cylinder rather than an oblate spheroid, and that it was somewhere in the region of 1.5 km (1 mile) long.

Allegedly, a Village Labs staff consultant, formerly with the National Security Agency (NSA) in a top-secret intelligence position, has classified the Edwards UFO as an 'Alien Visitation Craft' or AVC, apparently an NSA term to designate a vehicle that is 'definitely not one of ours'.

People who encounter UFOs/aliens more than once always have a rough time at the hands of skeptics, and Tim Edwards is no exception. However, he maintains that the objects he has seen and filmed are not natural phenomena, and weight has been added to his claims by numerous other witnesses who have seen similar objects in the Colorado skies. Edwards says:

> This time, with dozens of witnesses here in Salida and many
> others that were hundreds of miles away who I have talked to
> over the phone, there is no denying that something very
> unusual is going on up there. It's not just me, my family and a
> few others here have seen it.

Whatever the true nature of the Edwards objects, ufologists all over the world are keeping a watchful eye on the ongoing Village Labs analysis of his video films.

SHATTERED CITIES IN THE SKY

The Face on Mars
In recent years, there has been a great deal of controversy regarding another type of photographic evidence. According to a number

of researchers, definite proof of extra-terrestrial activity *is* available in the form of photographs taken by American and Russian space probes. On the surfaces of Mars, the Moon and other planets in the solar system there are said to be artificial structures that could only have been built by intelligent alien beings.

The best-known and most vocal of these researchers is Richard Hoagland, head of the Mars Mission, which has recently been renamed the Enterprise Mission after the famous starship in *Star Trek* (their motto being 'To boldly go where maybe someone has gone before'). To label Hoagland a starry-eyed crank would be unfair; his qualifications are impressive. Since 1965, he has held several high posts at science museums and planetariums, and has also been a space consultant to NBC and CBS News. He was editor-in-chief at *Star and Sky* magazine, and conceived (with Eric Burgess, co-founder of the British Interplanetary Society) the plaque on the Pioneer space probe. Therefore, Hoagland is probably a man to be taken seriously, or at least not to be dismissed out of hand.

Anyone with the slightest interest in the subject of alien contact (and many with none whatsoever) will be aware of the so-called 'Face on Mars', also known as 'the Martian Sphinx', a 1.6-km (1-mile) long protruberance first photographed by the Viking probe as it passed over the region of Cydonia in 1976. In addition to this, Hoagland's analysis of the Viking images revealed several pyramid-like structures, and 'the Tholus', a circular mound featuring what looks suspiciously like a spiral ramp.

When the Viking pictures were first released by NASA, interest briefly centred on frame 35A72, which showed a landform resembling a humanoid face. NASA was quick to dismiss this interpretation, insisting that the curious image was nothing more than a 'trick of light and shadow'. However, Vince DiPietro and Greg Molenaar, engineers at the Goddard Space Flight Centre and computer-imaging experts, were so impressed that they searched the other 60,000 Viking frames until they discovered another photograph of the same image, but taken 35 orbits later and with the Sun at a different angle. With the aid of various computer-enhancement techniques, they were able to increase the resolution of the 'Face'. The results were stunning. It seemed that the Face had eye sockets complete with eyeballs, a mouth with discernible teeth and regularly spaced stripes that appeared to be a kind of headdress.

Since the orientation of the Face was directly upwards, Hoagland concluded that, if it had indeed been intelligently constructed, its function must have been to draw the attention of someone looking down from a great height, perhaps even from orbit. An examination of the surrounding landscape yielded even more amazing results: the presence of yet more apparently artificial structures, including a colossal five-sided pyramid (now known as the DiPietro Molenaar Pyramid) and the Tholus. In fact, an observer standing in the centre of what Hoagland has christened 'the City' would have a fine view of the Face across the Martian desert.

Hoagland suggests that not only are the structures artificial, but some may be hollow, raising the possibility that they were once living-quarters. In support of this theory, he cites the environmental conditions on Mars, for example the very low atmospheric pressure (about a hundredth that at sea-level on Earth). In order for any complex life-form to live in such a place, he reasons, some sort of artificial environment would have been essential.

Large, self-contained 'arcologies' or architectural ecologies have been proposed by Paolo Soleri. These would contain everything needed by a technological society, including factories, greenhouses, living and recreation areas and energy-generating equipment. An example of this kind of self-contained community can be found in Biosphere II in Arizona (Biosphere I being the Earth itself). The Martian structures are somewhat larger than Biosphere II (some of the 'pyramids' are 1.5 to 3.5 km (1 to 2 miles in diameter), but their vast size does suggest that they may have housed millions of inhabitants, perhaps the last representatives of a dying race.

Hoagland also discovered a complex geometric pattern linking many of the structures, one that further reinforces the notion that they were built with a definite purpose in mind. According to Hoagland, the geometry expresses two fundamental constants of nature: pi (the ratio of the circumference of a circle to its diameter) and e (the base of natural logarithms). Pi divided into e gives the ratio 0.865, a ratio that is present throughout the structures in the Cydonia complex. Hoagland states that the mathematical data encoded in the complex confirm certain predictions made by astrophysicists, in particular that spinning objects such as stars and planets should display energy upwellings at specific latitudes (19.5 degrees north or south). This angle is repeated throughout the Cydonia complex.

Hoagland then discovered a pattern ranging throughout the solar system, based on latitude 19.5 degrees. At this latitude on Earth lies the Hawaiian chain of volcanoes; on Mars we find the gigantic shield volcano Olympus Mons, the largest mountain in the solar system; on Jupiter there is the Great Red Spot, a storm system larger than the Earth. Hoagland therefore predicted that Voyager would reveal a spot on Neptune at latitude 19.5 degrees two weeks before the probe arrived at the planet. He was proved correct.

According to Hoagland, these discoveries represent the existence of a 'new physics', based on 'hyperdimensional mathematics'. As he reminds us, energy flows 'downhill' (from hot to cold, from higher to lower levels). He maintains that a spinning object, such as a star or planet, will exhibit energy anomalies as a result of its connection to higher and lower dimensions. The implication here is that whoever built the Cydonia complex was well aware of hyperdimensional physics, and was capable of utilizing the 'free energy' arriving from higher dimensions.

Given the state of apparent decay of the Martian complex, it seems almost certain that it was built a long time ago. Curious as to just how long ago, Hoagland experimented with a possible connection between the ground plan and the positions of the Sun and stars over the Cydonia plain. He projected a line of sight from a point at the exact centre of the city towards the eastern horizon, and discovered that the Sun would have risen on the summer solstice directly over the eyes of the Face approximately 500,000 years ago. Was this, then, the date of construction of the Cydonia complex? If so, does it mean that the Red Planet is now deserted?

The Mars Observer spacecraft was launched from Florida on 25 September 1992, and was to conduct a photo-reconnaissance of the entire planet from a near-polar orbit at 376 km (234 miles) above the surface. In order for the craft to enter the correct orbit, its thruster fuel tanks had to be pressurized; this necessitated temporarily shutting down the radio transmitter, so that its fragile components would be protected during pressurization. When this had been achieved, the mission controllers on Earth tried to switch the radio transmitter back on. Nothing happened. Neither was there any response from the Observer when instructed to activate its back-up transmitter. In desperation, the mission controllers decided to wait for five days, after which the spacecraft was programmed to signal Earth automatically with a request for commands. After five days, a hollow silence remained in the vicinity of Mars, where the the Observer had been.

Despite the decades of fierce competition between America and the Soviet Union, the Russians could feel only sympathy for NASA's loss of the Mars Observer. It was a disaster they themselves had experienced in March 1989, when their probe Fobos 2 was lost in Mars space. The Russian craft, however, managed to transmit some very intriguing – and unsettling – information before it was lost, information that might shed some light on what actually happened to the Mars Observer. While it was near the Martian moon Phobos, the probe photographed a large shadow on the surface. Moments later, it photographed the object that was casting the shadow, a bright, cigar-shaped object that was computed to have a length of 25 km (15½ miles)! The last images transmitted to Mission Control in Kaliningrad were of the thing altering its attitude so that it was facing the Fobos 2 probe. Contact was then permanently lost.

If we take this information at face value, it becomes at least possible that Fobos 2 was disabled by the gigantic, anomalous object it had photographed, either because it had entered the region of Mars, or of Phobos itself. It is tempting to speculate that the beings who built the Cydonia complex are still present in the solar system; but, given the nature of the complex and the information it apparently contains, this conclusion makes no sense. The Face on Mars seems to have been designed to draw attention (perhaps ours) to itself, implying an invitation to investigate. Why, then, would the Cydonian architects attack our spacecraft when we accepted that invitation? My own feeling is that the Cydonians are long gone, whether to elsewhere in the galaxy or to extinction is anyone's guess, and that the activity that seems to be continuing in the region of Mars indicates the presence of someone else.

In fact, Phobos itself is something of a mystery. First discovered, along with its companion Deimos, in August 1877 by the astronomer Asaph Hall at the United States Naval Observatory in Washington, DC, the Martian satellite does not behave in quite the way a natural object should. Nearly 70 years later, in 1944, B.P. Sharpless, who also worked at the United States Naval Observatory, attempted to determine the orbits of Phobos and Deimos. He discovered that the orbit of Phobos (the inner moon) was gradually decaying, a phenomenon, also known as 'secular acceleration', whereby an object's speed gradually increases until it enters the atmosphere (see Curt Sutherly, *Strange Encounters*, page

66). Natural bodies such as moons do not undergo secular acceleration; however, artificial satellites do.

The idea that Phobos might be an artificial satellite was first put forward by the Russian astrophysicist I.S. Shklovskii in 1960. After re-examining the work done by Sharpless, the Russian came to the conclusion that the density of Phobos is a thousandth that of water. His reasoning was that, since Mars has no magnetic field that could influence the moon, its orbit must be decaying due to atmospheric drag from Mars. But the planet's atmosphere is negligible, and nowhere near dense enough to produce a dragging effect; hence Phobos must have an unnaturally low density. Shklovskii realized there was a serious problem with this conclusion: no natural solid object could possibly be a thousand times less dense than water. Therefore, he concluded, Phobos must be hollow; and, since this likewise could not have occurred naturally, it must be artificial, the product of a gigantic engineering project.

When Viking I went to Mars, it was able to approach Phobos and measure the moon's mass. Shklovskii's calculations were shown to be very inaccurate: the moon was far denser than he had stated, although its density was still very low. As Curt Sutherly states in his book *Strange Encounters*, while this damages the Russian astrophysicist's theory that Phobos is hollow, it nevertheless fails to explain the decaying orbit (Sutherly, page 69).

Lunar Structures

While Mars and its moons hold many fascinating mysteries, we needn't travel so far from home to find bizarre cosmic puzzles hinting at alien activity. Richard Hoagland has recently turned his attention to Earth's Moon, and has discovered intriguing evidence of vast, ruined cities rising from the dead, grey surface of our nearest neighbour.

The next time you look up at the full Moon, concentrate on the very centre of the disc. You will be looking at the region known as *Sinus Medii*, or Central Bay. It is here that some very strange things have been found. Although you won't see it without a good telescope, there is a 10-km (16-mile) diameter crater here called Ukert, at the centre of which lies a perfect equilateral triangle. No one knows exactly what this feature is, or whether its presence has anything to do with the fact that Ukert is at the sub Earth point, the central point on the Moon's disc as seen from Earth, and thus the point on the Moon closest to Earth.

Just southwest of the *Sinus Medii* region stand two objects that are simply staggering in their implications, not to mention their physical size. In 1967, NASA launched the unmanned Lunar Orbiter III to conduct a photo-reconnaissance of the Moon, in preparation for the Apollo landings. During the mission, the probe photographed the objects that have come to be known as 'the Shard' and 'the Cube'. The Shard is a vertical column nearly 1 km (½ mile) high, with a peculiar bulge about half-way up the central section. Within this bulge is a geometric detail that gives the impression of being hexagonal in shape. There is no plausible geological explanation for the presence of this eerie object.

Even more impressive – although less easy to see without the aid of computer enhancement – is the Cube, a glass-like structure about 1.5 km (1 mile) wide, apparently composed of a large number of smaller sub-cubes, all suspended in a darker, meteor-eroded matrix. This matrix forms what seems to be a near-vertical tower 11 km (7 miles) high, connecting the Cube to the Lunar surface. Computer-enhanced false-colour images of the original photographs show that the most intense light scattering is within the interior of the Cube, not its exterior as one would expect from a natural, geological feature. This implies that the Cube and its tower are not geological features, but are constructed of semi-transparent, meteor-eroded glass.

In the spring of 1994, the Pentagon sent an unmanned military probe, Clementine, to photo-reconnoitre the entire Lunar surface. The craft carried state-of-the-art multi-spectral cameras, capable of analysing the composition and distribution of minerals. The results of that mission were allegedly leaked to Hoagland and his colleagues. They apparently show that the Mars Mission was correct in its interpretation of the original Lunar Orbiter images. The titanic structures on the Moon do not appear to correspond to the laws of Lunar geology, and seem to have been badly eroded by millennia of meteoric bombardment. This of course, implies that they were once part of far larger and more extensive structures, which probably included vast domes to protect the now-ruined complexes below.

The theory that domes once extended some kilometres above the Lunar surface seems to be borne out by the presence of an object known as 'the Castle', which Hoagland describes as a 'geometric, glittering glass object hanging more than nine miles [14.5 km] above the surface of the Moon'. The fact that this object seems to be hanging implies that it is being supported by some sort of framework.

During their researches, Hoagland and the renamed Enterprise Mission uncovered a 36-year-old government report, commissioned by NASA from the Brookings Institute in Washington DC. The report, entitled 'Proposed Studies on the Implications of Peaceful Space Activities for Human Affairs', dealt with:

> . . . the need to investigate the possible social consequences of an extra-terrestrial discovery and to consider whether such a discovery should be kept from the public in order to avoid political change and a possible 'devastating' effect on scientists themselves – due to the discovery that many of their own most cherished theories could be at risk.

The report concluded that any discovery of extra-terrestrial artefacts on the Moon, Mars or Venus should be kept from the public in order to preserve our civilization, citing the numerous cultures here on Earth that had been undermined and ultimately destroyed through contact with technologically superior societies. With this in mind, Hoagland has claimed that the true purpose of President Kennedy's rush to get to the Moon by the end of the 1960s was inspired by an urgent desire to get American astronauts to the derelict Lunar cities before the Soviets.

Did the Apollo astronauts succeed? Did Alan Bean of Apollo 12 really walk amid 'tiers of glasslike ruins', as Hoagland claims one photograph shows? Bean himself says not. When questioned by reporters from CNN and the Associated Press, the veteran astronaut replied: 'I wish we *had* seen something like what he's describing. It would have been the most wonderful discovery in the history of humankind – and I can't imagine anyone, in my wildest dreams, not wanting to share that.' According to Hoagland, however, Alan Bean and others like him are simply being loyal to NASA, which still doesn't want the truth to be revealed to the world.

As might be expected, Richard Hoagland's discoveries have been ridiculed by officialdom. Experts in geology like Paul Lowman of the Goddard Space Flight Center believe the Lunar structures are no more than image-processing effects. However, Hoagland has his own circle of equally eminent experts who support his findings. (This calls to mind the Fortean dictum 'For every expert, there is an equal and opposite expert'.)

It seems that, until another unmanned mission to the Moon is launched, and its findings released to the public, the debate will continue to rage. Apparently, Richard Hoagland is at present seeking funding for just such a mission. Let us hope that he succeeds.

THE RIDDLE OF AREA 51

No study of alleged extra-terrestrial artefacts would be complete without an examination of the controversy that continues to surround Area 51, also known as 'Dreamland', in the Nevada desert. Already well known and bearing a sinister reputation among UFO researchers, Area 51 came to international public attention in 1996 with the release of the blockbuster film *Independence Day*, which has ironically been described as the most expensive and successful B-movie ever made. The part played by the Nevada base in the film bears scant resemblance to the facts familiar to ufologists, perhaps because the 'truth' is too bizarre even for a science-fiction film!

The real Area 51 occupies Groom Lake, a dry lake-bed in the remote and inhospitable Emigrant Valley, about 200 km (120 miles) northwest of Las Vegas. It is here that peculiar aerial objects, displaying astonishing speed and manœuverability, have been spotted on countless occasions by both ufologists and aviation enthusiasts. But this is far from being the whole story, for, according to UFO lore, Groom Lake is the place where human pilots test-fly aircraft based on extra-terrestrial technology.

As one might expect of a top-secret government flight-test area, security around Groom Lake is quite astonishing: the place is not even listed on Federal Aviation Administration pilots' charts, nor can it be found on US Geological Survey maps. Officially, it doesn't even exist, and yet on every day of the week at least ten Boeing 737 aircraft fly workers and supplies into the Groom Lake area. The special terminals are operated by the EG & G Corporation, and are located at McCarran Airport in Las Vegas and Palmdale, California. The number of aircraft making this daily trip implies that between 1500 and 2500 people work there.

The ultra-secret test facility at Groom Lake was constructed in 1954; its main purpose was to be the home of the U-2 spyplane. The contract to develop and build the high-performance aircraft was awarded by the CIA to the Lockheed Aircraft Corporation. Groom Lake was chosen as the ideal place where such a sensitive

project could be carried through to a successful conclusion, away
from the eyes of the public. Lockheed constructed the runways,
hangars and support buildings for the U-2 near the site of the
Atomic Energy Commission (later the Department of Energy).
Groom Lake was also to be the home of the U-2's replacement, the
SR-71 Blackbird, and more recently, the F-117A stealth fighter.

Tempers flared in Nevada when, in 1984, the US military made
an application to seize 36,000 hectares (89,000 acres) of public
land, to consolidate further the base's isolation. In spite of public
opposition, the application was approved by Congress in 1986, on
grounds of national security. However, whether because of bad
luck or incompetence, this seizure of public land failed to take into
account three vantage-points, from which the Groom Lake facility
can be seen. Thus a further request for a another 1600 hectares
(4,000 acres) was made, resulting in even more public attention.
The journal *Popular Science* requested permission from the US
Government to give 'a reasonable overview of the defence
research the government conducts there, without jeopardizing the
security of sensitive technologies'.

This brought an unsympathetic response from the Pentagon,
saying that, in spite of the end of the Cold War, tight security had
to be maintained on certain military projects. This view was not
shared by Representative Robert S. Walker, vice-chairman of the
House Science, Space and Technology Committee, who stated:

> We now have a re-shaped world. When we had a super-power
> confrontation, it made sense to run the programs the way we
> ran them. Now, we ought to re-examine how we handle
> 'black' programs. It makes little sense to withhold technology
> from public entrepreneurship, if in fact it allows us to leapfrog
> the rest of the world.

Another Congressional source, allegedly with the highest level of
security clearance, has visited Groom Lake and has stated that a
'mysterious technology' is being developed there, one that is 'not
part of the official programme of the US Government'.

There is little doubt that unconventional aircraft are being tested at Groom Lake. Remotely Piloted Vehicles (RPVs) and
Unmanned Aerial Vehicles (UAVs) have very impressive flight
characteristics which could account for the innumerable UFO
sightings in the area.

However, the riddle of Area 51 is a good deal more complex than that, based as it is upon an intricate network of rumours, leaked documents and the testimony of those who claim to have seen what is 'really' going on at the facility.

The following information (original source unknown) is available on the Internet, and describes the various alleged top-secret projects that have been, and are being, conducted by the US military. It makes extraordinary reading, since it reveals that contact has already been established with a variety of alien races.

DISCLOSURE OF THIS INFORMATION IS AN ATTEMPT TO PROTECT AND PRESERVE THE CONSTITUTION OF THE UNITED STATES OF AMERICA. THE GROUP KNOWN AS MAJESTIC TWELVE HAS ENGAGED IN A VILE CONSPIRACY THAT HAS IGNORED THE LAW OF THE LAND AND THE PRINCIPLES OF FREEDOM THAT THE UNITED STATES WAS FOUNDED UPON. THEY HAVE TAKEN IT UPON THEMSELVES TO INSTITUTE UNLAWFUL AND DANGEROUS PROJECTS WHICH HAVE ENDANGERED THE NATION AND THE HUMAN RACE. THE DISCLOSURE GROUP CONSISTS OF INDIVIDUALS WHO HAVE SWORN TO UPHOLD AND PROTECT THE CONSTITUTION OF THE UNITED STATES. WE HOPE AND PRAY THAT THIS DISCLOSURE WILL ENCOURAGE OTHERS CONNECTED WITH THIS CONSPIRACY TO MAKE SIMILAR DISCLOSURES. WE ASK THAT THIS STATEMENT REMAIN ATTACHED TO THIS INFORMATION. WE SEEK NO REWARD OR PUBLIC ACCLAIM. WE ONLY SEEK TO EXPOSE THIS ACT AS A CRIMINAL ASSAULT UPON THE UNITED STATES AND THE HUMAN RACE.

MAJESTIC TWELVE (PROWORD) MAJIC

MAJESTIC TWELVE, MAJESTIC 12, MAJESTIC-12, MJ-12, MAJIC, are all forms of the code name for the control group authorized by President Truman on 09/24/47. The Director of the Central Intelligence Agency (CIA) is the Director of Majestic Twelve, MJ-1. The control group was formed to oversee a TOP SECRET Research and Development & Intelligence Operation and was responsible only to the President. The need for this group was dictated by the finding of a downed FLYING SAUCER scattered over 2 sites near the town of Roswell New Mexico in July 1947. The dead bodies of 4 very small human like ALIENS were also found. MAJESTIC TWELVE is the most highly classified secret in the United States and its existence has never been divulged to Congress. The funds for MJ-12 and Aquarius are CIA confidential (non-appropriated).

DOCUMENTS

MAJESTIC TWELVE documents can be identified by the following:
TOP SECRET/MAJIC/RESTRICTED DATA EYES ONLY COPY — OF — TOP SECRET/MAJIC/RESTRICTED EYES ONLY COPY — OF — TOP SECRET/MAJIC EYES ONLY COPY — OF —

One of the above will appear both at the top and bottom of each page. You will never see one version in a document along with any other version. Also on each page will appear: T52-EXEMPT (E) or just EXEMPT. T52 is the publication outlining procedures for automatic downgrade of all security classifications and the time period for declassification of each security level. This information is never to be declassified. Each page of each document will be numbered consecutively and the number of pages will appear upon the cover sheet. Copies of MAJESTIC TWELVE beyond the original number are forbidden.

PROJECTS under MAJESTIC TWELVE

The operations listed here were current as late as 1976 with absolute certainty and are still operational to the best of our knowledge. The names of the original operations were changed several times over the years and eventually evolved into those listed.

PROJECT SIGN (PROWORD) MAJIC

The first project under MAJESTIC TWELVE. The mission of Project Sign was essentially the same as that which PROJECT AQUARIUS evolved into. PROJECT SIGN referred to aliens as Extra-terrestrial Biological Entities. The reasons for the absorption of PROJECT SIGN by PROJECT AQUARIUS were mainly of a political and security nature. PROJECT AQUARIUS stripped the Air Force and Army Generals of their historic

control of the UFO/IAC projects and placed most of it under
the Intelligence umbrella.

PROJECT AQUARIUS (PROWORD) MAJIC

Established in 1953 by President Eisenhower under control of
MJ-12 and PROJECT SIGN. The Project contains all
information collected by the United States since it began
investigating UFO's (Unidentified Flying Objects) and IAC's
(Identified Alien Craft). At the time we saw this information it
existed in approximately 15 or 16 volumes. This project
became an independent project when PROJECT SIGN was
eliminated in 1960. PROJECT AQUARIUS referred to aliens as
Alien Life Forms. The mission of PROJECT AQUARIUS was to
gather all scientific, technological, medical, and intelligence
information from UFO & IAC sightings and contacts with Alien
Life Forms. The information was to be used in the space
program.

PROJECT SIGMA (PROWORD) AQUARIUS

Established in 1954 as part of PROJECT SIGN. The mission of
PROJECT SIGMA was to establish communication with the
aliens. First communication was established in 1959 through
binary computer language. On April 25, 1964 a USAF (OSI)
officer met with aliens at a prearranged desert location in New
Mexico. Information was exchanged and a basic
understanding was reached after several hours. It was learned
through this effort that several species of alien life existed.
Communication was eventually established with all of them.
Through communications it was determined that 3 categories
existed. The three categories are MALEVOLENT
(DANGEROUS), BENEVOLENT (GOOD-HELPFUL), and
NEUTRAL (OBSERVERS ONLY) The project has been
extremely successful.

PROJECT PLATO (PROWORD) AQUARIUS

Established in 1960 after the United States established
communications with the aliens. The mission of PROJECT
PLATO was to establish diplomatic relations with the aliens.
Project Plato made agreements in order to prevent hostilities
between the United States and the aliens. An agreement was
made with the MALEVOLENT aliens whereby they could

abduct humans. The purpose of these abductions was to provide blood and other biological fluids as food for the aliens. The aliens agreed to furnish a list periodically to MJ-12 of the names of those abducted. PROJECT PLATO took whatever steps necessary to prevent public disclosure.

PROJECT PLUTO (PROWORD) AQUARIUS

Established in 1947 after the Roswell incident. The mission of PROJECT PLUTO was to recover all crashed or downed alien craft, to recover all evidence of alien presence or technology, and to recover all alien bodies (alive or dead). PROJECT PLUTO developed cover stories to satisfy press and civilian curiosity. PROJECT PLUTO was authorized to use deadly force and/or relocation to insure secrecy. PROJECT PLUTO was responsible for biological intelligence of the Alien Life Forms.

PROJECT POUNCE (PROWORD) AQUARIUS

Established in 1968. The mission of PROJECT POUNCE was to evaluate all UFO/IAC information pertaining to space technology. The goal was to duplicate the technology and/or improve upon it. Ultimate use of the technology would establish the United States as the dominant world power and close the gap in any confrontation with the aliens.

PROJECT REDLIGHT (PROWORD) AQUARIUS

Established in 1954. The mission of REDLIGHT was to test a recovered alien craft. The mission was accomplished in part only. PROJECT REDLIGHT was terminated in 1963 after every (flyable) recovered craft exploded during test flights. There were no survivors among the human test pilots.

PROJECT SNOWBIRD (PROWORD) AQUARIUS

Established in 1972. The mission of PROJECT SNOWBIRD was to test fly a recovered alien craft. The project was ongoing the last time I saw this information.

PROJECT ???????? (PROWORD) AQUARIUS

(NOTE . . . We are unable to recall the name of this project nor have we been able to get response from anyone on it. At the time we saw the information the project was ongoing. It cannot be determined if this project is still in existence.) The mission of this project was to develop a low frequency pulsed sound generator. The energy produced from this generator was to be concentrated so that it could be aimed and used as a weapon in order to destroy the alien craft and beam weapons. The alien beam weapons were described as able to incapacitate or destroy any weapons system known to date (1972). The aliens also possess a beam weapon which is described as being able to paralyze any human within range. Tests were described as having shown that the alien craft and weapons were extremely sensitive to low frequency pulsed sound waves. This weapon was to be used to incapacitate the alien defenses in order to allow PROJECT EXCALIBUR to succeed in its mission. The initial technology used in this project was captured from the Germans during WW-II. The German sound generators were described as being able to knock down reinforced concrete buildings and shatter 4″ thick armour from a great range. This technology is believed to further substantiate that Germany had recovered alien craft and had possibly had some dealings with the aliens prior to or during WW-II. Documents captured during and after WW-II indicated that an alien craft had been recovered by Germany in 1939. A German-built flying saucer was captured during the last few months of WW-II.

PROJECT EXCALIBUR (PROWORD) AQUARIUS
Established in 1972. The mission of PROJECT EXCALIBUR is to develop a weapons system capable of destroying the alien underground base after the alien beam weapons have been incapacitated or destroyed. The alien underground base is located beneath an Indian reservation near the small town of Dulce, New Mexico. The device must be capable of penetrating 1,000 meters of tufa/hard pack soil and sustain no operational damage. This type is commonly found in New Mexico where the alien base is located. Missile apogee must not exceed 30,000 feet AGL. Impact deviation will not exceed 50 meters. The device will carry a 1 megaton warhead.

PROJECT BLUE BOOK
A U.S. Air Force project established to determine whether UFO's pose a threat to the security of the United States and to determine whether UFO's exhibit any unique scientific information or advanced technology which could contribute to

scientific or technical research. PROJECT BLUE BOOK was successful in its primary mission outlined above. PROJECT BLUE BOOK was not quite so successful in its secondary mission which was to publicly explain away the UFO phenomenon as natural or known phenomenon in order to eliminate public interest. To completely fulfill the secondary mission it was decided that an outside commission of distinguished scientists would be convened in order to permanently lay the issue to rest. After this 'study' was completed (Condon Commission) the Air Force stated the continuation of Project Blue Book could not be justified, either on the ground of national security or in the interest of science. PROJECT BLUE BOOK was abandoned and its mission and information was consolidated under PROJECT AQUARIUS in 1969.

SCIENTIFIC STUDY OF UNIDENTIFIED FLYING OBJECTS

Contracted to the University of Colorado in 1966 and Chaired by Dr Edward U. Condon. The results of the panel were dictated before the first meeting. Despite objections of the other panel members, Dr Condon was able to fulfill the mission. The general conclusion was that 'nothing has come from the study of UFOs in the past 21 years that has added to scientific knowledge.' A panel from the National Academy of Sciences agreed. The press and the public were satisfied. Except for a hard core element of UFO believers the issue died in the public forum.

OPERATION UFO (NSA OPERATION IN SUPPORT OF PROJECT PLUTO)

The mission of Operation UFO was to form intelligence teams versed in all of the knowledge learned which would be the first on scene of any UFO crash site in order to secure the technology and prevent it from falling into foreign hands. Several teams existed over the world. The United States was specifically concerned that it did not fall into Soviet hands. This mission was to be accomplished no matter the country of occurrence. Many subsequent ALIEN CRAFT recoveries would occur in foreign countries as well as the United States. UFO was also used to recover downed space hardware (especially

Soviet and to recover nuclear weapons which became lost
(usually by accident).

OPERATION MOONDUST

The mission of Operation Moondust was to provide a cover
which would neutralize public curiosity while recovery of an
ALIEN CRAFT was being conducted. The teams that made up
the complement of Moondust were the same teams that made
up UFO. Moondust was made public and its mission (to the
public) was to identify and recover United States space
hardware which might fall to earth. It was a bonafide mission
when circumstances dictated.

OPERATION BLUEFLY (SUPPORTED UFO & MOONDUST)

The mission of operation Bluefly was to provide QUICK
REACTION COMBAT TEAMS known as ALPHA teams (fight
for technology if necessary), mechanical and technological
support in recovery, rapid and secure transport to secure
storage and examination areas. There are several of these
storage and examination areas in order to limit distance
traveled and thus limit the possible chance of an accident that
could expose cargo to public knowledge. Several teams existed
over the world. Recovery and transport of both EBEs (dead or
alive) and Alien craft were accomplished. Bluefly was also
utilized in event of recovery of space objects (of terrestrial
origin), and event of recovery of lost nuclear weapons (usually
due to accident).

NOTE . . . This account of the history and current status of
MAJESTIC TWELVE and the Alien Life Forms has been kept
brief. We believe that the intent, however, has been served
with the data provided. The whole story would fill several
hundred volumes. We realize that even with the combined
effort of several memories we have probably made some
mistakes. We have tried to minimize the mistakes and feel that
what is represented is true and correct to the best of our
combined knowledge.

Over the years since Area 51 first came to public attention via the
claims of Robert Lazar, who had allegedly worked on various

'reverse-engineering' projects on captured alien spacecraft, a vast network of conspiracy theories has blossomed like one of Baudelaire's flowers of evil. Indeed, what researcher John Lear has called 'the horrible truth' is far too big for a context as straightforward as the extra-terrestrial hypothesis, i.e. the arrival on Earth of a scientific expedition from another planet. As we shall see in the chapters that follow, the concept of alien presence has grown into a colossal, malformed beast whose tentacles extend through the darkest realms of human paranoia and mythology.

In these benighted realms, characterized by the flickering light of contradiction, absurdity and terror, we will look at the processes by which perhaps genuinely unexplained occurrences have contributed to the development of, to borrow J.G. Ballard's phrase, 'the myths of the near future'. The outrageous tales of crashed UFOs, secret treaties with sinister aliens, and hidden struggles between extra-terrestrial races for the future of the Earth are liberally seasoned with rumours and legends from decades and even centuries ago. The history of alleged alien presence on Earth has come to include the nefarious activities of secret societies in every corner of the globe; the existence of lost civilizations far underground; vicious, unknown predators that decimate cattle and other animals across the United States and Europe; top-secret research projects that have conquered the problems of time travel and teleportation; and even a plan to evacuate selected humans from a dying Earth and take them to a new life on the planet Mars.

SIX

Journey to the Underworld

THE IDEA THAT there is a mysterious civilization living deep beneath our feet has a rich provenance in both mythology and the literature of the unexplained. This includes both scientific and cultural sources, which have combined in the crucible of the human imagination to produce a modern system of beliefs which, whether based on truth or not, is peculiarly suited to our post-industrial world.

The so-called 'Hollow Earth' theory was first mooted by highly respected men of science as far back as the seventeenth century, among them the Astronomer Royal, Edmound Halley, who suggested that the planet's interior contained three additional spheres. A plethora of weird and wonderful variations on this theory have appeared since, including that of Cyrus Teed, who maintained that the Earth is actually a hollow bubble set in an infinity of rock, and John Cleeves Symmes' notion that the Earth's interior can be reached via a pair of vast openings at the North and South Poles.

In 1968, a satellite called ESSA-7 took a series of photographs of the North Pole, minus the usual cloud cover, which showed a very large circular dark area. Adherents of the Hollow Earth hypothesis immediately claimed this as categorical proof that they were correct. These photographs still show up from time to time in books by writers insisting that the Earth is hollow. The truth, however, was somewhat less exciting: the area around the North Pole was dark because, due to the satellite's orbital trajectory, it had not

been included in the photo-mosaic that made up the whole picture
– it had simply not been photographed.

From the viewpoint of the present, where little grey miscreants
are said to follow their nefarious agendas while the US
Government turns a blind (but increasingly apprehensive) eye, we
can trace a path back through this strange offshoot of ufology
which makes occasional whistle-stops in the fields of popular
rumour, paranoid fantasy, literary occultism, genuine scientific
enquiry and traditional folklore.

THE SHAVER MYSTERY

That the vast majority of races allegedly living beneath our feet
have our worst interests firmly at heart there can be little doubt.
Perhaps the most sinister of them all were first brought to the
world's attention by Richard Sharpe Shaver, who wrote a number
of 'factual' accounts of his experiences for the American magazine
Amazing Stories in the 1940s.

Shaver was a crane operator and welder at an auto-body shop
in Detroit. He maintained that the underworld is populated by the
descendants of an ancient race of highly advanced extra-terrestrials who colonized Earth in the distant past, calling the planet
'Lemuria'. At some point in prehistory, the Sun underwent a radical change and began sending out harmful radioactive rays,
which forced some Lemurians to leave the planet in search of
more hospitable environments, while others chose to retreat into
the sheltering innards of the Earth. However, the harmful rays
had already done their damage, reducing most of the Lemurians
who stayed behind to a state of unthinkable deterioration and
savagery. These became known as the 'Deros' (a contraction of
'abandon*deros*' or '*de*trimental *robots*'). The Deros are in constant
conflict with another group of Lemurians, the much more benign
'Teros' ('constructive' or '*in*tegrative *robots*'), who do their best to
counteract the harmful energy rays projected to the surface by
their enemies. These rays, produced by ancient machinery left
behind by the original Lemurians, poison our minds and force us
to do evil. The fiendish Deros also use them to cause all manner
of upheavals, such as earthquakes and violent storms.
Fortunately, the Teros have their own versions of these machines,
which transmit beneficial 'telaug' rays, promoting goodness and
tranquillity.

Shaver had come by this knowledge in a suitably novel way. He had been sent to prison as punishment for an 'enforced escapade' (apparently, the Deros had been beaming their rays at him through his welding gun), and was languishing in his cell one night when a beautiful young woman appeared before him. Her name was Nydia and she was a Tero. She explained the history of the Dero–Tero conflict, and later took him on a trip into the underworld to consult the Teros' ancient telepathic records.

When he submitted his bizarre manuscripts to *Amazing Stories*, Shaver insisted to its managing editor, Ray Palmer, that every word was true. In view of the fact that the magazine's circulation went through the roof whenever a Shaver story appeared, Palmer saw no reason to disagree. In fact, he began to receive letters from people claiming to have undergone experiences similar to Shaver's. The concept of the subterranean world had struck a popular chord, and was reinforced by Kenneth Arnold's subsequent sighting of spaceships above Mount Rainier in June, 1947. For Shaver, Palmer and their tens of thousands of readers, this was confirmation that the Deros and Teros really existed. The craft were said to belong to the descendants of the Lemurians who left the Earth in the distant past. According to Shaver, the oscillating motion of flying-saucer flight was actually a defensive manoeuver to avoid the Deros' attempts to shoot them down.

OCCULT ANTECEDENTS

There is a striking parallel between the Shaver Mystery and *The Coming Race*, a short novel by the Victorian novelist Edward Bulwer-Lytton. First published in 1871, it describes a vast subterranean world inhabited by a technologically superior master race. The source of their power is an energy source called Vril, which sounds rather like the powerful ray machines used by the Deros for their ghastly ends. Lytton's novel was hugely popular, and the mysterious Vril power became so closely associated with energy and vitality that it was used in the name of a famous beverage that is still produced today: Bovril.

Lytton himself was deeply involved with occultism, and it has been suggested that he may have been drawing on a genuine body of occult knowledge when he wrote *The Coming Race*. In his fascinating book *The Lost World of Agharti*, Alec Maclellan tells us that Bulwer-Lytton was evidently deeply interested in the Rosicrucians (or the Order of the Rosy Cross), the oldest secret society in the Western world, which has its origins in the ancient Egyptian and Greek mystery schools. Bulwer-Lytton wrote to his friend Hargrave Jennings in 1854 that Rosenkreuz, founder of the Rosicrucian Fraternity, born in 1378, 'found his wisdom in a secret chamber. So will we all. There is much to be learned from the substrata of our planet.' And, in a comment concerning the communicative powers of the pentacle, the novelist again refers to subterranean races: 'The pentacle itself has an intelligible meaning, it belongs to the only universal language of symbol, in which all races that think – around, and above and below us – can establish communion of thought' (Maclellan, page 90).

Maclellan sees a link between Bulwer-Lytton's tale of an adventurer who stumbles upon a thriving, highly advanced civilization deep underground, and the legendary subterranean kingdom of Agharti, which is said to lie beneath Tibet, and is connected to other underground cities and cave systems by a tunnel network circling the Earth. The legend of Agharti holds a central position in the history of the occult, and played a major part in the philosophy of a woman who is regarded by some as being the founder of modern occultism: Helena Petrovna Blavatsky.

Madame Blavatsky was born in Russia in 1831, and co-founded the Theosophical Society, an organization dedicated to the dissemination of Eastern religious and occult philosophy in the West. Her first book, *Isis Unveiled*, which appeared in 1877, was a treatise on Hermetic philosophy, 'the ancient universal wisdom', which, she believed, was guarded by 'the Masters', a group of wise men who have 'always existed', and who have 'total command over the forces of nature and make themselves known only to those persons who are deemed worthy of knowing and seeing them'.

Her second and greatest book, *The Secret Doctrine* (1888), purports to be a vast commentary on an ancient manuscript called *The Book of Dzyan*, the oldest manuscript in the world, several million years old, in fact. *The Book of Dzyan* is, in turn, said to be a fragment of the *Mani Koumbourm*, a repository of the sacred writing of a vanished race known as the Dzugarians, who once inhabited northern Tibet (see Robert Turner's commentary in *The Necronomicon*, published by Skoob Books, 1992). The Dzugarian texts tell of the arrival on Earth in the remote past of monstrous, chaotic beings from other dimensions, and of how they were ultimately expelled from our universe by the forces of order. As anyone familiar with the work of H.P. Lovecraft will quickly realize, the implications of *The Book of Dzyan*'s existence are shocking and far-reaching, and well beyond the scope of this book.

WHAT HAPPENED TO COLONEL FAWCETT?

Colonel Percy Fawcett disappeared in the Amazon more than 70 years ago. The most widely held belief is that he was killed by Calapalo Indians, ancestors of the same tribe that recently attacked an expedition searching for Fawcett's remains. But what was the explorer looking for in the mysterious and all but impenetrable Amazonian rainforests, and what really happened to him?

The recent 16-man expedition that had hoped to discover Colonel Fawcett's fate set off from Cuiaba, the capital of Mato Grosso, in mid-June 1996. Led by James Lynch, a Chase Manhattan banker, and René Delmotte, a Mercedes-Benz executive from Sao Paulo, the expedition was not the first to attempt to unravel the mystery of Fawcett's disappearance. Over the years, at least 13 expeditions have tried – and failed.

The aim was to cover the 2400-km (1500-mile) stretch of jungle Fawcett is known to have traversed, and which he described in letters home. With Fawcett on his ill-fated trip were his son, Jack, and a friend, Raleigh Rimmel. Although historians assume that the men were killed by Calapalo Indians and their possessions stolen, no evidence has ever been found to corroborate this theory.

In fact, it was only thanks to twentieth-century technology that the 1996 expedition was saved from a similarly ignominious fate. Whereas Fawcett's family were alerted only by the sudden absence of mail from him, James Lynch's radioed SOS signals to Brazilian government officials in Cuiaba brought a speedy response from search parties.

Lynch reported that the expedition had encountered Indians from the Calapalo and Camaiura tribes, who had promptly stolen three Jeeps and two boats. Once safely back in Cuiaba, Lynch reported on what had happened to them while in the hands of the Indians:

> After days of trekking in the jungle we were met by Indians
> who threatened us with their bows and arrows. They
> kidnapped 12 of our men and demanded that we hand over
> Jeeps and boats and all the things in the rucksacks. We had
> to barter with them and succumb to their bribes.

They threatened to kill our men unless we handed everything
over. We eventually gave them what they wanted, and when
we had our men back, I radioed for help. It was a long ordeal
and we tried to stay calm. I feared for the lives of those men
because the Indians were armed with poisonous arrows and
kept making angry threats.

The other leader of the expedition, René Delmotte, said he
thought it ironic that they came so close to suffering the same fate
that everyone thinks befell Colonel Fawcett.

When Colonel Fawcett's letters stopped arriving from the
Amazon, several adventurers set out to discover what had happened to him. In 1927, a US Navy commander met Indians, one of
whom was wearing a glass ornament, which turned out to be a
name-plate from one of Fawcett's cases. Brazilian anthropologists
Orlando and Claudio Villas Lobos subsequently said they had spoken to the Calapalos, who had told them that Fawcett had been
clubbed to death by a particularly 'courageous' chief named Izazari.

According to *O Globo* newspaper, the members of the latest
expedition 'were kept for five days in a village, had their bodies
painted and were spat on and constantly pushed around'. They
were also forced to eat ants and worms in an Indian ritual.
However, the team were undaunted by their terrifying experience,
and they hope to try again to unravel the enduring mystery of
Colonel Fawcett's disappearance.

But why did Colonel Fawcett undertake his doomed expedition, which apparently came to an end in 1925? In short, he was
looking for the very first cities built by humanity. 'It is certain,' he
wrote, 'that amazing ruins of ancient cities – ruins incomparably
older than those of Egypt – exist in the far interior of the Mato
Grosso.' Of his impending journey, he wrote:

Whether we get through and come out again, or whether we
shall leave our bones to rot inside, one thing is certain: the
answer to the riddle of South America – and perhaps of the
entire prehistoric world – may be found when the site of those
ancient cities is fixed and made accessible to scientific
exploration. This much I know: the cities exist . . . I have not a
moment's doubt on that score. How could I have? I myself
have seen a part of them . . . The remains appeared to be the
outposts of greater cities.

Some commentators on ancient mysteries believe that Colonel Fawcett did not die at the hands of the Indians, but actually found what he was looking for, and a great deal more besides.

Fawcett was convinced that there exists in the Mato Grosso a highly advanced white race (light-skinned Indians *are* found there) living in a vast network of subterranean caverns and passages. Before setting off for Brazil, Fawcett said:

> I have but one object: to bare the mysteries that the jungle
> fastnesses of South America have concealed for so many
> centuries. We are encouraged in our hope of finding the ruins
> of an ancient, white civilisation and the degenerate offspring
> of a once cultivated race.

Alec Maclellan describes how Fawcett was fascinated by a historical document discovered in Rio de Janeiro and preserved in the Biblioteca Nationale in that city. The document tells how a Portuguese expedition came across a small passage in one of the mountains of the Mato Grosso. Crawling through the passage, they discovered the ruins of a city that had apparently been destroyed by some enormous cataclysm. They allegedly encountered two white-skinned men with golden hair, and promptly despatched a native runner to Rio de Janeiro to tell of their discovery. However, the Portuguese were never heard of again.

Fawcett familiarized himself with the legends of Brazil, which told of fabulous cities dating back 60,000 years. In a letter written in 1924 to Lewis Spence, he speculated that this mysterious race of white-skinned people might be the remnants of the Atlanteans, who had fled their doomed continent in the distant past.

As the years following Fawcett's disappearance passed, some people, including his wife Nina, grew more and more convinced that the explorer had not met with foul play, but was still alive, somewhere beneath the mountains of the Mato Grosso. In *The Lost World of Agharti*, Maclellan quotes a monograph written by Dr Raymond Bernard in 1960:

> Many Brazilian students of the occult share with the wife of
> Colonel Fawcett the belief that he is still living with his son
> Jack as residents of a subterranean city whose entrance is
> through a tunnel in the Roncador Mountain range of
> northeast Mato Grosso where he was heading when last seen

after leaving Cuiaba. The writer met in Cuiaba a native who
claimed that his father was Fawcett's guide and who offered to
take him to a certain opening leading to the Subterranean
World in the region of Roncador, which would indicate that
Fawcett's guide believed in the existence of subterranean cities
and brought Fawcett to one, where he was held prisoner lest
he reveal the secret of its whereabouts, which he might be
forced to do on his return, whether he wished to or not.
(Maclellan, page 143–4)

According to the American naturalist Carl Huni, the Roncador
entrance is said to be guarded by a particularly fearsome tribe of
Indians called the Murcego, or Bat. In his essay 'The Mysterious
Tunnels and Subterranean Cities of South America', he states that
these people are small in stature, and possess great strength. If they
approve of you, they might just allow you to enter the tunnel; but
it will be a one-way trip, since they will almost certainly not allow
you to leave.

Huni goes on to say:

There are also caverns in Asia and many Tibetan travellers
mention them. But as far as I know, the biggest ones are in
Brazil and they exist at three different levels. I am sure I
would get permission if I wanted to join them and they would
accept me as one of theirs. I know they use no money at all,
and their society is organised on a strictly democratic basis.
The people do not become aged and live in everlasting
harmony. (Maclellan, page 145)

Dr Raymond Bernard has spent many years researching the legends of subterranean tunnels beneath Brazil, and claims that in
Santa Catarina in the south of the country, the 'choral singing of
Atlantean men and women has been repeatedly heard'. According
to Dr Bernard, a group of scientists entered a tunnel in a mountain
near the boundary of Parana and Santa Catarina, and descended
to a subterranean city. Suddenly seized with fright, they fled without further investigation.

The most famous of these tunnels is the so-called 'Roadway of
the Incas', which is said to stretch for hundreds of kilometres from
Lima to Cuzco, Tiahuanaco, and on beneath the Atacama Desert.
Other tunnels beneath Brazil are said to extend out under the

Atlantic Ocean in the direction of what was once Atlantis, implying that the Atlanteans (assuming they existed) had established colonies in South America.

Madame Blavatsky's Theosophists (see Chapter 3) have long believed in the existence of a subterranean world, populated by a superior race. Dr Bernard claims to have been in contact with a group of Theosophists at Sao Lourenço, who told him that one of their members had found the entrance to a tunnel and succeeded in travelling from Peru to Brazil underground. Another Brazilian told Bernard of a journey he had made through a smoothly cut, illuminated tunnel for three days, travelling 20 hours a day, in the company of two subterranean men he had met at the entrance. Eventually he came to a colossal illuminated cavern containing buildings and a fruit orchard. According to Bernard's informant, the sexes of the cavern-dwellers live apart. Women produce children through the process of parthenogenesis, which results in all the people looking exactly alike, with no individual variation. The man eventually succeeded in escaping through an exit tunnel.

If unequivocal proof of such a network of subterranean cities and tunnels still eludes us, we nevertheless have a considerable amount of witness testimony, not mention extensive research by people such as Raymond Bernard, Harold T. Wilkins, Lewis Spence and Alec Maclellan. In addition to this, of course, there is an extensive mythological system that has, over the centuries, developed around the basic notion. For instance, there is said to be an entrance to the subterranean kingdom of Agharti behind the Red Door in the Potala (the palace of the Dalai Lama) in Lhasa. Indeed, according to legend, the capital of Agharti, Shamballah, lies directly beneath Tibet.

The author and Buddhist teacher Robert Ernst Dickhoff maintains that the tunnels and caverns that extend throughout Asia and South America also extend beneath North America, an assertion that calls to mind rumours that have recently arisen concerning sinister underground facilities in the American southwest, said to be operated by alien beings. This region of the United States is said to have a large number of entrances to this realm, including Mount Shasta in California and the Superstition Mountains in Arizona. As already mentioned above, the members of the 1996 expedition to the Amazon have said that they would like to make another attempt. Perhaps they should head out to the American southwest instead.

THE WYOMING MUMMY

Although categorical proof of unknown subterranean races has not been forthcoming, there have been some intriguing discoveries over the years which are difficult to explain in conventional terms. There have been many reports (especially in the nineteenth century) concerning strange artefacts found in places where logically they should not have been. Discoveries range from a small metallic sphere with a number of parallel lines etched around its equator, said to have been found in 2.8 million-year-old strata in South Africa, to shoe-prints preserved alongside dinosaur tracks. Such finds should, of course, be treated with caution, especially in view of the lengths to which opponents of Darwin were known to go in order to discredit his theories of evolution. However, if any of those anomalous artefacts are genuine, and not placed in their archaeological contexts by nineteenth-century religious zealots, they would offer powerful evidence in support of a pre-human technological presence on – and perhaps also *in* – Earth.

One of the most interesting discoveries was made in October 1932, in the Pedro Mountains, about 100 km (60 miles) west of the town of Casper, Wyoming. Two gold prospectors were exploring a gulch at the base of the mountains, when they came across what they thought was an indication of gold in one of the walls. After setting explosive charges in the wall and blasting away part of it, they saw that they had exposed a cave about 1.2 metres (4 feet) square and 4.5 metres (15 feet) deep. Inside the cave they discovered something that should not have been there: the tiny figure of a man sitting cross-legged on a ledge. His arms were also crossed, his body was dark bronze in colour and he was only 35 cm (14 inches) high.

The two astounded prospectors promptly took their curious find back to Casper. The initial mutterings of 'hoax' were dispelled when the tiny, mummified man was X-rayed by anthropologists, and was found to contain a skull, spine, rib-cage and bones, virtually identical to those found in a normal man. The mummy also had a full set of teeth, weighed about 340 grams (12 oz) and, by the anthropologists' estimates, was about 65 years old when he died. According to the Wyoming State Historical Society, the tiny man was undoubtedly human – a view shared by anthropologists from Harvard. Dr Henry Shapiro of the American Museum of Natural History declared that the mummy was 'of an extremely great age, historically speaking, and of a type and stature quite unknown to us'. The mummy was also examined by the Boston Museum Egyptian Department, which supported the earlier contention that it was a fully grown adult, not a child; and also that the method of preservation seemed to match that of the Egyptian Pharaohs.

It could be suggested that the two gold prospectors had stumbled on the burial-place of an ancient and (presumably) long-dead humanoid race, one whose habitat lay beneath the surface of the Earth. Certainly, although they declared the Casper mummy to be genuine, the anthropologists who investigated the case were somewhat reluctant to commit themselves as to its possible origin.

THE DEEP BIOSPHERE

Perhaps unsurprisingly, orthodox science has never been particularly sympathetic to the idea of complex life-forms existing far beneath the Earth's surface. The main reason for this is the harshness of the conditions, including pressures hundreds of times greater than at sea-level, and searing temperatures. Scientists have assumed that no life of any description could survive in such an environment.

Recently, however, drilling operations reaching 4000 metres (13,000 feet) below the Atlantic Ocean have yielded some surprising discoveries. Core samples were taken from a depth of 760 metres (2500 feet) below the ocean bed, lying in turn beneath 3350 metres (11,000 feet) of water. The International Ocean Drilling Programme, which took the samples from its research ship off the east coast of the United States, brought to the surface microscopic organisms that have evolved in an environment completely separate from the surface, an environment in which the pressure is 400 times that at sea-level, and where the temperature is 170°C (380°F).

According to John Parkes, professor of geo-microbiology at Bristol University, England, the discovery of these microbes overturns conventional ideas about the resilience of life. Parkes stated, 'This is a big conceptual leap because the idea of life being confined to the surface of our planet has been shown to be incorrect.' The core samples produced an even greater surprise: the numbers of bacteria actually *increased* with depth. 'Normally you would expect bacterial populations to decrease with depth, commented Parkes. Instead we found bacterial populations can increase with depth.'

Of course, the primitive bacteria discovered by the scientists of the Ocean Drilling Programme are a far cry from the technological civilizations described by Bulwer-Lytton, or the inscrutable Masters of Theosophy. And yet the idea that life could arise in complex forms far beneath the Earth's surface was raised five years ago by Thomas Gold, an astronomer at Cornell University, New York. His 'deep biosphere' theory proposes that subterranean life could evolve in parallel with life on the surface, and he suggested that future space missions should search for life *inside* other planets.

Moreover, if we remember that the interior of the Earth's crust is actually more like a honeycomb than a solid layer, it now seems more feasible that large caverns, containing the fundamental necessities of life, could exist. And if they do exist, perhaps they could also be inhabited by intelligent beings who fled underground in the distant past.

'THEY DON'T LIKE US'

We can speculate wildly and endlessly about ancient, lost races dwelling underground, but, in the absence of absolutely unequivocal evidence, it will remain mere speculation. However, the idea refuses to go away, having like the notion of non-human visitors to our world, undergone gradual alterations in context over the years. As discussed in Chapter 2, an argument can be made that the 'alien beings' encountered today are essentially the same as the 'good people' of folklore, having changed their appearance and behaviour in order to interact with us in a context familiar to us: that of deep-space exploration.

As we shall see, deep space is now home to the various legends of subterranean civilization. The two strands of belief have converged to form a single, unified and complex scenario, in which the subterranean realms have become vast, artificial environments, and their inhabitants an occupying force of malevolent aliens.

If we look back over the history of UFO sightings, it is easy to see how such a system of belief could have developed. One of the most bizarre and least explainable aspects of the entire phenomenon is the apparent ability of UFOs literally to vanish into thin air. This has led some ufologists, most notably John Keel, to theorize that they and their operators may originate in another dimension of space – time (see page 204). Even more bizarrely, some witnesses claim to have seen UFOs plunging into solid ground, or beneath the waters of lakes and oceans. This suggests that the UFOs are returning to underground bases, which have been constructed by the aliens for the purpose of easy concealment while on Earth.

Although the southwestern United States has become the centre for rumours of such bases, they are said to exist all over the world, connected to each other by a tunnel system, through which hurtle ultra-fast trains, carrying both aliens and humans in a kind of commuter's LSD nightmare. This sounds rather glib, but as we shall soon discover, it is absolutely essential to maintain a healthy sense of humour when examining UFO-related conspiracy material. The 'horrible truth' is indeed horrible, and more than one researcher has been driven to the edge of madness by the apparent implications.

Even the most ardent UFO conspiracy buff will readily admit that there is a large amount of disinformation floating around; so much, in fact, that it is virtually impossible to say with any degree of accuracy what is actually happening. All we can do is weed out the absurdities and inconsistencies in the mass of data available, and attempt to evaluate whatever is left. No one in the field of ufology is doing more to aid this process than Jacques Vallée, and I direct the interested reader to his books, particularly *Revelations: Alien Contact and Human Deception*. Vallée's attitude is commendable in that, while he maintains that UFOs represent a genuine mystery, quite possibly originating from the activities of a non-human intelligence, he is nevertheless unwilling to accept uncritically the rumours and allegations of rampant alien activity that threaten to take over the subject.

It is often said that every legend is based on a kernel of truth, and the theory of underground alien bases is no exception. It is an indisputable fact that governments all over the world have constructed underground complexes for a variety of reasons. The United States Space Command's Space Surveillance Center was built 800 metres (half a mile) underground, inside Cheyenne Mountain near Colorado Springs, Colorado. Here the Space Detection and Tracking System monitors all known objects in near-Earth space, and can instantly pinpoint any object entering US airspace. Experiments in high-energy physics are conducted underground with colossal, ring-shaped particle accelerators, such as the one at CERN (the European Organization for Nuclear Research) in Geneva, Switzerland. In the United States, a plan known as

'Continuity of Government' (COG) has been developed in order to protect and ensure the survival of the administration in the event of a national catastrophe. There are allegedly 50 underground command posts scattered around the country, to which the president and key officials could be evacuated, should the need arise.

Experiments are constantly being conducted to find more and more efficient ways of constructing tunnels. In September 1983, *Omni* magazine included an article on a nuclear tunnel-boring machine, called the 'Subterrene'. This remarkable device is capable of heating rock to melting-point and then passing through it. As it moves on, the molten rock cools to form a smooth, tough glass-like wall lining the tunnel, thus dispensing with the need to strengthen it with concrete (the method used in the Channel Tunnel).

Secret military-industrial technology is years ahead of that put into official use. A prime example is the stealth technology used in the Northrop B-2 bomber and the F-117A fighter aircraft. According to the British *UFO Magazine*, the first test prototype of the F-117A was built in 1975, more than ten years before it was revealed to the public. It would not be too far-fetched to say that the technology is already in place for what we will be seeing around the year 2010

If this is the case, the extensive underground tunnel network which allegedly criss-crosses the United States is entirely feasible, and could constitute the kernel of truth around which have grown the rumours of subterranean alien activity. Before we attempt to assess the possible validity of these rumours, let us examine their essential elements in some detail.

One of the strangest and most frightening cases of UFO abduction contains all these elements, and is thus useful as a template for the general scenario. It concerns an unnamed woman who encountered a UFO and its crew on a stretch of road near the town of Cimarron, New Mexico. Concerned about a missing time period of about four hours, she underwent regressive hypnosis with Dr Leo Sprinkle on several occasions between 11 May and 3 June 1980. Also present was Paul Bennewitz, investigating for APRO (the Aerial Phenomena Research Organization).

The encounter got off to an explosive start, with the woman seeing brilliant lights which revealed the horrific sight of a cow being mutilated by strange creatures. While the poor beast was still alive and struggling, the beings plunged a long, tapered knife into

• Close-up of UFO photographed by Paul Trent at McMinnville, Oregon, USA, May 1950. This astonishing object, with its strange, off-centre tower, has resisted all attempts at explanation. According to analysis carried out by Ground Saucer Watch in the USA, it is metallic, 30.5 metres (100 feet) in diameter, and is approximately half a mile from the camera. *Fortean Picture Library*

• Saturn-shaped UFO photographed by newspaper-man Almiro Barauna, as it flew over Trindade Island in the South Atlantic Ocean, 16 January 1958. The object was also witnessed by 100 sailors. *Fortean Picture Library*

• UFO photographed by Dan Fry at Merlin, Oregon, USA in May 1964. Modern ufologists tend to discount the claims of Fry and other contactees since they sound more like bad science fiction than true encounters. *Fortean Picture Library*

• Casper, the Wyoming mummy. This bizarre little man was discovered after two gold prospectors dynamited a mountain in Wyoming in 1932. When examined, it proved to be the body of a man measuring 35.6 cms (14 inches). He was about 65 years old when he died. Is this the proof of an unknown civilization dwelling on Earth? *Fortean Picture Library*

• *(left)* Captain Thomas Mantell was the first human being to be killed while actively pursuing a UFO. Today it is widely accepted that his P51 Mustang aircraft crashed while chasing a high-altitude balloon. *Fortean Picture Library*

• *(below)* Face and pyramids in the Cydonia region of Mars. Many researchers claim that these intriguing features are artificial constructions. NASA, whose Viking spacecraft took this photograph in 1976, maintain that the face is merely a trick of light and shadow. *NASA*

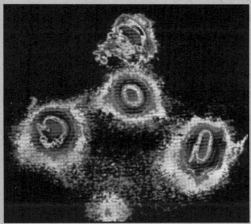

• *(above)* The Shard. This half-mile-high object was photographed on the far side of the moon by NASA's Orbiter 3 in 1967. Researcher Richard Hoagland believes that this is additional evidence to support the theory that extra-terrestrials were active in the Solar System thousands or even millions of years ago. *Quest Publications*

• Belgian triangle UFO, 1990. Throughout the late 1980s and early 1990s, northern Europe was plagued by UFOs such as this. It is conceivable that these strange craft were actually highly advanced Remotely Piloted Vehicles (RPVs) being tested by the US military.

• Numerous farm animals, like this unfortunate cow discovered in Newry, Northern Ireland, have been mutilated by unknown agencies over the years. Some claim that aliens are the culprits, while others suggest that sinister government agencies may be testing biological weapons on farmers' property. *Quest Publications*

• The harsh landscape around Roswell, New Mexico, where an alien spacecraft allegedly crashed in July 1947. Rumours still abound that the US government has engaged in a 50-year cover-up of the crash. *Fortean Picture Library*

• *(below)* An impression of a grey alien by artist Rod Dickinson. These malevolent and militaristic beings have been held responsible for a huge number of alleged abductions since the 1960s. *Fortean Picture Library*

• *(left)* Disc-shaped craft built by AVRO Aircraft Ltd. of Canada, 1960. The project was abandoned in 1965 because it could not rise more than a few feet with stability. *Fortean Picture Library*

One of the famous Cottingley fairy photos taken by Francis Griffiths and Elsie Wright in 1917 and 1920. Although these photos were hoaxed, the interaction between fairy-like beings and humans remains a possible alternative Extra-terrestrial Hypothesis for 'alien' contacts. *Fortean Picture Library*

its chest, then proceeded to excise its genitals with a single, swift cutting motion. The beings then captured the woman and her son, who was travelling with her, and took them to a number of different locations, some of which appeared to be spaceships. Under hypnosis, she reported that, despite her struggling, the beings forcefully disrobed her and gave her the standard physical examination, including a vaginal probe, to which she attributes a subsequent life-threatening infection. Despite their rough treatment of her, the beings seemed to be fascinated and delighted by her hair, eyebrows and eyelashes (they themselves were totally hairless).

At this point, the encounter became truly bizarre, with the appearance of a 'tall, jaundiced-looking man, dressed in white and looking different from the others', who seemed to be very angry and declared that the woman's abduction should not have taken place. After apologizing to her, he informed her – telepathically – that her son was all right, and that the other beings (apparently of the Grey type) would be punished for their mistake. This is how she described the scene:

> I remember seeing them naked, waist up, thin, ribs, clavicles, more ribs than we have – I don't know. The thinness of them, their hands and yet they could pick me up . . . Not claws, long fingernails, knotty and gnarled. Harsh-looking, so small, thin, bones . . . One has a nose that's crooked, turned up and crooked. They shuffle and drag their feet.

The beings' clothing was as odd as their behaviour, at once strange and familiar. One had 'a Franciscan monk's collar', together with 'a belt, military type boots [and] patch'. A feminine being had 'a collar, gathered at the neck like a pilgrim, with ruffles'. That fact that she had a square head, two holes instead of a nose, and was pea-green made the entity's get-up even more incongruous.

The woman was taken on a tour of a number of weird places, full of control panels, television monitor screens and, at one point, a 'window' through which could be seen a starscape with a planet in the foreground. The planet did not seem to be Earth. 'It's big, white, black, white here and black,' she said.

According to the percipient, one of the most frightening aspects of the encounter at this point was the apparent confusion and incompetence of the entities. Of the man in white, who ordered the punishment of the other beings, she said: 'He seems agitated, but not with me . . . I'm scared, not of him, but his confusion. It worries me that they don't know what they're doing.'

After the ship landed, she was taken out by another group of beings similar in appearance to the man in white; she remarked on how kind they seemed, and how beautifully they moved: 'They all shuffle their feet, long strides. Taller than me. Six feet [1.8 metres] or taller.' These beings were also hairless, but were 'attractively dressed', and three of them looked human.

It seems that, during the encounter, certain 'necessary alterations' were made to her, in the form of implants that were placed in her body and which (it is alleged) were later found by means of CAT scans.

Outside the ship, the woman immediately recognized the surrounding landscape as that of New Mexico – more specifically, the Roswell region. She was then taken into an elevator which led down to an underground complex, which she described under hypnosis as 'the base city of operation'. The complex was vast, and densely populated with the strange entities. She also remembers the roaring of water from an underground river.

When she briefly saw her son and was separated from him yet again, she broke away from her captors and found her way into a room full of tanks containing fluid of some kind. When she looked down into one of the tanks, she saw something unbearable:

> Something is horrifying me . . . Top of a bald head. Light is dim . . . I think I see an arm with the hand – human! Other something red and bloody-looking. Oh, God! I'm so scared at seeing this. Ahh! Tongues, huge; they look real big. They're under liquid, real dark . . . They found me, but when they found me, I was in the corner on the floor crying.

After the woman was recaptured, it seems that her memories of the abduction were erased by means which involved painful flashes of brilliant white light. Her son also experienced this traumatic treatment. In the woman's eyes, the beings were no longer kind and beautiful. 'You know something' she commented, *they don't like us*. They are something monstrous to me now. I feel like I've been in Auschwitz.'

When their ordeal was over, she and her son were flown back to the point of their abduction in one of the ships. Their car was also stored on board. The car was transferred back to earth, and she and her son continued on their journey home with no conscious memory of their experiences.

This encounter displays all the hallmarks of the modern UFO conspiracy scenario: not only did it involve abduction and implantation, but also cattle mutilation, and an underground base, apparently jointly operated by humans and aliens. The now world-famous Robert Lazar claims that, while working at the top-secret S-4 military test site in Nevada, he was given access to approximately 120 briefing papers, some of which described the point of origin of these beings. Their home star system is Zeta Reticuli, a binary system that is roughly 37 light years from Earth. Astronomers believe the stars to be much like our Sun. They are approximately 560 billion km (350 billion miles) apart. The so-called 'Extraterrestrial Biological Entities' (EBEs) come from Reticulum 4, the fourth planet out from Zeta Reticuli 2.

The professional pilot and UFO researcher John Lear believes that between 1969 and 1971, the US Government forged a secret treaty with these beings, whereby they would be allowed to conduct human abductions without interference from the military, in exchange for items of alien technology. The mutilation of cattle on a regular basis allegedly for the extraction of enzymes and other material desperately needed by the aliens, was also part of the deal. (Interestingly, other researchers have stated that cattle mutilation is a necessary element in the aliens' monitoring of pollution levels in the Earth's biosphere.) Although the aliens themselves are reported to have given the reason for human abduction as the monitoring of our physical and intellectual development, their true purpose seems to involve experimenting on us to perfect a method of producing a new race, composed of human/alien cross-breeds.

As if this were not frightening and sinister enough, some researchers, such as John Lear and William Cooper, believe that the tiny devices that are routinely inserted into victims' bodies are designed to act as receivers for commands transmitted by the aliens. This was the conclusion arrived at by Paul Bennewitz, who investigated the Cimarron case described above. (It is also the reason for my earlier comment about maintaining a healthy sense of humour when dealing with material of this kind.) Bennewitz's researches revealed a realm of utter nightmare, in which the Earth was being fought over by several groups of aliens: the evil and destructive Greys and the benevolent Highs, which included the

Nordics, the Talls and the Blonds. The Greys are allegedly a highly advanced, militaristic society who are on the point of succumbing to a genetic defect that causes their digestive systems to atrophy. In order to sustain themselves, they extract enzymes and hormones from both humans and cattle.

Although, according to Bennewitz, a secret treaty was drawn up between the Greys and the US Government, the aliens reneged on it by abducting many more humans than the agreement stipulated; also, the equipment they gave to their human hosts (mainly in the form of weapons technology) turned out to be intentionally defective, leaving humanity without an adequate defence against them. This accounts for the development of the low-frequency pulse generators to shoot down UFOs, and also for Project Excalibur, which it utilizes ground-piercing nuclear missiles to destroy underground alien bases.

The nature of the information he was making available ultimately began to unbalance Paul Bennewitz; he became more and more paranoid, claiming that the Greys were invading his house at night and injecting him with strange substances. Eventually, his terror caused him to have a mental breakdown.

THE DULCE BASE

The small town of Dulce in northern New Mexico was already the site of some unexplained cattle mutilation activity in the mid-1970s, before it became the undeclared capital of the aliens' subterranean colony on Earth. Actually, the terrible secret lies not beneath this little town of 900 souls, but under the nearby Archuleta Mesa.

The base first came to the attention of researchers in the late 1980s, after a series of reported abductions in the area. In the intervening years, a body of information has been accumulated from eyewitness accounts and 'official' documents, such as the so-called 'Dulce Papers', allegedly compiled by a high-level security officer known as 'Thomas C.', who made notes, took photographs and shot videotape footage of the base before fleeing and going into hiding. Every six months, so the story goes, he makes contact with each of the five people with whom he left copies of the material. In the event of his failing to contact them four successive times, his instructions are that they are to do whatever they wish with it.

In December 1987 a description of the contents of the Dulce Papers was released to researchers. Among other things, it contains discussions of the following: copper and molybdenum, magnesium and potassium, ultraviolet and gamma rays, the true purposes of the EBEs, the use of cow blood, DNA manipulation, 'almost human beings' and 'the creation of a nongender being'. The primary function of the Dulce Base appears to be that of a genetics laboratory, which is connected to the atomic weapons research centre at Los Alamos by an underground tube shuttle.

According to 'Commander X' a self-styled 'retired military intelligence operative now on the side of humanity', the 'aliens' who operate bases such as the one near Dulce consider themselves natives of Earth. They are themselves hybrid beings, their race having resulted from the cross-breeding of an ancient 'reptilian humanoid species' with 'sapient humans'. However, the secret agenda for planet Earth is not theirs, for they are actually no more than what they call 'Mercenary Agents' for a genuinely extra-terrestrial group known as 'the DRACO', who consider Earth to be their ancient 'outpost'. At this very moment, (according to Commander X), the DRACO are hurtling towards our unsuspecting world inside a planetoid starship.

Thomas C. reported on the interior arrangement of the facility and the research being conducted there. As we shall see, the information he presents in the Dulce Papers extends beyond the range of science and enters the realm of the occult and paranormal. This development now casts its shadow across the entire field of ufology.

While Levels 1 and 2 of the base contain garages for the maintenance of tube shuttles, tunnel-boring machines and flying discs, the contents of the deeper levels are far more sinister and frightening. Level 4 is where the paranormal research is conducted. This includes the utilization of telepathy, human auras and dreams. According to Thomas, the aliens know how to separate the 'bioplasmic body' from the physical body, so that an alien soul can be transplanted into a human body. They can also implant information and programmed reactions directly into the mind. This level is known as 'the Dream Library', and is just one aspect of what Commander X calls 'the Technologicalization of Psychic Powers'.

Level 6 is known as 'Nightmare Hall' by the human operatives who work there, and is the location of the main genetics laboratories. Thomas C. stated:

I have seen multi-legged 'humans' that look like half-human/ half-octopus. Also Reptilian-humans, and furry creatures that have hands like humans and cries [*sic*] like a baby, they mimic human words . . . also huge mixtures of Lizard-humans in cages.

Thomas C.'s experiences on Level 7 finally made him realize that things could not continue as they were:

I frequently encountered humans in cages, usually dazed or drugged, but sometimes they cried and begged for help. We were told they were helplessly insane, and involved in high-risk drug tests to cure insanity. We were told to never try to speak to them at all. At the beginning we believed the story. Finally, in 1978, a small group of workers discovered the truth. It began the Dulce Wars.

He may be referring to an incident in which 66 human personnel are said to have been killed by the aliens after a dispute over weapons. Apparently, the aliens warned the military and scientific personnel not to carry loaded weapons into a certain room, since they would have to pass through an energy field that would make the bullets explode. The personnel attempted to do so anyway, and paid the price. Although this event resulted in a deterioration of human – alien relations at the base, it remains fully operational today.

According to Thomas C., who held an 'Ultra 7' security clearance, there are far more than seven levels in the Dulce Base, and the very lowest levels feed directly into natural cavern systems deep beneath New Mexico.

BUT IS IT TRUE?

Such stories are bizarre and fantastic, to say the least. A skeptic would dismiss them completely as unworthy even of the effort required to refute them. However, I believe this would be a mistake. As I mentioned in the Introduction, stories like these are worthy of study for two reasons: we should examine them to search for whatever kernel of truth they may contain, and we should also accept that they spring from the mythopoeic faculty of the human mind, which tries to find logical explanations for mysterious events. Each of these viewpoints is valuable in understanding humanity and its relationship to wider reality.

Nevertheless, there are a number of questions we have to ask ourselves when assessing the possible validity of the claims made by people like John Lear, William Cooper and others. It has been said by some researchers, particularly with regard to the alien-abduction phenomenon and its science fiction-like overtones, that there are no precedents for the imagery found in victims' reports. Also, the various elements in alien encounters display a striking similarity from report to report. However, if we look at the history of science fiction, we can see that there are, in fact, a number of precedents for the activities of the aliens, and even for their appearance.

The most obvious correlation, as regards physical appearance, is undoubtedly with Steven Spielberg's splendid 1977 film *Close Encounters of the Third Kind*, in which the alien visitors are depicted as diminutive, large-headed beings with enormous eyes and pasty, grey skin. If we look at the phenomenon in the context of cultural feedback, it is clear that the aliens in Spielberg's film are a kind of prototype for subsequent descriptions of the Greys that now appear in virtually all reported alien encounters. It is as if the Greys have usurped the position formerly occupied by the 'Venusian' humanoids as the archetypal alien in the public mind. The humanoids linger on as a kind of vestigial presence, sometimes seen by themselves, and occasionally with the Greys. In films such as *Invasion of the Saucer Men* (made in the mid-1950s) the aliens have huge heads and large, bulging eyes, features culled from the 'bug-eyed monsters' of the pulp science-fiction magazines of the 1930s and 1940s.

There are also precedents in science fiction for the reported activities of the Greys, the most obvious being the 1950s film *Invaders from Mars*, in which the aliens abduct both adults and children and implant them with tiny electronic devices, enabling them to be controlled. The Greys are now regarded by many ufologists as invaders from a dying planet; this idea has been a staple of science fiction since the genre's creation. In perhaps the most famous story of alien invasion, H.G. Wells' *The War of the Worlds*, the Martians were a dying race which set its sights on Earth as a new home, with the human race as a convenient source of food. Had he been writing a few decades later, Wells would doubtless have taken advantage of the science of genetic engineering, and woven it into his story as well.

The alien invasion scenario as envisaged today, and presented as 'the horrible truth' by many ufologists, owes much to the science fiction of yesteryear, in terms not only of visual imagery, but of plot. Unfortunately, the plot seems to have been written by a scientifically illiterate hack. Absurdities and inconsistencies abound. For instance, it is scarcely feasible that an alien life form could sustain itself by ingesting the life-forms of this planet, whether cows or humans. One of the greatest dangers humans will face when they finally explore distant planets will be that posed by the contents of the planets' biospheres. Just as the Martians in *The War of the Worlds* were ultimately defeated by the bacteria in the Earth's atmosphere, so the microscopic life-forms on other planets will be a big problem for our own future explorers.

Their problems would not end there. Even if a survey team followed the obvious strategy of constructing a long-term habitat on an Earth-type planet's surface, complete with all the machinery necessary to filter the air so that it could be breathed without serious risk to life, they would be prevented from nourishing themselves on any indigenous vegetable or animal life for the very same reason. The microbes filtered from the surrounding atmosphere would still be present in the food sources. And, even assuming that the food could somehow be treated to ensure the eradication of these annoying microbes, it would almost certainly not sustain our intrepid descendants.

The reason for this involves the ways in which the chemistry of life-forms develops during the course of evolution. As Edward Ashpole explains in his book *The UFO Phenomena*, all life on this planet arises from the same 20 amino-acids. Since there are many more amino-acids which are *not* used by Earth-based life-forms, it is a fair bet that life on other planets will be composed of proteins arising from amino-acid groups that do not feature in our metabolism. In other words, the chances of our explorers finding a planet on which life is based on identical amino-acid groups to those on to Earth, are minute, perhaps non-existent. If humans attempted to eat anything they found on another planet, they would probably die rather quickly; and even if they survived, their metabolisms, geared to terrestrial amino-acid and protein groups, would be unable to process the food in their stomachs. The food simply would not provide any nourishment.

Those who claim that sinister aliens are mutilating cattle and people in order to ingest the enzymes necessary for their survival seem unwilling to tackle this fundamental flaw in their hypothesis. These believers in 'the horrible truth' might argue that a sufficiently advanced culture would be able to treat the biological materials extracted from their victims, so that they could be processed by alien metabolisms. However, if this were the case, surely they would be able to synthesize all their own food, without going to the trouble of making unwelcome visits to distant planets.

This raises the question, why would they need bodies at all? Our own computer scientists and cyberneticists are even now discussing the possibility of one day downloading the entire personality of a human being into a mechanical container, an artificial body that would, for all practical purposes, be virtually immortal. Indeed, these cyborgs would be the ideal future explorers of far-flung worlds, unhindered by the dietary requirements of fragile human flesh.

Some extra-terrestrial theorists have suggested that the Greys, with their insect-like movements and total lack of individuality, are actually sophisticated 'robots', controlled by an unseen intelligence. Whitley Strieber has said that these entities often walk in 'lock-step', with no variation in their movements. The Greys are often described as having no discernible musculature or bone structure, as if fashioned from a single, undifferentiated substance. These descriptions actually make a lot of sense, in view of the difficulties of planetary exploration outlined above. If the Greys do exist, and are here on Earth now, it is much more sensible to conclude that they are not 'living' creatures in the familiar sense, but resilient biological machines designed to operate autonomously in our biosphere.

However, this would run counter to the claims of John Lear and his colleagues, since it is unlikely that the power requirements of sophisticated biological robots – the products of a technology said to be 'a billion years' ahead of our own – would include fresh meat. Even if they did, would it make much sense to raid the farms and ranches of humans, who would instantly see that something sinister was going on? The Greys would surely be better off conducting their rustling activities on the sparsely populated plains of Africa, far from the prying eyes of avid alien-spotters.

There is a great deal that does not make sense in the scenario we have been examining. As Jacques Vallée notes in *Revelations*, many of the essential elements can be traced back to the unfortunate Paul Bennewitz, who was driven to breaking-point and beyond by the information he received. Some of this information was revealed by the Cimarron, New Mexico, case described earlier, a case that depended entirely on the use of regressive hypnosis, a technique that is considered extremely dubious by some ufologists, particularly in the United Kingdom. (BUFORA, the British UFO Research Association, have introduced a moratorium banning the use of regressive hypnosis in abduction investigations, citing the potential dangers to witnesses' mental and emotional well-being, particularly at the hands of inexperienced and unqualified practitioners of the technique, of whom there are, unfortunately, a great many.)

Bennewitz was also the target of a great deal of elaborate disinformation, provided by the Los Angeles-based researcher Bill Moore at the instruction of the US Air Force Office of Special Investigations. According to Moore, Bennewitz had constructed a piece of electronic receiving equipment, with which he was trying to eavesdrop on extra-terrestrial transmissions. When he actually succeeded in receiving unusual signals, he immediately assumed they were of alien origin. At a MUFON (Mutual UFO Network) meeting in Las Vegas in 1989, Moore claimed that Bennewitz had unwittingly tuned in to signals related to a secret Air Force experiment that had absolutely nothing to do with UFOs (Vallée, 1991, page 79). When he was visited by Air Force security officers, who asked him to stop listening in on their sensitive transmissions, Bennewitz refused. Since his paranoia was already firmly established, he took the Air Force's quite legitimate concern over his activities to mean that they really were engaged in UFO-based activities.

At this point, said Moore, AFOSI changed their tactics and decided to go along with Bennewitz, feeding his deluded fantasies (with Moore's willing assistance) to the point where his credibility, not to mention his mental health, became utterly compromised. AFOSI hoped that, even if Bennewitz leaked sensitive information about the Air Force experiment, no one would believe him. Unfortunately, many people in the UFO community did believe him, and the bizarre disinformation he received at the hands of AFOSI and Bill Moore became the foundation of the occupying alien force scenario.

As mentioned earlier, the underground alien base near Dulce, New Mexico occupies a central position in this complex network of rumours. It is said to be a truly colossal facility, comparable to the island of Manhattan in area. Again, we have to ask, just how feasible is this? And again, the answer has to be: not very. In principle, the building of underground facilities is well within the scope of current technology, especially using the sophisticated tunnel-boring machines discussed earlier. Ironically, however, that very technology proves that a base as vast as Dulce is claimed to be simply cannot exist in practice, although it is theoretically possible. An underground facility the size of Manhattan would produce an infra-red heat signature that would be impossible to hide from the many remote-sensing satellites that constantly orbit the Earth. Jacques Vallée reminds us that state-of-the-art military satellite technology would not be required to detect such a base; the equipment on board the now-obsolete LANDSAT, with its 30-metre (100-foot) resolution, would be quite sufficient. And LANDSAT images are available to 'hundreds of civilian geographers, planners, students, and geologists throughout the US and the world' (Vallée, 1991, page 57).

THE LAND OF SUPERNATURAL PEOPLE

Dubious data such as those revealed by regressive hypnosis and blatant disinformation have created a nonsensical scenario. And yet, no matter how much of the illogical detail we strip away, we are always left with the core mystery, represented by unexplained UFO sightings and encounters with non-human beings that are experienced and recalled in full consciousness, without the aid of hypnosis.

While UFOs and non-human entities continue to be reported throughout the world, the most significant activity seems to be centered on an area enclosed by the Nellis Test Range in southern Nevada, the Sedona region of north central Arizona, the Roswell area of southern New Mexico and the San Luis Valley in southern Colorado. If we look at contemporary reports, we can see a number of reasons for this. First, there is the genuine mystery of Roswell and the thing that crashed there (discussed in Chapter 5). To the northwest lies the ultra-secret Nellis base, where unconventional aircraft have undoubtedly been seen, regardless of their possible origin. The Sedona region of Arizona has been the setting for some truly bizarre events, involving UFOs, ghosts, Bigfoot and other strange creatures. In fact, according to researcher Tom Dongo, approximately 80 per cent of all UFO activity in Arizona occurs within Sedona. Similar events have also been reported for many years in the San Luis Valley; these include a large number of cattle mutilations, mysterious helicopters and UFO abductions.

That something very strange is happening in the southwestern United States seems beyond dispute. The questions we have to ask ourselves are as follows: is it wise to confine investigation of this activity to the present? Are there any answers to be found in the rich and legend-haunted history of this region? And do the persistent rumours of subterranean realms have an identifiable origin in the powerful myths of the indigenous peoples, myths that continue to find expression even today?

The Creation legends of the Native Americans are particularly rich in subterranean imagery, telling of humanity born deep inside the Earth and dragging itself to the surface. For instance, the Mandan tribe, who are related to the Sioux, believed they originated in an underground village near a vast lake. According to the legend, their remote ancestors climbed up the roots of a tall grape-vine that extended into the world above. Finding this new world well stocked with plants and animals, the first explorers returned to the underworld to tell the others of the delightful realm they had discovered. The entire population of the village decided to leave and seek a new life on the surface, but only half of them made it before the grape-vine root gave way under the weight. This gave rise to the Mandans' afterlife belief, in which the dead return to the underground village to rejoin the ancestors who were left behind.

A common motif in Native American underworld legends is that of a spiritual race which continues to live in tunnels and caverns. This realm is known as 'the Land of Supernatural People', whose existence largely mirrored that of the surface-dwellers.

In his examination of these legends, Alec Maclellan points out the most striking feature of these 'Supernatural People': the fact that they were white-skinned and fair-haired, traits shared with the Incan civilizer-god, Viracocha. He also states that the Apaches believed these people to have migrated underground after leaving 'a great island'. This, together with the widespread Native American story of an ancient Deluge, calls to mind the legend of Atlantis. The connection is strengthened (although far from proved) by the Mandans' belief that the very first men to emerge from the subterranean realms did so too soon, and were drowned in the great flood, which had not yet subsided.

A NEW SHAMANISM?

We have seen that a belief in subterranean realms, and the mysterious beings that inhabit them, is not confined to the late twentieth century context of technological facilities and the sinister beings who operate them. The core belief is common to many Native American peoples, and almost invariably involves the arrival on the surface of ancestors who came from far underground. There seems to be a link between these two systems of belief, the traditional and the technological, but what is that link? What is the essential factor in our own cultural and spiritual development that might connect people today (particularly those living in the modern United States) with the belief systems of ancient peoples?

As we saw in Chapter 4, humanity's relationship with that which lies beyond the mundane and material has always been mediated by a special group, existing within society and yet apart from it. Shamans, priests and other holy men are the middlemen in the commerce of the soul. Although it might appear that in our modern, secular, cynical world we have less and less need of such people, this is a delusion; it seems that the more we delude ourselves that we do not need them, the greater that need becomes.

The rise in the popularity of so-called 'New Age' thinking may be a reflection of the greater social uncertainties with which we are all increasingly having to deal. The implication of these developments is a growing perception of the need for the individual to take responsibility for his or her relationship with the spiritual. In the United Kingdom, New Age consciousness looks to the pre-Christian past, and the importance placed by the Celts upon communication with and understanding of the spirits of nature (although, contrary to popular opinion, the Celts were not a shamanic people). In the United States, New Age consciousness has much the same goals, and places an emphasis on Native American shamanism and mythology in its own search for ultimate answers to the problems of conscious existence.

It could thus be argued that the link between the modern legends of strange beings living underground and the Native American creation legends, with their stories of the original subterranean home of their ancestors, shows that this aspect of the alleged non-human presence on Earth is firmly grounded in the mythology of ancient America. Whether that mythology is in turn grounded in a demonstrable reality will, perhaps, become clear in time.

SEVEN

Cow-cutters and Goatsuckers

IN A SUBJECT WHERE there is so little concrete evidence which could be regarded as unequivocal proof of a genuine alien presence on Earth, the phenomenon of cattle mutilation would seem to be exactly what ufologists are looking for. The fact that so many animals have met this mysterious and ghastly end, coupled with the various apparently related phenomena that have also been reported in areas which are particularly prone to so-called 'mutes' ('mutilated'), strongly implies the involvement of an intelligent and very stealthy agency. And yet, as we shall see, the various researchers who have investigated the mutes are far from agreed as to their origin and purposes.

EARLY REPORTS

The animal-mutilation phenomenon first came to public attention with the case of Snippy the horse. As Christopher O'Brien reminds us in his exhaustive study of anomalous phenomena in the American southwest, *The Mysterious Valley*, the horse was mistakenly called 'Snippy' by the press who initially reported on the incident; the animal's actual name was Lady.

Her body was discovered on the morning of 9 September 1967 by Harry King, the son of her owner, Nellie King. The filly had been missing for 24 hours when Harry King went searching for her. He eventually found her 400 metres (a quarter of a mile) north of the main ranch house. The animal's head and neck had been stripped completely of all tissue; the bones were white and glistening, as if they had been exposed to the sun for many years.

King carefully examined the surrounding ground, which was still soft from the rain that had recently fallen. The tracks of the horses (the Kings had three of them; the other two were safe and well) told the experienced rancher a strange story. He concluded that all three horses had been running at full gallop toward the ranch house, but that Lady had for some reason left the other two and headed off in a different direction. After several hundred metres, her tracks stopped in mid-stride.

A week later, Harry King, his mother Nellie and some friends and family examined the entire area of the meadow in which Lady had been killed, and discovered four 'burned areas' at 4, 9, 13 and 21 feet (1.2, 2.75, 4 and 6.4 metres) away from the carcass, in the direction of the northwest. Extending in the opposite direction, to the southeast, they found eight more burned patches, between 12 and 15 metres (40 and 50 feet) from the body (see O'Brien, *The Mysterious Valley*, pages 66–7).

The death of Lady was merely the prelude to a spate of reported mutilations of cattle and other livestock throughout the United States in the following years. In each case, parts of the hide and various organs appeared to have been excised with surgical precision: eyes, tongues, udders, anuses, rectums and sexual organs were all missing. The explanation that might first spring to mind – that these were all soft body parts that predators or scavengers would be expected to devour first – seemed to be undermined by the nature of the incisions, and also by the reported absence of tracks around the carcasses. In the early to mid-1970s, mutilations were reported throughout the Midwestern states, in Ohio, Iowa, Minnesota, Kansas, Nebraska and Oklahoma.

The law-enforcement agencies were as mystified as the unfortunate ranchers and farmers whose animals were being slaughtered, and it remains a curious fact that no one has yet been apprehended or prosecuted for this crime.

A TRANSATLANTIC PHENOMENON?

In the July/August 1995 issue of *UFO Magazine*, Quest International Investigations Director Anthony Dodd wrote an article entitled 'The Invisible Predators' in which he states that animal mutilations have been on the increase for some years in the United Kingdom, as well as in Europe. The animals are typically found in much the same condition as those in America, sometimes with internal organs apparently having been sucked out through small incisions in the skin.

According to Dodd, the village of Kinlochewe, Scotland, suffered an outbreak of sheep deaths in March 1991. The carcasses were discovered with a small hole bored into the head; there was apparently no sign of blood, either in the animals, or on the surrounding ground. An (unnamed) veterinary surgeon was called in to investigate, and was at a loss to explain what had happened to the sheep.

Strange animal deaths have also been reported in the Orkney Islands, where more than 30 seals were found on beaches, minus their heads. The Scottish RSPCA (Royal Society for the Prevention of Cruelty to Animals) had never seen anything like it before. The seals' heads, a spokesman said, had been removed 'almost surgically', which would appear to rule out predators such as sharks or killer whales. Anthony Dodd interviewed the veterinary surgeon who performed post-mortems on the seals. She informed him that the cuts were so clean that they had penetrated between the vertebrae without damaging the bones.

More sheep and lambs were found in 1993 on the east coast of England. Their brains and rectums had been removed. Understandably upset by this, a group of local farmers decided to stake out one of the hardest-hit fields. A number of cameras were also set up, which would be triggered by infra-red sensors. Something evidently entered the field on one occasion, triggering the cameras. When the films were developed, they revealed a curious white 'cloud' in an area where a mutilated lamb was later found.

When Anthony Dodd wrote to the National Farmers' Union and the National Veterinary College, they replied that they were unaware of any such cases. As Dodd points out, the questions raised by the mysterious deaths of livestock across the country ought to be seriously addressed by the authorities, although this has yet to happen.

THE ALIEN CONNECTION

In the previous chapter, I criticized the more extreme theories associated with animal mutilations, pointing to the absurdities inherent in the notion of alien beings feeding on terrestrial life-forms. However, no matter how convincingly one refutes such theories, the fact remains that UFO sightings are closely associated with mysterious animal deaths.

The alien connection was not immediately apparent within the context of the mutes, and did not become so until Linda Moulton Howe produced her ground-breaking documentary *A Strange Harvest* in 1980. An extra-terrestrial explanation was mooted in the programme to account for some very bizarre aspects of the mystery; these included the total absence of tracks around muti-lated animals, even when there was snow or soft mud at the site. Also, the nature of the wounds themselves suggested that an instrument operating at extremely high temperatures had been used, altering the structure of the cells in the tissue. The implica-tion here was that the animals had been cut with a laser or laser-like device, although such a device would have been prohibitively large and unwieldy, and certainly would have left evidence of its presence on the ground.

The ranchers Howe interviewed were in little doubt as to the other-worldly nature of the mutilators. They had worked the land for many years, and were familiar with mundane predator activi-ty. While such activity certainly explained some mutilations, there were still many that defied a solution in these terms.

Not only have strange lights been sighted in the skies just before mutilations, but unusual ground traces have been discov-ered in the vicinity, as mentioned earlier in the Lady case. Richard L. Thompson cites the case of a 180-kg (400-pound) heifer found on 1 December 1974, in a field in Meeker County, Minnesota, by farmer Frank Schifelbien. The animal was discovered in a snow-covered field, although the ground was bare in a perfect circle around the carcass. There were no footprints in the snow around the site, and photographs taken from the air revealed a collection of discoloured circles in the nearby pasture (see Thompson, *Alien Identities*, pages 340–41).

Linda Moulton Howe reported on a case in April 1980, near Waco, Texas, in which a cattle-rancher was searching for a missing cow, when he encountered two strange-looking creatures, who were in the act of carrying off a calf. The creatures were about 1.2 metres (4 feet) tall, and were about 90 metres (100 yards) away from the witness, who described them as being green (or perhaps wearing green garments), having large heads and eyes that were 'like big, dark almonds'. The witness fled in fear, but returned to the scene two days later with his wife and son. There they found the calf's hide, which had been pulled inside out over its skull, along with its intact backbone. As with many other mutes, there was no sign of blood anywhere at the scene.

One of the most famous cases of alleged alien involvement with cattle mutilation is that of Judy Doraty who, along with four members of her family, encountered a bright light while out in her car. Pulling over to the side of the road, Judy got out of the car and walked to the rear. She then returned and climbed back in, telling the others that she was thirsty and felt nauseous. There was also a missing time period of one and a quarter hours, which was later filled in during a hypnotic regression session, conducted on 3 March 1980 by Dr Leo Sprinkle (who conducted the hypnosis in the Cimarron, New Mexico case, described in Chapter 6).

Judy's hypnotic regression revealed a so-called 'bilocation' experience, in which the percipient seems to occupy two places simultaneously. In this case, Judy reported standing beside the car, while simultaneously being on board the UFO they had seen earlier. She was dismayed to realize that her daughter was also in the craft, and was being examined by a group of beings similar in appearance to Greys. The beings reassured her, by means of telepathy, that they would not harm her daughter. Elsewhere in the UFO, a calf, which had been taken up by a beam of yellow light, was being mutilated. Its organs and bodily fluids were taken and placed in various receptacles before its carcass was lowered to the ground via the light beam. The creatures informed Judy that they were monitoring the presence of an unspecified poison that was apparently spreading through the environment, and would eventually affect humans (Thompson, page 343).

A TESTING GROUND FOR BIOLOGICAL WEAPONS?

An early theory about the causes of animal mutilation, and one that has not been entirely displaced by the more popular extraterrestrial theory, involves the secret testing by the US Government of race-specific biological weapons. The so-called 'VX toxin' programme was allegedly initiated in 1961, as a result of growing US involvement in Vietnam. Biological weapons were banned in 1970, so the programme descended even deeper into the murky realms of secrecy.

The VX toxin was supposedly tested on the property of unfortunate ranchers, by 'rogue researchers', who killed the animals and took away various organs – eyes, lymph glands, sexual and excretory organs, etc. – in order to monitor how the toxin spread through the body. According to the mutilation researchers who came up with this theory, cows were ideal test subjects, since their eyes and mucous membranes are chemically similar to those of Orientals (Peebles, page 261).

However, this was discovered to be a complete fabrication by Daniel Kagan and Ian Summers, who published their findings in their book *Mute Evidence* in 1984. The source of these allegations, one 'Dale Edwards', was actually a petty criminal and conman. It need hardly be said that the alleged similarity between cow eyes and the eyes of Orientals is utterly absurd, as is the very idea of a race-specific biological weapon. The various races of humanity are nowhere near different enough genetically to make such a weapon feasible.

THE MYSTERY OF THE BLACK HELICOPTERS

The theory that the US Government is somehow involved with cattle mutilations has been put forward by many researchers, who point to the high incidence of reports of black or grey helicopters, which are either unmarked or have their registration numbers obscured, so that their origin cannot be verified.

Writing in the April 1996 issue of *Fate* magazine, Jim Keith reports that on 7 May 1994, a teenager in Harrahan, Louisiana, was chased by an unmarked black helicopter for 45 minutes. The helicopter's crew allegedly pointed strange, 'scope'-like instruments at the boy, who reported the incident to the local police. The police chief said that, since the helicopter was owned by the federal government, no further action could be taken.

There seems to be an important connection between whoever is piloting these helicopters, and the mysterious animal deaths. There have been a number of reports of the craft spraying livestock and vegetation with unknown substances that have an immediate and disastrous effect. In addition to this, some mutilated cattle have been found sprayed with fluorescent paint, which implies that they have been pre-selected for dissection.

It seems likely that an experiment of some kind is being conducted, although its precise purpose is still far from being established. Researchers such as Jim Keith have suggested that some form of biological warfare agent is involved, and that the helicopter crews are monitoring its distribution and effectiveness. And yet, other activities – such as the apparently pointless harassment of innocent individuals with no prior interest in the subject – indicate a more subtle and insidious programme of experimentation, more along the lines of psychological than bacteriological warfare. Sadly, there is a dreadful precedent for such a programme, one that gives skeptical accusations of paranoia a hollow ring.

UNCONVENTIONAL OPERATIONS

The project known as MKULTRA is often cited in support of government conspiracy theories, whatever their nature. While their veracity may be open to debate, and subject to verifiable evidence, the initial premise – that people in positions of power have occasionally involved themselves in the top-secret perpetration of atrocities against their own civilians – cannot be dismissed with the supercilious chuckle that usually greets the allegations of conspiracy theorists.

MKULTRA had its origins in the CIA's (perhaps understandable) ambition to be able to control and manipulate the human mind at a distance. According to Brian Freemantle's 1983 book *CIA: The 'Honourable' Company*, neither the Director of the CIA, nor Congress, was aware of the experiments being conducted during project MKULTRA (see below); even the President himself was kept in the dark. And, since almost all the documents relating to it have been destroyed, in direct contravention of CIA regulations (Freemantle, page 80), we shall all continue to be kept in the dark.

The original rationale for MKULTRA was to remain ahead of the Soviet Union in mind-control methods. By 1952 the Soviets were believed to be experimenting along these lines, and it was suspected that they might even be ahead of the CIA. One of the areas in which the Agency showed most interest was known as 'depatterning', in which the subject's memories would be completely erased through the use of intense electroshocks and powerful drugs such as Thorazine, Nembutal, Seconal, Veronal and Phenergan. Once the mind had been 'wiped', experiments in 'repatterning' were conducted, in which the test subjects received tape-recorded instructions (Freemantle, pages 82–3).

Other experiments in mind control were conducted using LSD with drug addicts at the rehabilitation centre at Lexington, New York. The drug addicts were led into an almost Faustian arrangement, whereby they would allow themselves to be experimented upon in return for supplies of the drug of their choice.

However, addicts were not the only guinea-pigs in the CIA's search for a method of mind control. Richard Helms, the then Assistant Deputy Director for Plans, wrote to CIA Director Allen Dulles:

We intend to investigate the development of a chemical
material which causes a reversible non-toxic aberrant mental
state, the specific nature of which can be reasonably well
predicted for each individual. This material could potentially
aid in discrediting individuals, eliciting information and
implanting suggestions and other forms of mental control.

In order to test their various drugs more fully, the CIA conducted Operation BIG CITY, in which the exhaust-pipe of a 1953 Mercury car was adapted so that it could emit mind-control substances in gaseous form. The car was then driven around New York City while emitting the gas. Other CIA operatives travelled on the city's subway, spraying LSD from specially adapted suitcases, while on the opposite coast, a disorientating biological gas was released from the Golden Gate Bridge in San Francisco, to see the effect it would have on the population of that city. The plan was foiled by the wind, which blew the gas out to sea where it couldn't do any harm (Freemantle, page 89).

At no time during this dark and tragic affair were the test subjects examined or supervised by qualified medical or scientific practitioners. The reason for this was somewhat ironic: there *were* no such individuals with sufficiently high security clearance to allow them to be told anything about MKULTRA. It was left to CIA operatives, who were totally unqualified in the administration of drugs, to conduct the experiments, and then follow up on the results as best they could.

Operation MKULTRA was eventually terminated in 1963. The Congressional investigatory committee headed by Senator Frank Church concluded that the operation 'demonstrated a failure of the CIA's leadership to pay adequate attention to the rights of individuals'. The Church Committee's report criticized the Agency for placing the lives of innocent citizens in jeopardy, and for continuing its programme for ten years, despite the fact that the laws of the United States were being violated.

In 1964, MKULTRA was replaced by MKSEARCH, which plumbed new depths in drug experimentation. Tests were now conducted on mentally defective patients at a hospital in Washington. The programme was carried out in co-operation with the US Army at its Fort Detrick installation, and included the use of various biological agents produced under contract by a laboratory in Baltimore, Maryland. Project MKSEARCH came to an end in 1972.

The CIA's fear of Soviet advancement in the field of mind control was shared by the Army, which conducted its own experiments with LSD and other psychoactive drugs. However, liaison between the two was so poor that the Army actually duplicated many of the experiments already conducted by the CIA, with the CIA spying on the Army to discover the results!

PSYCHIC ESPIONAGE

During the 1970s, while skeptics and debunkers scoffed at all aspects of the paranormal, the CIA were becoming very interested in psychic abilities for espionage and mind-control purposes. The KGB were also conducting parapsychological research, and once again, the CIA feared that their Soviet counterparts were ahead in the race.

The artist and psychic Ingo Swann is perhaps the most famous practitioner of 'remote viewing', the mysterious process of visualizing what lies at a particular set of map co-ordinates from an entirely different location. One such experiment took place in a laboratory at the Stanford Research Institute in Menlo Park, Palo Alto, California. Swann was given a set of coordinates: 48 degrees, 30 minutes south, 69 degrees, 40 minutes east. The sketch he drew was compared with what actually lay at those co-ordinates: Kerguelen Island (which he had never seen or even heard of) in the Indian Ocean, where the French and the Soviets were jointly conducting research into upper-atmosphere meteorology. The two outlines were a perfect match.

If the thought-transference talents of people like Ingo Swann could be utilized, the benefits to any intelligence service would be self-evident. Hence the CIA's interest in parapsychology. During the Cold War, laboratories had been established throughout the Soviet Union. In the early 1980s, I.M. Kogan, chairman of the Bioinformation Section of the Moscow Board of the Popov Society, was investigating the applications of mental suggestion over long distances, intercity telepathy and awakening subjects from hypnotically induced sleep by beamed suggestion. At the Leningrad Institute for Brain Research, L.L. Vasiliev attempted both telepathy and hypnosis over long distances, while in Moscow, Viktor Adamenko successfully trained Alla Vinogradova to use psychokinesis to move objects without physically interacting with them. Other researchers examined the possibility of 'reading' (and perhaps controlling) the electrical fields produced by the human brain.

The conclusion reached by the American researchers was that the left side of the brain controls verbal and analytical thought, while the right side is responsible for intuition and the understanding of patterns. An additional conclusion was that the most successful psychics tend to be 'non aggressive extroverts tending towards holistic world views, capable, both subjectively and empirically, of high interest in psi processes' (Freemantle, page 99). The CIA were interested in a number of applications of parapsychology, including 'remote viewing, [psychokinesis], telepathy, instant hypnosis, thought reading through interception of the brain's electrical energy and precognitive remote view (seeing into the future)' (Freemantle, pages 99–100).

The US research programme into parapsychology began in the early 1970s, and during its 23 years cost about $20 million. The realization that the Soviet Union was investing heavily in its own experiments resulted in near panic at the Pentagon; many officials feared that the Russians would be able to commit 'thought theft' and steal America's most sensitive secrets directly from the minds of its most important military and secret service personnel.

The US remote-viewing group was known as 'Project Scanate' (Scan by Co-ordinate), and while there were many spectacular successes, there were also tragic failures and casualties. For some subjects, the mental pressures that resulted from constant testing became too much. According to Noel Koch, a high-ranking Pentagon official, some people had out-of-body experiences, and it was hoped that 'they might be able to travel distances and perhaps enter someone else's mind. But people had been having trouble getting back into their bodies and some had to be taken to hospital.'

One of the first psychic recruits to be employed was a former Army intelligence officer named Joe McMoneagle, who explained the experimental process:

> We would empty our minds of everything and get into a
> centred meditative state. We might write the information as it
> came to us, or sketch. What's important to remember is that
> this information was never used alone. It was always in
> concert with other information. So those who say there isn't
> one instance where remote viewing could stand alone as a
> way to solve something are probably right.

The talents of McMoneagle and his colleagues weren't confined to the experimental laboratory. During the Iranian hostage crisis of 1979, when the American embassy in Tehran was seized by militants who took 63 diplomats prisoner, the remote-viewing team were brought in to help establish the exact location of the hostages. McMoneagle, describes how he was given photographs, inside a double envelope, of hostages:

> Then I would concentrate and sketch the room where that
> person was being held, or maybe just the contents of the
> room. My rate was and is about one in four. I would consider
> it effective that I could describe the location where three of
> the hostages had been taken.

Notwithstanding the tragic destruction of the rescue aircraft at Desert One, south of Tehran, the remote-viewing exercises met with considerable success in other areas. One viewer accurately described an airfield with a gantry and crane at the Soviet nuclear test site at Semipalatinsk, his vision being corroborated by a spy satellite which photographed the area the following day. Another psychic successfully located Colonel Gadaffi just before the 1986 air-strike on Tripoli (which nevertheless failed to kill him).

As one might expect, the remote viewers' success rate was not 100 per cent. When General James Dozier was kidnapped by the Italian Red Brigade in 1981, it took a tip-off to the police to get him released. The psychics had come up with plenty of locations for him, including a yacht on Lake Como, but they all proved to be wrong.

Opinion is split over whether the CIA's research into parapsychology was worth while. According to Ray Hyman, a psychology professor at the University of Oregon and co-author of a CIA study into the value of such research, 'There's no evidence these people have done anything helpful for the government.' But Edwin May, a former director of Stargate (a later version of Project Scanate), declared:

> Statistically speaking, we are exactly correct 50% of the time with viewing. [. . .] The average person will guess correctly 20% of the time, so some say that's a difference of only 30%. But in statistics, 30% is a lot.

However, the CIA now wants to discontinue the programme, citing money and 'the giggle factor' as reasons. But if remote viewing works as well as its defenders claim, it seems unlikely that the Agency would lose interest in this field altogether.

PSYCHIC UFO TRACKING

In his 1990 book *Out There*, journalist Howard Blum cites an example of just how important remote viewing might be to governments anxious to monitor UFO activity, bearing in mind that conventional radar is not always useful in this respect. During a remote-viewing experiment at the Stanford Research Institute in 1985, the viewer was asked to scan for a Soviet Delta-class submarine, having been shown a photograph of the craft.

While he was informing the scientists of the submarine's coordinates (it was patrolling the waters between Maine and Nova Scotia), the viewer stumbled, apparently having encountered some sort of trouble. His confusion was rapidly replaced by what the scientists present realized was fear. When asked what was wrong, the viewer replied that while he was scanning for the Soviet submarine, he had also 'seen' something at the same coordinates, something hovering above the craft. The scientists asked him if he thought it was an aeroplane; the viewer merely shrugged. When asked to draw what he had seen hanging above the submarine, he drew a circular, wingless craft.

The scientists studied the drawing, trying not to make the obvious comparison. Eventually, one of them said to the viewer: 'Well, what else could it be? I mean, you're not going to tell me it's a flying saucer.' The remote viewer replied, 'Yes, that's it exactly.' (Blum, *Out There*, pages 37–8.)

If the CIA, not to mention other intelligence agencies in the United States and throughout the world, are really monitoring the UFO phenomenon (and there is very strong documentary evidence to support this), obtaining information by parapsychological means would surely be helpful. This is especially true if a team of remote viewers could tell them, with a 50 per cent rate of accuracy, precisely where a UFO is and what it is doing. In view of the enormous sums of money that are routinely channelled into the various 'black projects' under development, the cost would be unlikely to be a problem.

MEANWHILE, BACK AT THE RANCH . . .

We seem to have come rather a long way from the subject of this chapter, and yet the digression is significant with regard to the distressing events that have been occurring on remote farms and ranches for the last three decades. Government involvement with research into psychological warfare and the paranormal has implications that extend far beyond the hapless ranchers of rural America.

For the moment, we must return to the question of animal mutilations and killings, and ask if there might be some connection between the CIA's nefarious activities, and the public perception that a top-secret conspiracy is responsible for these deaths. The subject of ufology in general is often examined in total isolation, without reference to the background of contemporary events. This is a serious mistake, since it ignores a significant amount of related data that might help explain those mysterious events.

Mutilation researchers Daniel Kagan and Ian Summers have discovered some intriguing correlations between the waves of cattle deaths and the state of contemporary American society, correlations that strongly imply the influence of one over the other. The public was first alerted at a national level in 1973, at the time of the Watergate scandal; the mutilation reports reached a peak the following year, when President Nixon resigned from office. Another wave of mutilations occurred in Colorado in 1975, just after the United States withdrew, in less than glorious circumstances, from Vietnam.

The helicopter came into its own as a weapon of war in that conflict, and remains perhaps its single most enduring image. (In *Watch the Skies*, his skeptical survey of the history of ufology, Curtis

Peebles reminds us that 'the last helicopter out of Saigon' came to epitomize America's defeat.) It was in 1975 that the first reports of mysterious unmarked helicopters began to surface, and this year also saw the Congressional investigations into the CIA's MKULTRA programme. It is therefore entirely understandable that the American public should begin to harbour intense fears regarding their government's secret use of chemical and biological weapons, and that their fears should be projected on to the discoveries of dead cattle on isolated ranches.

The following year, 1976, saw a marked decrease in mutilation reports; this might seem puzzling until one remembers that this was the year of the Bicentennial celebrations in the United States, obviously a time for intense pride and a powerful sense of nationhood.

The lack of faith in government, coupled with a suspicion of sinister agendas, returned two years later with the poor performance of the economy, rising unemployment and further speculation over the conspiracy theory of the Kennedy assassination. There were plenty of possible culprits for the alleged cattle mutilations: aside from the CIA and its execrable MKULTRA programme, there was the military, an object of public contempt since Vietnam; the energy companies, which were hated for the destruction they visited upon the land; and the various cults that had been growing up throughout the 1970s, whose leaders (especially Jim Jones, whose followers committed mass suicide in 1978) were seen as sinister, almost demonic figures (Peebles, pages 266–7).

The skeptical stance adopted by Peebles and other so-called 'debunkers', such as Philip Klass, may be more useful than many ufologists would care to admit. Even if one does not accept the majority of their conclusions, it is important to keep in mind that an initial event, whether or not it is amenable to a mundane explanation, can generate a number of subsequent reports of similar events, influenced by political and social factors prevalent at the time. We can see this mechanism at work in the numerous cattle-mutilation reports that were later found to have rational explanations, such as predator action. For example, when researcher Ken Rommel pointed out to ranchers on a number of occasions that the injuries on their animals had not been inflicted with 'laser-like' precision, but were actually jagged (implying predators' teeth), the ranchers agreed, and explained that they 'had read about livestock mutilations', and had reported the deaths as such because they had 'wanted to make sure that this wasn't one of them', (Peebles, page 264).

I mentioned earlier that, no matter how much absurdity, illogicality or misidentification is stripped away from the UFO phenomenon, the core mystery remains, constantly eluding all attempts to solve it finally and unequivocally. It is the same with the mystery of the cattle mutilations: the fact remains that *some* animals have met dreadful ends in very puzzling circumstances. The frequent and unquestionable presence of unmarked helicopters, which are sometimes reported to have sprayed unknown chemicals on animals and crops (shades of MKULTRA?) is an additional enigma that refuses to surrender to the anodyne assurances of the debunkers.

Like so many other elements in the UFO phenomenon, unexplained livestock mutilations have recently undergone a metamorphosis of their own. The public imagination world-wide has been galvanized anew by the appearance of a terrifying predator that attacks without mercy, leaving its victims, like those of the supposed cattle mutilators, utterly drained of blood.

PART BAT, PART INSECT, PART UFO

At the beginning of 1995, on the Caribbean island of Puerto Rico, the animals started dying. Unlike the mutilations in the United States, the killings were not confined to livestock, but included domestic cats and dogs, as well as cattle, sheep, goats and hens. A common factor in all the deaths was the complete absence of blood in the carcasses: it seemed to have been drained through a single puncture wound.

For the first six months of the epidemic, which spread across the entire island, the killer remained unseen. Then, in September, the first reports of its appearance came in. They made extremely bizarre reading. The creature was initially described by witnesses as 'part bat, part insect, part UFO', probably because it had huge, bulging red eyes and was apparently capable of flight.

The highly respected UFO researcher Jorge Martin, who edits the Puerto Rican magazine *OVNI Evidencia*, has been investigating the phenomenon of the so-called *'Chupacabras'* (Spanish for 'Goatsucker'). He believes that the mysterious animal deaths have been caused by what he calls an 'Anomalous Biological Entity' (ABE). Having collected many eyewitness reports of the creature,

Martin has built up a kind of photo-fit picture. The Chupacabras has a large, oval head (reminiscent of the typical Grey alien), and the body of a tailless, bipedal dinosaur. Some witnesses have reported small, pointed ears, although this is not common to all sightings. Its body is said to be covered with short, black coarse hair, which can apparently change colour, like a chameleon. Indeed, the creature's ability to camouflage itself has been described on a number of occasions: at night, it will be black or dark brown, while in daylight it will change to green or greenish-brown. The Chupacabras has very powerful hind legs, which enable it to leap enormous distances.

First reported in the town of Orocovis in the interior of the island, the killings continued to grow in frequency throughout 1995, prompting municipal authorities to lead large search parties out into the night in an attempt to capture the vampiric monster. At the beginning of 1996, there was a lull in activity, which led some investigators to speculate that the unseasonably cold weather had driven the Goatsucker into a temporary hibernation, possibly in the El Yunque rainforest.

This 'hibernation' was short-lived, however, for in March the predator returned to slaughter 30 fighting cocks and hens on the farm of Arturo Rodriguez, in Aguas Buenas. All of the animals bore the trademark puncture wounds and were found drained of blood. In the same month a boy, Ovidio Mendez, encountered the creature in his back yard. According to Ovidio Mendez, it was 1.2 metres (4 feet) tall and walked upright on two legs. Its eyes were elongated and bright red; it had large fangs and claw-like hands. Despite its fearsome appearance, the creature made no hostile moves towards the boy, and eventually ran away.

Like their counterparts in the United States, the Goatsucker killings have been treated with great concern by the farmers who have lost valuable livestock. According to Jorge Martin, writing in the British *UFO Magazine*, the President of the Puerto Rico House of Representatives Agricultural Commission, Juan E. Lopez, has introduced a resolution asking for an official investigation into the situation.

One of the most curious aspects of the Goatsucker phenomenon is that it seems to be culture-specific, being confined to Spanish-speaking communities. The animal deaths quickly spread from Puerto Rico to the United States, especially to the large Latin communities in Florida, Texas and other parts of the southwest.

Early on the morning of 1 May 1996, José Espinoza of North Palomas Avenue on the west side of Tucson, Arizona, played unwilling host to the Goatsucker, which broke into his house and hopped into the bedroom of his seven-year-old son. Espinoza, a construction worker, said he awoke at 3:30 am to strange noises outside his home. He went outside to investigate and found the creature at his front door. Later, it managed to get into the house and into his son's bedroom. Espinoza claimed that the creature slammed the bedroom door, sat on his son's chest, then hopped out through the bedroom window. Espinoza reported that the creature had 'big red eyes, a pointy nose, pointy ears and a wrinkled face. It mumbled something at me and hopped away.' Several hours later, searchers in Agua Prieta, Sonora, reported seeing a strange beast flying north.

Espinoza said that the animal smelled like a wet dog, and left footprints and handprints all over his house, which his aunt later identified as those of a Goatsucker. (On what previous knowledge she based this conclusion is not clear).

Tales of the Goatsucker have spread through the Spanish-speaking communities of the United States as quickly as they did through Puerto Rico. Keoki Skinner, owner of a fruit shop in Agua Prieta, Sonora, told investigators, 'It's like a mania. My kids were scared to come out of the house last night.'

In Texas, Sylvia Ybarra found her pet goat dead, with three puncture wounds in its neck. Her first thought was of the Chupacabras. She said she believes the creature 'is watching over us', and that nobody knows when it's going to return.

According to Tony Zavaleta, an anthropologist at the University of Texas at Brownsville, the spreading of the Goatsucker 'legend' is typical of mass hysteria. 'In the technical world [of television and Internet websites]', he explains, 'it spreads almost instantaneously. I would call it pop hysteria.'

To Sylvia Ybarra, however, the fate of her goat had little to do with 'pop hysteria'; and her mother, Maria, became increasingly afraid for the safety of the children playing outside in the area. Like the unfortunate ranchers whose cattle have been mysteriously killed by unknown predators, claims of hysteria ring hollow for people like Sylvia Ybarra.

And yet it seems very likely that hysteria is at work with regard to some of the more outrageous Goatsucker sightings. For instance, people in San Juan have testified that they have seen the creature walking down the street in broad daylight, while others in Miami swear that they have seen it at the airport, waiting for a flight to its next destination!

Unlike the cattle mutilations, the Goatsucker attacks have entered the popular imagination in a less than serious context. For instance, the creature has been recruited by political cartoonists in Puerto Rico. 'Do you believe in the political agenda of President Zedillo?' a pollster asks a man in a cartoon in the newspaper *El Imparcial*. 'No,' the man replies. 'Do you believe in the Chupacabras?' the pollster asks. 'Yes!!!' the man replies.

In Spanish-speaking areas of Florida and Texas, one can find restaurants named 'Chupa Cabras', and also Salsa bands called 'Los Chupacabras'. The creature can be found on everything from T-shirts to golf-club covers, spawning a lucrative souvenir industry.

Although the Goatsucker mystery is taken in a much more tongue-in-cheek way than the earlier cattle mutilations, the theories on its origin nevertheless arise from similar beliefs and suspicions. Some people have claimed that the Goatsuckers are a race of vampires which can only be killed by laser beams and silver bullets, while others believe they are aliens bent on spreading deadly viruses. Puerto Rico itself is believed to have been the site for much testing of dangerous chemicals and radiation weapons, leading to the theory that the Goatsucker is the freakish result of genetic engineering, whose movements are being monitored by the authorities.

The possible alien origin of the Goatsucker provides a further correlation with the cattle-mutilation phenomenon. Like the southwestern United States, Puerto Rico is considered to be a highly significant area in terms of UFO activity, and this has led researchers to assume a connection between the Goatsucker's presence and the high incidence of UFO sightings. And, as with the US government and the cattle-mutilation phenomenon, the Puerto Rico Government does not seem to be terribly interested in what is going on, preferring to take the word of veterinarians who assure them that the animal deaths are the result of nothing more sinister than predation by dogs, cats and coyotes. However, this begs the question, why has nothing like this happened before?

Researcher Scott Corrales reports that, although the Goatsucker has been encountered in Mexico, these sightings are even more bizarre than those reported in Puerto Rico or North America; Corrales even likens them to the work of H.P. Lovecraft. People in

Mexico have told of being 'overcome by shadows', and awakening from unconsciousness later on to discover puncture wounds on their bodies (see Corrales' article 'How Many Goats can a Goatsucker Suck?' in the August 1996 issue of *Fortean Times*).

According to Jorge Martin, at least two Goatsuckers have actually been captured by US and Puerto Rican 'Government officers'. The creatures were allegedly apprehended around 6 or 7 November 1995, one of them in the town of San Lorenzo, Puerto Rico, the other in the rainforest of El Yunque. Both were taken to the United States by 'special personnel'.

Martin and his colleagues succeeded in obtaining a sample of Goatsucker blood after one of the creatures was allegedly shot while escaping by a policeman in Camp Rico. Although analysis of the blood continues in the United States, preliminary findings show that the blood is not genetically compatible with any blood type belonging to any human or animal known to science (*UFO Magazine*, March/April 1996).

Jorge Martin believes that serious investigators of the Goatsucker phenomenon have been subjected to a subtle programme of debunking and ridicule by the intelligence community in an attempt to prevent the situation from being seriously addressed by the media and the authorities. Whether or not this is true, the Goatsucker phenomenon has entered the realms of popular folklore, which, as we have seen, is capable of generating events out of the substance of belief itself. It is worth noting that many witnesses have described the Goatsucker as producing a sulphurous odour, which is traditionally associated with demonic entities and other denizens of the underworld.

While numerous theories have been put forward to account for the origin of these bizarre reports, the fact remains that thousands of animals have been mysteriously killed and many have been found drained of blood through a single puncture wound. If we accept that *some* people have indeed seen an unusual animal in connection with these animal deaths (skeptics would contend that that is a very big if), then, once again, we have a collection of core events that, while they have undoubtedly spawned a number of spurious secondary reports, have yet to be explained by orthodox science.

The Human Operators

A CHAPTER ON THE theory that UFOs are actually built and flown by human beings might seem out of place in a book dealing with the alleged presence of aliens on Earth. The fact is, however, that any examination of ufology would be incomplete without it, since it forms an integral part of the history of the subject, both as a theory worth investigating, and also because it has become incorporated into a much wider network of alien conspiracy theories.

The idea of human-built flying saucers can be traced back to the end of the last century. As we shall see in this and the following chapter, the monstrous conspiracies it embodies have recently received greater attention from ufologists, who speculate that it will have serious implications for the future of humanity.

PROPELLER-DRIVEN UFOS?

The first true UFO wave occurred in the United States in the late 1890s. Between November 1896 and May 1897, thousands of people reported seeing large 'airships' gliding through the skies, occasionally shining powerful beams of light on the ground below. Judging from the descriptions given of these craft, they were indeed airships: they were said to be long and cigar-shaped, with motor-driven propellers that pushed them at a leisurely pace through the air. They often displayed the undulating motion typical of craft buffeted by winds, and their occupants (all of them human in almost every reported case) sometimes asked for assistance with their engines from bemused witnesses.

The great puzzle of the airship sightings is that, while they were clearly primitive contraptions, they were still ahead of the aviation technology of the time. Even the state-of-the-art machines being built in Europe at that time, by the likes of Charles Renard, A.C. Krebs and David Schwartz, were rather pitiful affairs capable only of very short flights. A machine comparable to the so-called 'Great Airships', capable of extended flight, was not constructed until 1904, when Thomas Baldwin successfully tested his dirigible *California Arrow* at Oakland, California.

However, since technological accomplishments are usually achieved years before they are officially unveiled to the public, it seems feasible that one or more inventors could have possessed sufficient aeronautical expertise to develop such a craft around 1896, a mere eight years before the flight of Baldwin's *California Arrow*. Many American inventors obtained patents for their airship designs, and were constantly on their guard against the theft of their ideas. It is therefore understandable that they should have wanted to maintain intense secrecy.

To obtain some idea of the airships' capabilities, and the behaviour of their occupants, let us look at an encounter that occurred in Deadwood, Texas on 30 April 1877, as described by W.A. Harbinson in his book *Projekt UFO*.

Alerted by the distressed sounds of his horse, a farmer named H.C. Lagrone went outside and saw a brightly lit object circling his fields before coming to rest in one of them. Lagrone went to the landing site to investigate, and there met the five-man crew of the craft, two of whom proceeded to collect water, while the other three engaged the astonished farmer in conversation. According to the crew, the airship in which they had arrived was one of five that had been designed and constructed in 'an interior town in Illinois'. They refused to give any more information concerning the machine, because they had yet to take out any patents on it.

FOO FIGHTERS

World War Two saw the development of numerous new weapons and support systems, including rockets, electronic guidance devices and jet-engine technology. There were also many reports of tiny unmanned aircraft that repeatedly harassed Allied aircrews on bombing missions over Germany. The so-called 'foo fighters' were described as brightly lit metallic spheres, no more than a metre or two (a few feet) in diameter, which flew alongside the wings of the Allied aircraft during night flights. The flight characteristics of these objects led the crews who encountered them to conclude that they were under remote control from the ground. This in turn led to the assumption that they were, in fact, Nazi (or perhaps Japanese) secret weapons designed to interfere with the electrical systems of aircraft, or merely to confuse the Allied pilots.

According to the Italian author Renato Vesco, the mysterious foo fighters were indeed German secret weapons, as the Allies had initially suspected. Powered by turbo-jets, the *Feuerball* ('Fireballs') were tiny devices used in both an anti-radar and psychological warfare capacity. The larger, manned flying disc was known as the *Kugelblitz* ('Ball Lightning').

In the years following the end of World War Two, the foo fighters were replaced by cigar- and disc-shaped 'ghost rockets', seen mostly in the skies over Scandinavia, which were capable of flying in all weather conditions, even those that would have kept conventional aircraft on the ground. The geographical location of these sightings led to feverish speculation that the ghost rockets were Soviet missiles, based on captured Nazi V-1 and V-2 rocket technology, on test flights into Scandinavian airspace.

NAZI SAUCERS?

In the early 1950s, a former Luftwaffe aeronautical engineer named Rudolf Schriever became the centre of intense controversy concerning the true state of German aero-technology during World War Two. In the spring of 1941, Schriever allegedly designed a prototype flying disc, which was test-flown the following year. He went on to build a larger, more sophisticated version of the disc in 1944, at the BMW factory in Prague. The craft was composed of a wide ring, which rotated around a fixed cockpit, and was powered by adjustable jets. According to some reports, Schriever's flying disc was an extremely formidable machine, which could reach an altitude of 12,200 metres (40,000 feet) and fly at speeds of up to 2000 kph (1,250 mph).

Rudolf Schriever maintained until the end of his life that he had worked on flying discs under the code name of Projekt Saucer. The large prototype had been destroyed in 1945 to prevent it from falling into the hands of the Allies, who were advancing into Germany.

There is little doubt that the Germans were in the process of developing some highly advanced weapons by the end of World War Two. W.A. Harbinson provides us with an impressive list, including plans for heat-seeking missiles, electric submarines, the Messerschmitt ME-262 jet fighter, vertically rising aircraft and a prototype atomic bomb.

When the Third Reich was finally defeated, the scientists and engineers who had been working on these and other projects were taken to the United States and the Soviet Union. The United States maintained a serious interest in the development of high-performance disc-shaped aircraft for several years after World War Two. Their main intention was to develop aircraft that could take off and land almost vertically, for use on aircraft carriers. One such machine was the US Navy's Chance-Vought Flying Flapjack, a near-circular, twin-turbo-prop aeroplane that was first revealed to the public in 1950. Perhaps because of the uneasy marriage between a radical shape and traditional propulsion, the Flying Flapjack performed disappointingly, and had serious stability problems. A new and vastly refined version was said to have been produced after the Flying Flapjack was abandoned. The XF-5-U-1 was rumoured to be 30 metres (100 feet) in diameter, and was powered by jet nozzles arranged around its rim.

Perhaps the most famous man-made flying disc was the Avro Car, developed in the early 1950s by the Avro-Canada aircraft company based in Malton, Ontario. Astounding claims were initially made for its performance, claims that later proved to be over optimistic. The Avro Car was intended to be capable of vertical take off and landing, and to have a cruising speed of 2400 kph (1500 mph). Its test flights, however, proved to be rather less impressive: it was actually capable only of lifting itself a metre or two off the ground and hovering pathetically for a few minutes. By 1960, the project had officially been dropped, and the Canadian and US governments claimed to have no further interest in flying-disc construction.

The rumours concerning man-made flying discs form a complex microcosm of the UFO controversy in general. While some researchers have suggested that the US Government's flying-disc development has continued in extreme secrecy, based on Nazi documents captured from their facilities at Nordhausen and Peenemunde at the end of World War Two, others have claimed that Nazi disc technology came from a captured alien spacecraft (as described in the Internet documents quoted in Chapter 5) – an apparent variation on the rumours of reverse engineering at Area 51 (see pages 113–4).

OPERATION HIGHJUMP

In May 1946, the majestic and utterly inhospitable land of Antarctica became the target of an expedition known as 'Operation Highjump', funded by the USA and headed by the distinguished aviator and polar explorer, Rear Admiral Richard E. Byrd. Although it comprised a formidable array of military personnel and equipment, including helicopters, flying boats and support ships, the expedition's presence in Antarctica was short-lived: the press in Chile published information alleging that it had run into trouble, and had sustained 'many fatalities'.

According to Rear-Admiral Byrd, Operation Highjump had been equipped to survive in Antarctica for between six and eight months, and yet the expedition fled the continent a few weeks after its arrival. Byrd is said to have told journalists that it was necessary for the US to take defensive action against potential enemy air fighters which might come from the polar region, and that, in the event of a new war, the US would be attacked by fighters able to fly from one pole to another at incredible speeds.

Much has been made of Rear-Admiral Byrd's pioneering flights over the North and South Poles in the early part of this century, particularly by proponents of the Hollow Earth theory. In his book *The Hollow Earth*, for instance, Dr Raymond Bernard maintains that when Byrd said, 'I'd like to see that *land beyond the Pole*. That area beyond the Pole is the centre of the *Great Unknown*,' he was referring to the entrance to the interior of the planet. It is, of course, more likely that Byrd was merely referring to the 'great unknown' of Antarctica's vast unexplored regions.

And yet the mystery of Operation Highjump endures. What did Byrd's expedition encounter in those frozen wastes? What caused the alleged deaths of so many military personnel? Why, for that matter, were so many (supposedly 4000) sent there in the first place?

When Operation Highjump set out for Antarctica, comments were made concerning the large numbers of personnel and the nature of the equipment they took with them. To many, it looked more like an assault force than a survey team. Its objective, Neu Schwabenland, had been taken by the Nazis from Norway (the area had originally been named Queen Maud Land). As soon as the expedition landed, it split up into three separate task forces, which headed into the interior. It was then that they had their alleged encounters with high-performance 'enemy aircraft'. When Operation Highjump came to an ignominious end only a few weeks later, the USA retreated from the continent for the next ten years.

A DARK SECRET IN ANTARCTICA?

Nazi interest in Antarctica began around 1938, when Hitler sent an expedition, led by Captain Alfred Rischter, to the continent's South Atlantic coast. After extensive aerial reconnaissance, the areas around the Princess Astrid and Princess Martha coasts were claimed for Germany. Throughout the war, German vessels patrolled the waters of the South Atlantic, seizing many Allied merchant ships.

On 25 April 1945, Captain Hans Schaeffer, commander of the German submarine *U-977*, began what W.A. Harbinson calls 'one of the most remarkable naval feats of the war' (Harbinson, *Projekt UFO*, page 219). Taking his ship out of Kiel Harbour in the Baltic, Schaeffer dropped off some of his crew on the coast of Norway near Bergen, and then embarked on a four-month-long voyage to the South Atlantic, eventually landing at Mar del Plata, Argentina, on 17 August.

The Argentine authorities who subsequently interrogated him wanted to know why he had turned up in the South Atlantic so long after the war in Europe had ended (on 8 May 1945). Their suspicion was that someone of 'political importance' had been smuggled away on board the *U-977*. Captain Schaeffer denied this, and maintained that he had merely wanted to avoid the attentions of the victorious Allied Command.

However, a group of high-ranking British and American officers flew to Argentina to conduct their own interrogation of Captain Schaeffer. According to Harbinson, they were anxious to investigate the possibility that the *U-977* had carried Adolf Hitler and

Martin Bormann to a secret Nazi base in Antarctica, having stopped off first in Patagonia. Schaeffer's interrogation by the Americans continued in Washington DC, and by the British in Antwerp, Belgium. After many months of questioning, Schaeffer was sent back to Germany, but soon left for Argentina and the large group of German ex-officers who live there.

According to the conspiracy theory known as 'Nazi Survival', Schaeffer's objective was indeed a secret base in Antarctica, which had been established during the years since the first reconnaissance in 1938, in an ice-free area hidden in the mountains. There, Nazi scientists continued their aeronautical research into disc-shaped craft, research unhindered by Germany's defeat at the hands of the Allies. It was this rumoured Nazi base that allegedly prompted the United States to launch Operation Highjump.

As mentioned earlier, when Operation Highjump failed, having sustained 'many fatalities', the Americans withdrew from Antarctica for ten years. They were not to return until 1957, with the start of the International Geophysical Year (IGY). This time they were accompanied by representatives from the scientific communities of no less than 67 countries. The official reasons for international interest in the Antarctic during the IGY were to take advantage of technological developments in the exploration of polar regions, and to observe the 'maximum sunspot activity' predicted for 1957–8. Observations of the ionosphere, the aurora and cosmic rays were also planned, and more than 50 stations were eventually established on the continent (Harbinson, page 221).

Conspiracy theorists who support the idea of Nazi survival in the Antarctic point out that the massive international scientific effort undertaken during the IGY centred on research into two areas: Antarctica and outer space. They also point to the huge increase in world-wide UFO sightings around this time. It is widely believed that many unexplained UFOs are actually craft originating from this secret Antarctic base.

From a logistical point of view, it is perfectly feasible that Germany could have transported the personnel and slave labour necessary to construct such a base to the Antarctic during World War Two. The vast underground rocket factories and laboratories at Peenemunde and Nordhausen testify to the Nazis' expertise in such ambitious engineering projects. The motive for locating the base in the Antarctic is obvious enough: its extreme isolation and harsh conditions would afford ample security and secrecy for the ongoing experiments to create an Aryan 'super race'. According to the Nazi Survival hypothesis, this impregnability is the very reason for the failure of Operation Highjump, whose actual mission was to destroy the base and capture its personnel.

These ideas about the true origin of UFOs are very intriguing, but how close to reality do they actually come? Much of the information that has given rise to the Nazi UFO theory can be traced, via the neo-Nazi publication *Brisant*, to the books of one Ernst Zundl, written under the pseudonyms Mattern Friedrich and Christoff Friedrich. The books, *UFO: Nazi Secret Weapons?* and *Secret Nazi Polar Expeditions*, contain much distasteful historical revisionism, including the now familiar claim that the Nazi death camps were a propaganda hoax perpetrated by the victorious Allies. The main thrust of these books appears to be an affirmation of Nazi technological prowess in constructing incredibly advanced aircraft.

However, as W.A. Harbinson reminds us (pages 249–51), Zundl based most of his ideas on a novel by Wilhelm Landig, entitled *Gotzen gegen Thule*, published in 1971, which contains all the elements of the Nazi Survival theory, the only difference being that in the novel the Nazis decamp to the North Pole instead of Antarctica. Like most theories and stories about the origin of UFOs, the Nazi survival idea, while based on rather unsound, circumstantial – or even completely fictitious – evidence, does nevertheless draw our attention to some unanswered questions and curious facts. For instance, why *did* Operation Highjump fail so miserably? Was it really rebuffed by a hidden Antarctic base populated by escaped Nazi scientists and engineers? The International Geophysical Year of 1957–8, with its emphasis on Antarctica and outer space, was a very rare example of Cold War co-operation between the United States and the Soviet Union. Were they actually co-operating properly to assess the continuing threat posed by a common enemy?

THE ETHICAL EVENT HORIZON

As I remarked earlier, the Antarctic continent can provide a great deal of privacy for anyone wanting to develop unconventional technologies. Harbinson, among others, has speculated that those technologies may rely on procedures that would be considered unethical by both the public and mainstream science. Indeed, one of the most horrifying theories currently being discussed is that the so-called 'ufonauts' are actually human beings who have been altered, both genetically and mechanically, in order to operate more effectively in outer space. This idea is not quite as outlandish as it sounds, if we remember that technological advances have a habit of occurring years – or even decades – before they are officially revealed to the public.

Encounters such as those reported by Judy Doraty and the woman in the Cimarron, New Mexico, case suggest parallels with the dreadful biological experiments conducted in the Nazi death camps. If experiments of this nature were still being conducted to develop a 'superhuman' being capable of existing in the harsh environment of outer space, they would clearly have to remain a very closely guarded secret. In effect, a kind of ethical event horizon would have been passed, beyond which no information could be allowed to escape into the public domain.

We have also seen from the CIA's MKULTRA programme that certain individuals within intelligence organizations are capable of ignoring ethical considerations in pursuing their objectives with or without the knowledge of their superiors. In fact, it has been suggested that the extra-terrestrial hypothesis for UFO encounters is considered a convenient diversion by various governments, who are party to these continuing crimes against humanity.

Whether or not we accept the idea that an occupying force of aliens really has taken up residence on Earth, or give serious credence to the man-made UFO hypothesis, the two theories are linked by a common factor: those in authority possess secret knowledge, which they have developed and are using for their own ends, at the expense of innocent people all over the world. This factor has contributed to the ever-increasing sense of paranoia and helplessness that permeates UFO research.

In the final chapter, we will look at some of the conspiracies regarding aliens on Earth that are said to have resulted from the irresponsible pursuit of scientific knowledge (a complex subject in itself). They are both surprisingly diverse and shockingly bizarre.

NINE

The Knowledge of the Damned

T HE UFO PHENOMENON cannot be considered in isolation from the contemporary events occurring in society. There is, of course, a strong case for the investigation of UFO sightings within an objective, scientific framework, in which we can still be guided by J. Allen Hynek's classification system, which covers close encounters of the first to third kinds. However, once we get beyond these, into the realms of close encounters of the fourth and fifth kinds, we find ourselves in different territory. (A close encounter of the fourth kind is a UFO abduction; encounters of the fifth kind involve ongoing communication between a human being and 'aliens'.)

As we have seen, the elements of these encounters form a complex interplay of psychological and cultural processes, many of which may have their origins in the psyche of the percipient, and which may be heavily influenced by the belief systems of the society in which the percipient lives. This is not to say that alien encounters are 'all in the mind', and have no existence in objective reality. Rather, it seems sensible to view these events from a deistic point of view; that is, to see them as representing the activity of an intelligence which we cannot understand through our accepted notions of what constitutes reality. The theological deist believes that God may not be known through recourse to orthodox religions, (these are, in effect, attempts to comprehend the incomprehensible). In the context of the alien-encounter phenomenon, the deist should accept that the beings who have revealed themselves to humans over the centuries may represent the activities of an agency that is beyond comprehension, and that the efforts of ufologists to identify them may not lead us to a complete understanding of the phenomenon.

Whatever the true nature of this immense mystery, it is undeniable that our interactions with it are experienced through the lens of the culture in which we live. Just as the child is father to the man, history is the father of our culture and the world-view it embodies; and it is by virtue of this fact that the central mystery of the supposed alien presence on Earth has given rise to the ideas and conspiracy theories discussed throughout this book.

As technology continues its assault upon the territory of science fiction, and secret organizations prove themselves capable of the most egregious violations of human rights, the theories arising from five decades of modern UFO and alien encounters have become more and more elaborate and bizarre. It is to these that we now turn our attention.

THE END OF DAYS: ALTERNATIVE 3

On 20 June 1977, the UK television company Anglia produced a documentary programme entitled *Alternative 3*. It sparked a controversy that has still not abated, 20 years on. After the programme had been aired, Anglia Television was inundated with calls from frightened viewers; more than 10,000 people were shocked by what they had seen and been told. So intense was the uproar that Anglia hastily issued a statement assuring the viewers that the 'documentary' had, in fact, been an April Fool's Day hoax, an admission borne out by the closing credits, which included the tell-tale caption: 'Anglia Television – April 1, 1977'.

Just before the programme's transmission, Anglia had issued a press release, which stated:

> A team of journalists investigating, among other topical
> subjects, the drought of 1976, and the changes in the
> world's atmospheric conditions, and also a disturbing rise in
> the statistics of disappearing people, follow a trail of
> information and scientific research through England and
> America.

A Cambridge scientist, an ex-astronaut living in
unpublicised retirement following a nervous breakdown,
are among links in their investigations, which comes together
finally in some strange discoveries about the future of life on
Earth and elsewhere in the Solar System.

As a result of private screenings a few weeks ago, this
programme has been acquired for simultaneous transmission
in Australia, New Zealand, Canada, Denmark and Iceland and
will be seen eventually in the majority of European and Asian
markets.

The programme's theme may seem extraordinary, but it is
scientifically possible. The question is, how far does it mirror
the truth?

Alternative 3 was screened as part of Anglia's *Science Report* documentary series which had, until then, featured factual programmes
on science and nature. There is no doubt that this accounted in
part for the furore: people who tuned in to *Alternative 3* were
expecting a factual programme, and assumed that was what they
were watching.

On the day the programme was transmitted, journalist
Kenneth Hughes wrote an article in the London *Daily Mirror*, having gained access to some of the material to be presented. Under
the heading 'WHAT ON EARTH IS GOING ON?' he wrote:

A science programme is likely to keep millions of Britons glued
to their armchairs.

ALTERNATIVE 3 (ITV [Independent Television] 9.0) is an
investigation into the disappearance of several scientists.

They seem simply to have vanished from the face of the
Earth.

Chilling news is read by former ITV newscaster Simon
Butler who gives a gloomy report on the future.

The programme will be screened in several other countries
– but not America. Network bosses there want to assess its
effect on British viewers.

According to Leslie Watkins and David Ambrose in their book
Alternative 3, based upon the television programme, the last para-
graph in Kenneth Hughes' article was not entirely true: the
American network bosses had not even been consulted about the

possibility of screening *Alternative 3* in the States. The programme
had been banned outright, as it had been in Russia (Watkins and
Ambrose, page 164).

The secret of *Alternative 3* was revealed in a series of interviews
with a Dr Carl Gerstein, who filled in the background to this
strange story. At a conference in Huntsville, Alabama in 1957, Dr
Gerstein had made it clear that industrial pollution was destroying
the biosphere of the planet. The so-called 'greenhouse effect'
(caused by high levels of carbon dioxide trapping heat within the
atmosphere) was steadily worsening. Although some efforts were
made to cut down on the production of fluorocarbons, this was not
nearly enough, and by the late 1970s, it had become too late to
reverse the damage. It was thought that, by about the year 2000
the Earth would undergo a complete environmental collapse, wip-
ing out virtually all life on the planet.

Three alternatives for survival were developed (by the shadowy
Jason Society, according to William Cooper). Alternative 1
involved positioning nuclear devices in the upper atmosphere, and
then detonating them in an attempt to blow holes in the carbon-
dioxide envelope, thus allowing the heat to escape into space. This
alternative was rejected, not least because it would have meant the
virtual destruction of the ozone layer, which protects the Earth
from deadly ultraviolet radiation.

Dr Gerstein regarded Alternative 2 as 'even crazier than
Alternative 1'. His explanation of it calls to mind some of the
strange legends discussed earlier in this book. In his interview for
the *Alternative 3* programme, Dr Gerstein described the theory that
humanity's distant ancestors, living 'millennia before what we call
Prehistoric Man, had progressed far beyond our present state of
knowledge'. As a result of some unknown cataclysm, they were
forced to evacuate the surface of the planet, and retreat into vast,
purpose-built cities far underground. As in the Agharti legend,
these cities were constructed beneath all the continents, and were
linked by a world-wide tunnel network. Life was maintained by
means of 'a green luminescence', which provided a substitute for
the Sun as a source of energy.

Eventually, though, these remote ancestors of humanity once
again experienced a great natural disaster – possibly an immense
flood – which gave rise to the stories of the Deluge, a legend common to virtually every culture on Earth. Gerstein speculated that
the flood waters seeped into the ground, drowning the people liv-

ing in the vast subterranean cities, except for a handful of survivors who returned to the surface 'the real children of Noah'.
These survivors had to begin human civilization all over again in a
devastated world.

Thus, Alternative 2 meant following in the footsteps of our distant, highly advanced ancestors and evacuating the most skilled
and talented members of our own civilization into the bowels of
the Earth, leaving the rest of humanity to take its (non-existent)
chances on the surface.

This alternative was also discarded, because it could not ensure
the permanent survival of the evacuees. The greenhouse gases in
the atmosphere would heat the surface of the planet until life
became impossible, and that heat would eventually permeate
down through the Earth's crust, making conditions equally intol-
erable for those living underground.

There was only one option left: Alternative 3. In short, this
alternative involved the evacuation of a very small proportion of
the human race from Earth to Mars. Dr Gerstein cited the theory
that at one time the red planet was inhabited, and as conditions
gradually worsened, transforming it into a barren desert, the
indigenous life forms adapted to enter a state of hibernation and
wait for the return of conditions conducive to life. (This speculation arose out of a theory that the Martian atmosphere had
become locked into the soil.) Gerstein went on to describe how, in
1961, after a particularly large and violent storm on the Martian
surface, astronomers discovered that the polar ice-caps had
decreased dramatically in size, while around the equatorial
regions, a broad, dark band had appeared, which some suggested
might be vegetation.

At a conference held shortly before this happened, Gerstein
said he had suggested that a nuclear explosion might just release
the atmosphere locked into the Martian surface.

Gerstein stated that the Russians suffered a terrible disaster in
1959, when one of their rockets exploded on the launch pad. The
explosion killed a large number of people and devastated the
entire area, leading to speculation that it might have been carrying
a nuclear device intended for detonation on Mars. Perhaps,
Gerstein suggested, the Russians were able to launch another
rocket, which succeeded in delivering a nuclear device to the red
planet. Maybe this was the cause of the huge storm, and its curious aftermath, later witnessed by astronomers.

The *Alternative 3* programme included some startling footage of an apparent joint USA/USSR unmanned mission to Mars in 1962. The film showed the barren Martian landscape as seen from an approaching spacecraft, accompanied by the sounds of American and Russian voices. Computer readouts in both English and Russian scrolled across the screen, as atmospheric conditions were tested. Near the end of the film, an American voice could be heard saying:

> That's it! We got it . . . We got it! Boy, if they ever take the wraps off this thing, it's going to be the biggest date in history! May 22, 1962. We're on the planet Mars – and we have *air!*

The *Alternative 3* commentator said there must have been a reason why the 'true' conditions on Mars were kept secret from the public, and why the mission had been sent jointly by the United States and Soviet Union. The commentator suggested that a sinister and ultra-secret interplanetary operation was in progress, adding, 'We believe that operation to be Dr Carl Gerstein's Alternative 3' (Watkins and Ambrose, page 207).

In support of their argument, the programme-makers pointed to the large number of disappearances that occur throughout the world every year. According to *UFO Magazine's* sister publication *The Unopened Files*, which cites both Interpol and the BBC World News as its sources, in 1982 over 2,000,000 people disappeared without trace in the United States, while in 1995, 100,000 children disappeared in the United Kingdom, 35,000 of whom were subsequently located. In Europe, it is estimated that approximately 1,750,000 men, women and children are reported missing each year. Of these, about 35 per cent can be accounted for (*The Unopened Files*, Number 1, page 39).

According to the Alternative 3 scenario, many of these people are actually being abducted and transformed, by surgical and chemical means, into mindless, compliant slave labourers, who are then shipped off, as 'Batch Consignments', to the now-established Martian colony (see page 188). The Alternative 3 controllers callously refer to these unfortunates as 'superfluous people', and consider it perfectly acceptable to treat them in this abhorrent way.

The other group of people in whom the controllers are interested is composed of academics from various disciplines within the arts and sciences. The so-called 'brain drain', whereby large numbers of scientists were leaving Britain's shores (apparently for better-paid posts overseas), which had originally prompted Anglia Television's researchers, was actually the result of the nation's best minds being recruited by the conspiracy and relocated to Mars.

The entire operation was supposedly co-ordinated from nuclear submarines under the polar ice-caps, in which the project planners frequently arranged for the assassination of those who were close to discovering the truth. Their favourite method was the 'hot job' – remote-controlled spontaneous human combustion.

The Apollo Moon-flights have received a great deal of attention from the ufology community, who believe that the astronauts encountered much more on Earth's satellite than the barren, life-less landscape with which most people are now familiar. Anyone who has read the more recent UFO literature will recognize the following reported exchange:

MISSION CONTROL: What's there?. . . . Malfunction (*garble*) . . . Mission Control calling Apollo 11.

APOLLO 11: These babies are huge, sir . . . enormous. . . . Oh, God, you wouldn't believe it! I'm telling you there are other spacecraft out there . . . lined up on the far side of the crater edge. . . . They're on the Moon watching us. . . .

This conversation was allegedly picked up by radio hams on their VHF receivers, which bypassed NASA's broadcasting outlets, according to former NASA employee Otto Binder.

In their book *Alternative 3*, Leslie Watkins and David Ambrose provide transcripts of other conversations between Apollo astro-nauts and Mission Control in Houston, Texas:

MISSION CONTROL: Could you take a look out over that flat area there? Do you see anything beyond?

GRODIN: There's a kind of a ridge with a pretty spectacular . . . oh, my God! What *is* that there? That's all I want to know! What the hell is that?

MISSION CONTROL: Roger. Interesting. Go Tango . . . immediately . . . go Tango. . . .

GRODIN: There's a kind of a light now. . . .

MISSION CONTROL (*hurriedly*): Roger. We got it, we've marked it. Lose a little communication, huh? Bravo Tango . . . Bravo Tango . . . select Jezebel, Jezebel. . . .

GRODIN: Yeah . . . yeah . . . but this is unbelievable . . . recorder off, Bravo Tango, Bravo Tango.
(Watkins and Ambrose, page 106)

Another transcript, supposedly of a conversation between astronauts Scott and Irwin and Mission Control, occurred during their Moon-walk in August 1971:

SCOTT: Arrowhead really runs east to west.

MISSION CONTROL: Roger, we copy.

IRWIN: Tracks here as we go down slope.

MISSION CONTROL: Just follow the tracks, huh?

IRWIN: Right . . . we're (*garble*) . . . we know that's a fairly good run. We're bearing 320, hitting range for 413 . . . I can't get over those lineations, that layering on Mount Hadley.

SCOTT: I can't either. That's really spectacular.

IRWIN: They sure look beautiful.

SCOTT: Talk about organization!

IRWIN: That's the most organized structure I've ever seen!

SCOTT: It's (garble) . . . so uniform in width. . . .

IRWIN: Nothing we've seen before this has shown such uniform thickness from the top of the tracks to the bottom.
(Watkins and Ambrose, page 214)

Unexplained 'tracks' on the lunar surface have long perplexed ufologists, who have speculated that they are evidence of large machines built by extra-terrestrials. The latest controversy regarding artefacts such as the Shard and the Castle (described in Chapter 5) are merely the latest developments in a puzzle that has tantalized researchers for decades. George Leonard, Fred Steckling and Don Wilson, who wrote *Somebody Else Is on the Moon*, *We Discovered Alien Bases on the Moon* and *Our Mysterious Spaceship Moon* respectively, have studied NASA close-up photographs of the lunar surface, and have come to the conclusion that certain unusual features are actually manufactured machines, including gigantic roving vehicles and mining facilities.

In the early 1950s, John O'Neill reported seeing what looked like an enormous bridge on the Moon. Although O'Neill was widely derided, support came in the form of the professional astronomer H. Percy Wilkins, who announced that he had turned his own telescope on the area described by O'Neill, and spotted the bridge also. Even the British astronomer Patrick Moore, well known for his skeptical attitude to UFOs, found the lunar 'bridge' a very intriguing object.

In the Alternative 3 scenario of Watkins and Ambrose, these strange features seen on the Moon are indeed artificial, but they were not built by extra-terrestrials; they are Moon-bases built by humans as staging-posts for the journey to the Martian colonies.

Towards the end of their book, they describe an incident at a Moon-base in the crater Archimedes, which lies on the western border of the *Mare Imbrium*. The Archimedes Base is supposedly a vast transit camp hermetically sealed beneath a transparent dome. Shuttle craft regularly arrive from Earth, carrying scientific personnel, and also the 'Batch Consignments' of surgically altered slave labourers.

Using information supplied to them by an inside source called 'Trojan', Watkins and Ambrose describe a disaster that befell the base as a result of the compassion of a marine biologist named Matt Anderson. Anderson, from Miami, Florida, had secretly visited a segregated area of the base, where the Batch Consignments of slaves were kept apart from the colonists, or 'Designated Movers'. Once inside the slave village, Anderson encountered a man whom he had known in his schooldays. At this point, Anderson had not yet undergone the psychological conditioning to which even Designated Movers were subjected, in order for them to accept the necessity of slavery for the success of Alternative 3.

Anderson then recruited Gowers, a NASA-trained aerospace technician, as part of his plan to evacuate the slaves from the base, release them from their miserable condition and expose the atrocities of Alternative 3.

After overpowering several personnel, Anderson and Gowers loaded 84 slaves on to a Moon-ship and headed for one of the giant airlocks in the hermetically sealed dome covering the base.

But a technician in the central control room noticed the unscheduled opening of the airlock, and activated a security system that instantly closed it. Gowers was flying the Moon-ship, but he was an inexperienced pilot. When he saw the airlock closing in front of him, he panicked, lost control of the craft and sent it crashing into the side of the dome. There was an immediate and cataclysmic depressurization, killing virtually everyone at the base, which was almost totally destroyed.

According to Watkins and Ambrose, an earlier transit base in the crater Cassini has now been redeveloped to replace Archimedes Base, and Alternative 3 is still proceeding.

Although, as mentioned, Anglia Television assured frightened viewers that the documentary was an April Fool's Day joke, and Leslie Watkins and David Ambrose subsequently declared that the book version of *Alternative 3* is fiction, interest in this bizarre conspiracy theory has not subsided. Instead, it has lingered on and undergone various alterations, notably at the hands of William Cooper, who maintains that it is a reality, and that official assurances to the contrary are no more than a smokescreen to prevent the public from panicking *en masse*.

According to Cooper, the spacecraft that ferry technical personnel and slave labourers to the Moon and Mars are actually supplied by aliens. While the original Alternative 3 scenario has it that there is a breathable atmosphere and vegetation on Mars, Cooper informs us that the same is true of the Moon. (As Curtis Peebles rightly says, this idea is straight out of George Adamski and the contactees of the 1950s and 1960s.)

The real controllers of Alternative 3, Cooper says, are none other than our old friends MJ-12 (see page 107), who have financed the operation by gaining control of the world-wide illegal drugs market. In addition to this, he claims that they were able to appropriate money earmarked for national defence, since the Cold War was a monumental con: the United States and the Soviet Union were actually the closest of allies.

In an age when faith in politics and politicians is at an all-time low, when every other day seems to bring a new scandal demonstrating the mendacity and venality of our leaders, it is easy to see how conspiracy theories of every description – from the plausible to the utterly outrageous – can develop and grow in the fertile soil of political extremism, both of the far right and the far left. The fact that such theories are increasingly finding their way into

mainstream thought, and being picked up and seriously considered by some members of the general public, is an indication of the
low esteem in which our governments are now held. We have
come to the point where more and more people are of the opinion
that, if our governments say something is nonsense, the opposite
is probably true.

There is something for all political persuasions within the subject of alien-related conspiracies. MJ-12 is the sworn enemy of the
far right, who believe that the Constitution of the United States is
under threat of suspension, owing to the proliferation of drugs and
the drafting of gun-control laws. Any right-wing militia leader will
tell you that the unmarked helicopters which cause so much havoc
in the Midwest are part of an advance United Nations force,
preparing to invade the US and declare martial law.

Likewise, the far left, as Curtis Peebles reminds us (page 335)
strongly believe that the CIA is heavily involved in the illegal sale
of drugs. This idea has recently been borne out, to a certain degree,
by revelations concerning the Agency's involvement in the trans-
fer of drugs from South America to Los Angeles. It has even led to
accusations that the US Government is targeting black communities for genocide by means of hard drugs. At any rate, the idea that
the world is secretly controlled by a small group of ultra-rich and
powerful people is very appealing to the far left.

George C. Andrews claims that the US Government has made
it illegal for citizens to engage in contact with extra-terrestrials or
their vehicles, citing a law which is already on the books.
According to this law – 'Title 14, Section 1211 of the Code of
Federal Regulations, adopted on July 16, 1969' – anyone found
guilty of extra-terrestrial contact can be jailed for one year and
fined $5,000 (Andrews, page 28). It is worth quoting several fair-
ly substantial parts of the law, since they are of considerable rele-
vance to the claims of the alien-related conspiracy theorists:

1211.100 Title 14 – Aeronautics and Space
Part 1211 – Extra-terrestrial Exposure

1211.100 Scope.
This part establishes: (a) NASA policy, responsibility and
authority to guard the Earth against any harmful contamin-
ation or adverse changes in its environment resulting from
personnel, spacecraft and other property returning to the Earth

after landing on or coming within the atmospheric envelope of a celestial body; and (b) security requirements, restrictions and safeguards that are necessary in the interest of national security.

1211.101 Applicability.

The provisions of this part apply to all NASA manned and un-manned space missions which land or come within the atmos-pheric envelope of a celestial body and return to the Earth.

1211.102 Definitions.

(a) 'NASA' and the 'Administrator' mean, respectively the National Aeronautics and Space Administration and the Administrator of the National Aeronautics and Space Administration or his authorised representative.

(b) 'Extra-terrestrially exposed' means the state or condition of any person, property, animal or other form of life or matter whatever, who or which has:

(1) Touched directly or come within the atmospheric envelope of any other celestial body; or

(2) Touched directly or been in close proximity to (or been exposed indirectly to) any person, property, animal or other form of life or matter who or which has been extra-terrestrially exposed by virtue of paragraph (b) (1) of this section.

For example, if person or thing 'A' touches the surface of the moon, and on 'A's' return to Earth, 'B' touches 'A' and, subsequently, 'C' touches 'B', all of these – 'A' through 'C' inclusive – would be extra-terrestrially exposed ('A' and 'B' directly; 'C' indirectly).

(c) 'Quarantine' means the detention, examination and decontamination of any person, property, animal or other form of life of matter whatever that is extra-terrestrially exposed, and includes the apprehension or seizure of such person, property, animal or other form of matter whatever.

(d) 'Quarantine period' means a period of consecutive calendar days as may be established in accordance with 1211.104(a).

1211.104 Policy.

(a) Administrative actions. The Administrator or his designee . . . shall in his discretion:

(1) Determine the beginning and duration of a quarantine

period with respect to any space mission; the quarantine period as it applies to various life forms will be announced.

(2) Designate in writing quarantine officers to exercise quarantine authority.

(3) Determine that a particular person, property, animal, or other form of life or matter whatever is extra-terrestrially exposed and quarantine such person, property, animal, or other form of life or matter whatever. The quarantine may be based only on a determination, with or without the benefit of a hearing, that there is probable cause to believe that such person, property, animal or other form of life or matter whatever is extra-terrestrially exposed. . . .

(5) Provide for guard services by contract or otherwise, as may be necessary, to maintain security and inviolability of quarantine stations and quarantined persons, property, animals, or other forms of life or matter whatever . . . .

(b) (3) During any period of announced quarantine, no person shall enter or depart from the limits of the quarantine station without permission of the cognizant NASA officer. During such period, the posted perimeter of a quarantine station shall be secured by armed guard.

(4) Any person who enters the limits of any quarantine station during the quarantine period shall be deemed to have consented to the quarantine of his person if it is determined that he is or has become extra-terrestrially exposed.

(5) At the earliest practicable time, each person who is quarantined by NASA shall be given a reasonable opportunity to communicate by telephone with legal counsel or other persons of his choice. . . .

1211.108 Violations.

Whoever wilfully violates, attempts to violate, or conspires to violate any provision of this part or any regulation or order issued under this part or who enters or departs from the limits of a quarantine station in disregard of the quarantine rules or regulations or without permission of the NASA quarantine officer shall be fined not more than $5,000 or imprisoned not more than 1 year, or both.

George Andrews points out that, with a little semantic manipulation, this law could be applied to anyone who makes physical contact with a spacecraft entering the Earth's atmosphere, *whether human-built or extra-terrestrial in nature*. To the conspiracy theorists, this makes perfect sense, and exemplifies the growing danger of the United States falling under martial law (through the actions of the United Nations or the occupying alien force).

Some theorists reject the alien invasion idea, maintaining that it is actually a hoax to create an artificial external threat. The United Nations will, they believe, at some stage draw attention to this threat through the long-awaited release of the truth about UFOs. They will offer proof that the alien visitors are extremely hostile, and this will provide an irresistible reason for the creation of a New World Order – actually a world-wide dictatorship, according to the conspiracy theorists. The so-called 'ET Law' partially quoted here would supply a perfect excuse for incriminating dissidents and other potential troublemakers by accusing them of extra-terrestrial contact, and then incarcerating them indefinitely in concentration camps, which (it is believed) have already been built, and are even now awaiting their first guests.

The vast conspiracy embodied in Alternative 3 shows that religious mysticism is far from being undermined by the mind-set of the late twentieth century. Concerned parties who fear that religion will cease to be a relevant framework for our spiritual development are ignoring the modifications to the underlying concepts that have created present attitudes to the possibility of celestial influences on our lives.

Whether or not we believe in the literal existence of Alternative 3 (I myself have my doubts), we cannot avoid the implication of a resurgence, in a context that corresponds to our technological world-view, of the concepts of Judgement Day, and the New Jerusalem, in which the Elect will join Christ. By co-operating with the new priesthood of Majestic 12 and its associated organizations, those lucky and useful enough to be favourably included in their plans will be welcomed to the New Jerusalem on Mars, to continue their lives in a brand new world.

In this new variation on an ancient theme, there is still a vast intelligence 'out there', an intelligence that does not always have our best interests at heart (with the demonic Greys versus the angelic Nordics). There is still a powerful priesthood that has access to knowledge of these monumental events (the Majestic 12 organization, and the so-called 'Whistleblowers', who would warn us of the hidden dangers). There are still the sacred texts: the MJ-12 briefing papers, the Project Stigma Memorandum (which contains descriptions of alien creatures), and Project Grudge Report 13. And there is still the concept of ultimate salvation for the Elect – a new life in the cities of Mars.

It is perhaps an unfortunate comment on the state of our modern, cynical, every-man-for-himself society that, within the context of this new religious mythology, a blameless life and spiritual rectitude are nowhere near enough to guarantee salvation. What is really needed is knowledge and high intelligence, qualities that can be utilized in the New Jerusalem, whether on Mars or an alien-controlled Earth. A lack of these qualities will consign the unworthy to a life of miserable slavery – or worse, to a hideous fate as the main course on an alien dining-table.

FROM LONG ISLAND TO THE PYRAMIDS OF MARS

We have seen how, over the past five decades, material relating to the alleged alien presence on Earth has steadily become more extreme and outrageous. It would have been difficult to imagine where the subject could go next, were it not for the splendidly bizarre conspiracy known as 'the Montauk Project'. Based near the quiet town of Montauk at the easternmost end of Long Island, New York, this ultra secret project apparently succeeded not only in opening portals to different times (echoing the CIA's interest in 'precognitive remote viewing'), but in teleporting people and equipment to other planets and dimensions.

This astounding breakthrough is chronicled in a series of books by Preston B. Nichols and Peter Moon, which includes *The Montauk Project: Experiments in Time* and *Montauk Revisited: Adventures in Synchronicity*. In view of the current public disillusionment with authority, it comes as no surprise that the experiments allegedly conducted at the secret base at Montauk constituted some of the most outrageous abuses of human rights imaginable.

Like the controversy surrounding secret human-built bases on the Moon and Mars, the Montauk Project cannot claim the soundest of provenances, having its roots in the legendary Philadelphia Experiment of October 1943. Although the Philadelphia Experiment is firmly entrenched in the mythos of ufology, it is worth a brief review for the sake of background.

The experiment took place aboard the USS *Eldridge*, which was berthed in the Philadelphia Navy Yard. The intention was to make the ship invisible to radar, through the manipulation of powerful magnetic fields. However, the results of this field manipulation were utterly unexpected: not only did the USS *Eldridge* become invisible to radar, but invisible to sight. And literal invisibility was not the only goal allegedly achieved, for the ship was reported to have suddenly appeared in the Navy yards at Norfolk, Virginia. It seemed that the US Navy had succeeded in teleporting the USS *Eldridge* a distance of 320 km (200 miles).

For the crewmen on board the ship, the results of the experiment were disastrous: when the ship returned to its berth in the Philadelphia Navy Yard, many of them had become fused with the decks and bulkheads, while those who survived were hopelessly insane. They spoke of meeting strange alien creatures while in the hyperspace between Philadelphia and Norfolk.

This information was first revealed to the astronomer and pioneer UFO researcher Morris K. Jessup by a man who called himself Carlos Allende or Carl Allen. In July 1955, a copy of Jessup's book *The Case for the UFO* was anonymously mailed to the Chief of the Office of Naval Research (ONR) in Washington DC. The book had been heavily annotated in three different colours of ink, apparently by the same person. The Special Projects Officer of the ONR, Commander George Hoover, was so intrigued by the information contained in these annotations, which included details of the origin and propulsion of the UFOs, that he called Jessup to Washington to discuss them.

Jessup was shocked by the annotations to his book because of their similarity to the information with which he had been supplied by Carlos Allende, information that referred to the invisibility experiments aboard the USS *Eldridge*. Subsequently, the ONR commissioned the Varo Manufacturing Company (based in Texas and involved in high-tech military research privately to print a limited edition of the annotated text of *The Case for the UFO*.

In the late 1960s, Jacques Vallée became involved with the case, through his correspondence with Carlos Allende, who claimed to have witnessed the Philadelphia Experiment at first hand. Vallée believes that, although this is probably true, the experiment actually involved making the ship invisible to radar – and *only* to radar. Vallée cites the case of a Canadian reported to have had an encounter with a UFO and its occupants in 1975 who was later visited by three 'military men'. They mentioned that contact, and subsequent co-operation, with aliens had already been established in 1943, the year of the Philadelphia Experiment. This case is to be found in the book *The Philadelphia Experiment* by Charles Berlitz and William Moore, who would later collaborate on *The Roswell Incident*. Vallée points out a striking contradiction:

> If the Navy had contacted live aliens in Philadelphia in 1943, why would the Roswell crash of four years later come as such a surprise? And why should Moore consider it as the first instance when the US military was faced with the alleged humanoids? (Vallée, 1991, pages 206–7)

While Vallée maintains that both the Philadelphia Experiment and the Roswell crash represent disinformation and not genuine alien activity, this is difficult to accept, in view of the large amount of recent corroborative testimony the latter case has received (see Chapter 5). However, if only because of the inconsistency mentioned above, to which Vallée draws our attention, the Philadelphia Experiment (as described by UFO conspiracy theorists) must be considered spurious.

What, then, of the astonishing events at Montauk? According to Preston Nichols, the project was the culmination of 40 years of experiments that followed the alleged teleportation of the USS *Eldridge* and the destruction, both mental and physical, of her crew. Nichols claims that these experiments included 'electronic mind surveillance and the control of distinct populations', and culminated in 1983 in the opening of a doorway through time to the Philadelphia Experiment in 1943 (Nichols and Moon, 1992, page 9).

The Montauk Project was conducted in the Air Force base on the grounds of Fort Hero, which had been officially decommissioned in 1969, but was subsequently reactivated 'without the sanction of the US Government'. In the early 1970s, Preston Nichols, an electronics engineer and resident of Long Island, had been experimenting with parapsychology with a group of psychics. Having come to the conclusion that telepathy operates on a principle similar to that of radio waves, he was intrigued to discover that all of the psychics with whom he worked suddenly and inexplicably lost their ability at the same time every day.

Nichols suspected that this was the result of some form of electronic interference, and set about finding its nature and source. He discovered that the psychics' abilities were being impeded by a transmission on the 410–420 MHz wavelength, which seemed to originate in the officially abandoned Montauk Air Force Base. When he visited the base, Nichols found it to be active and tightly guarded, and he couldn't get anywhere near the large radar antenna that was broadcasting the disruptive transmissions.

In 1984, Nichols was informed by a friend that the base had now been abandoned, so he went back with one of his psychic colleagues, and found large amounts of equipment strewn around, as if the personnel had left in a hurry. They also found a man living rough in the abandoned buildings who had apparently been a technician involved in the Montauk Project. He told them that there had been an important experiment a year earlier that had resulted in the appearance of a strange, violent 'beast' which had frightened away all the personnel and forced them to abandon their programme. He also said that he recognized Nichols as his boss on the project. While they were there, the psychic said he had some very strange feelings about the Montauk Base. After carrying out a 'reading' of the place, he spoke about mind-control experiments, strange weather patterns and 'a vicious beast'.

Following their visit to the base, Nichols was unnerved when a stranger arrived at his house and insisted that Nichols had worked on the Montauk Project as Assistant Director. He also had several puzzling lapses in memory, involving the sudden appearance of sticking plasters on his hands, which implied that he had somehow injured himself without realizing it. He began to speculate that he might have been living on an alternate 'time-line', of which he had been consciously unaware.

Acting on a hunch, Nichols went to the basement of the building in which he worked (he was employed by a defence contractor on Long Island), which contained a high-security area. He had been experiencing strange, unsettling feelings while in certain parts of the building, and was anxious to find out why. To his surprise, when he walked up to the security guard and handed in his low-level pass, without a word the guard exchanged it for a high-level pass that would enable him to enter the area. Once inside the high-security area, he discovered an office which provoked an unpleasant visceral response, and entered. On the desk was a name-plate with his name on it, and the title Assistant Project Director.

Later, Nichols constructed what he calls a 'Delta Time antenna' on the roof of his laboratory, which brought an explosion of memories from the alternate time-line in which he had been working at the Montauk Project. With the help of these rediscovered memories, Nichols was able to establish that the main thrust of the project had been to manipulate time in order to open up doorways between distant places and times using technology based on designs provided by aliens from the Sirius star system. This was achieved by means of a psychic, who sat in what was known as 'the Montauk Chair'. The chair was hooked up to a battery of advanced computers which decoded his thoughts and projected them to the required location. The psychic would then open up a tunnel through time and/or space through which people could walk.

The controllers of the Montauk Project began to explore time, opening doors to the past and the future. The tunnel, or 'vortex', was shaped like a corkscrew which, Nichols said, 'twisted and took turns until you'd come out the other end'. The people sent through the vortex would observe their surroundings and then return to Montauk. According to Nichols, 'winos or derelicts' were frequently grabbed off the streets, sobered up for a week or so, and then sent into the vortex. The reason for this was that if there was a power failure while a vortex was open, the person inside would be lost forever, cast adrift in time with no hope of ever returning. Since this was a not infrequent occurrence, the 'explorers' had to be people who would not be missed if anything went wrong.

Many of these explorers were adolescent boys, who were enticed away from large cities, such as New York. Nichols maintains that they were all tall, blond and blue-eyed, conforming to the Aryan stereotype (Nichols briefly alludes to a neo-Nazi connection at Montauk). These boys were invariably sent into the future, to AD 6037. They would arrive at a ruined city, at the centre of which was a square containing a statue of a golden horse on a pedestal. Each recruit was required to read the hieroglyphic inscriptions on the statue, and report any impressions he got from them. Nichols suspects that there was some form of technology in the statue which had to be investigated.

Nichols also describes an attempt to reach the interior of the alleged city in the Cydonia region of Mars to investigate the ancient civilization that built the Face and the colossal pyramids discussed in Chapter 5. Apparently, a secret human colony on Mars (echoes of Alternative 3) had been investigating the huge city, but had been unable to find a way into it, so the Montauk scientists decided to open a portal directly into the underground region beneath the DiPietro Molenaar Pyramid. An effort was also made to search the past for the builders of the Martian monuments. Apparently, they were encountered in about 125,000 BC, although Nichols says he has been unable to discover anything else about this experiment.

The expedition into the the DiPietro Molenaar Pyramid yielded the discovery of technology that came to be known as 'the Solar System Defense', in which the DiPietro Molenaar Pyramid acted as a kind of antenna. Apparently, this technology was interfering with the research being conducted on Mars, so the scientists at Montauk had it shut off 'retroactive to 1943'. As Nichols points out, it was at about this time that UFO sightings began to increase, starting with the foo fighters that plagued aircraft in the closing years of World War Two.

Nichols says that he and several other scientists on the Montauk Project were becoming increasingly apprehensive about the irresponsible nature of the space-time experiments. For this reason, they decided to go ahead with a contingency plan to sabotage the entire project. A psychic sitting in the Montauk Chair was given a secret signal, whereupon he released a terrifying monster from his subconscious. The monster was transmitted into three-dimensional reality, and proceeded to smash parts of the base to pieces. The controllers attempted to banish the beast from normal space-time by completely shutting down all the generators on the base.

This was apparently the end of the Montauk Project. The base was decommissioned in 1983; all the personnel, including Nichols, were debriefed and brainwashed to forget everything that had happened. However, the beast itself was unwittingly photographed on the base in 1986. The photograph, which is included in the book *The Montauk Project*, shows a dark, hulking, Bigfoot-like shape, which apparently was not present when the photograph was taken.

As with other conspiracy scenarios, there is a powerful element of occultism at work here. The idea of alien influence is combined with parapsychology and the paranormal, so that the boundaries between them are obscured. To the disinterested observer, this is both fascinating and irritating, because a large number of additional elements are brought into play which, at first glance, ought to have nothing to do with UFOs and the alleged alien presence on

Earth. In the Montauk Project the basic premise – teleportation and the manipulation of time – mixes uneasily with the idea of alien-supplied technology, operated with the aid of psychics and their paranormal gifts. The whole scenario is shrouded in the strictest secrecy, and includes perhaps the ultimate in ill-treatment of innocent human beings: men abandoned for ever beyond the present.

There is an additional factor in all this, which needs to be mentioned, since it further illustrates the fusion of apparently contradictory ideas with the general theme of alien contact. In *Montauk Revisited*, the sequel to *The Montauk Project*, Nichols and Moon describe how the experiments at Montauk had a powerful antecedent in the form of the so-called 'Babalon Working', which was a magical operation allegedly conducted in 1946 by the rocket scientist John Whiteside 'Jack' Parsons and L. Ron Hubbard, the founder of the Church of Scientology. According to Nichols and Moon, the Babalon Working was 'an exhaustive operation which was designed to open an interdimensional door for the manifestation of the goddess Babalon (which means understanding), the Mother of the Universe'. Like the Montauk Project, the Babalon Working was an attempt to open a doorway to another dimension, to master the secrets of space and time; in effect, to usurp the role of God. Nichols and Moon believe that the success of the Babalon Working resulted in 'infiltration from another dimension'; that the way was opened for an inimical alien force to enter our universe. They cite the increase in UFO sightings around this time as corroboration for their theory. Although this is inconsistent with the assertion in their previous book – that the UFOs entered our solar system as a result of the deactivation of the device inside the DiPietro Molenaar Pyramid on Mars – it retains the idea of some form of defence being undermined. (Perhaps the deactivation of the pyramid device is what allowed the Babalon Working to succeed!)

Nichols and Moon include a chapter on 'Magick and Psychotronics' in *Montauk Revisited*, which throws some light on these confusing developments in the subject of UFOs and alien encounters. The writers quote the magician Aleister Crowley's famous definition of Magick: 'the Science and Art of causing Change to occur in conformity with Will'. (Crowley added a 'k' to the word to distinguish it from the bogus magic of conjurers.) They see a similarity between Magick and science, in that both systems recognize that cause precedes effect, without reference to super-natural elements: 'the entire order and uniformity of nature underlie both systems' (*Montauk Revisited*, page 83). While both systems are concerned with quantity (the empirical measurements upon which scientists base their theories), Magick extends beyond this, into the idea of quality or the mysterious and unquantifiable nature of the human mind and its capacity to transcend mundane experience. It is the ignoring of this unquantifiable aspect to human beings that, according to the authors, results in 'techno-logical nightmares' like the Montauk Project, in which science becomes the persecutor of humanity, instead of its benefactor.

Although the idea of Magickal operations is used to cast light on the principles behind bizarre and outrageous experiments like the Montauk Project, with its associated rumours of technological co-operation between humanity and alien beings, it also serves to explain how such elaborate scenarios arise. In *The Montauk Project* Nichols and Moon include a 'guide to the reader' which describes the book as 'an exercise in consciousness'. A distinction is made between 'hard facts', which are backed up by physical or docu-mented evidence; 'soft facts', which are not untrue, but which are not amenable to verification; and 'grey facts', which are plausible, but not as verifiable as 'hard facts'. Of course, what one person calls plausible, another calls outrageous nonsense; and conspiracy theories like the Montauk Project contain much that is plausible! This dichotomy between the concrete and the ambiguous is to be found throughout the field of ufology and alleged alien contact.

In fact, the authors say that their books may be read as science fiction, if it makes the reader more comfortable – an ambiguity, reminiscent of the *Illuminatus* novels of Shea and Wilson, which occupies a strange, nebulous realm between what is real and what is fiction. Like Alternative 3, which some conspiracy researchers have claimed represents an underlying reality, in spite of the fact that it was originally a hoax, the Montauk Project – whether or not it is true – provides a focus for public apprehension regarding the perceived moral and ethical dangers that arise from scientific progress.

In common with much UFO-related imagery, conspiracy theo-ries such as these often contain elements drawn from popular cul-ture, particularly science fiction. Anyone who has seen the film *Total Recall* will have noticed its parallels with the descriptions of alien machinery underneath the DiPietro Molenaar Pyramid on

Mars. Nichols and Moon draw attention to the similarity, and maintain that the film is 'fancifully based' on some of the events that happened in the Montauk Project!

As mentioned earlier, material of this type frequently incorporates fact as well as fiction, in order to increase its apparent feasibility. For instance, as we saw in Chapter 4, alien abductions almost always involve the harvesting of genetic material from human beings, a development that seems to have arisen from our own advances in this particular branch of science.

As we have seen over the course of this book, the idea of alien visitation has undergone a constant metamorphosis throughout its long history, and the same is true of conspiracy theories, whether they be political (the Kennedy assassination, the planned UN invasion of America, etc.), scientific (the secret testing of biological weapons on cattle), or a bizarre mixture of both (Alternative 3). In fact, many elements within conspiracy theories have become interchangeable. For instance, mutilated cattle are seen by some people as the victims of human scientists engaged in biological weapons research, and by others as the victims of hungry aliens. The mystery helicopters are seen as an advance UN invasion force, and as UFOs in disguise. The alien presence on Earth is seen as real, and as an elaborate hoax to make us tolerate the formation of a repressive, one-world government.

Whether or not we follow Nichols' and Moon's suggestion, and regard the Montauk Project as science fiction, it is clear that it comprises virtually all preceding theories. We have the secret manipulation of human beings (as with MKULTRA), and the manipulation of history itself (as with the now-famous Illuminati conspiracy); there is UFO involvement; irresponsible research into parapsychology and the unknown powers of the human mind; collaboration between aliens and human beings, and the use of Magick in association with physics to solve the mysteries of matter, space and time.

How have we arrived at a situation where all these diverse elements can coalesce into a single, all-embracing concept? I believe that the answer has a number of strands. As we have already seen, public faith in the rectitude of politicians and leaders is at a very low point, partly because of their apparent inability to solve the major problems of our times (poverty, famine, crime, etc.), and partly because of their documented history of ill-treating their citizens in a number of unpleasant ways. Not only has this given rise to the frightening theories of researchers who, judging from the previous bad behaviour of governments and intelligence services jump to extreme conclusions; it has also made the general public willing to believe that these stories are (or may be) correct. It seems that the price of freedom is no longer eternal vigilance, but eternal paranoia.

This is not the whole story, however. We must also look at the role science has played in our lives. Of course, science is a wonderful thing, and has brought innumerable comforts and improvements to our lives. But, as media people are fond of telling us, good news doesn't sell, mainly because good news is usually less dramatic than bad news. And there is no doubt that science has, over the years, provided us with some very bad news indeed. We now take for granted the fact that we can fly to the other side of the world in a few hours, or even have various organs replaced, should the need arise. Yet we shake our heads in horror and disbelief at the mechanized killing that we see occurring in distant countries. We switch on the lights in our houses without a second thought, but many of us regard the nuclear power stations that produce some of the energy for those lights with fear and suspicion, and remain unconvinced by official assurances that they are safe.

The 'down side' of science, the negative and destructive uses to which it has been so frequently put, makes a far more profound impression on us than its positive uses, which familiarity has made mundane and even rather boring. Therefore, when astonishing advances are made – whether in the field of astronomy, aeronautics, physics or medicine – they are perceived in a way that is heavily influenced by our subconscious distrust of science.

As I have continually maintained, no matter how much spurious material we manage to dispense with, the most impressive cases of alleged non-human contact represent a genuine core mystery that cannot be explained by orthodox science. Thus, when the US Air Force reveals its high-tech Stealth Fighter, rumours abound that it incorporates reverse-engineered UFO technology. When the idea of genetic engineering becomes established in the popular imagination, fears grow that sinister aliens are stealing the genetic material of their hapless human victims.

It is perhaps inevitable that this mystery, this great icon of the twentieth century, should combine with a mistrust of both science and government to produce the overriding impression that the answers are known by our leaders – and that those answers are terrible.

But what of the Magickal operations, the so-called 'Babalon Working', which allegedly opened up a doorway to another universe, allowing strange and hostile alien forces to persecute us? How have these anachronistic elements of superstition entered the equation?

It may be that science is, in this respect, the victim of its own success. Theoretical physicists have descended to the very foundations of the universe, studying and interpreting the blueprints of reality itself. And yet their conclusions have led one of the great popularizers of science, John Gribbin, to include a quote from John Lennon in his book *In Search of Schrodinger's Cat*: 'Nothing is real.' It seems that at the very core of matter, on the far side of the gulf between Newtonian and quantum reality, common sense breaks down, revealing a strange, chaotic world in which nothing exists in a particular place at a particular time, where fundamental particles flit like timid ghosts through realms of high or low probability.

Much has been made of the apparent similarity between quantum physics and the mystical philosophies of the Far East, most notably in Fritjof Capra's book *The Tao of Physics*, in which he likens the interactions of fundamental particles throughout the universe to the dance of the Hindu god Shiva. Whether or not this is a valid comparison (and opinion is somewhat divided on the matter), the effect on the millions of people who encounter such ideas, through books or television programmes, should not be underestimated. When a respected theoretical physicist tells us that the discoveries made on the cutting edge of science bear a striking resemblance to ancient ideas hitherto relegated to the realms of naive superstition, we cannot help but view those ideas with a renewed respect.

However, although most of us (myself included) are not terribly well versed in either quantum physics or the Hindu scriptures, the underlying concept seems to have gripped the popular imagination. We have taken to heart the notion that, not only does science not have all the answers to the mysteries of the universe, but some scientists themselves marvel at the similarities between science and mysticism. The inevitable result of this is that mysticism *per se* has been elevated in the public mind to a point where it can compete with orthodox science on its own terms.

This may have contributed to the present situation, in which all aspects of mysticism, from shamanism to Magick, from ghosts to angels, have come to be regarded with equal awe, and where there is a readiness to believe that their great enemy, orthodox science, cannot deny that they represent ultimate reality. It should therefore come as little surprise that these anachronistic mystical concepts should align themselves with scientific conundrums like parapsychology, UFOs, possible alien artefacts on our neighbouring planets, and the alleged non-human presence on Earth.

In the final analysis, we find ourselves returning to the concept of deism in our search for a framework within which to examine these curious and contradictory elements. It may be that the vast diversity of ideas to be found in the field of alien contact merely reflect an honest attempt to comprehend the incomprehensible. Perhaps the future will reveal whether this attempt is doomed, or whether it will give rise to a new era of miracles.

Beyond the Fantastic

THEORIES ON THE ORIGIN OF INTELLIGENT NON-HUMANS

VISITORS FROM THE UNIVERSE

IN SPITE OF the large number of theories that have been put forward over the years about the origin of 'aliens', by far the most popular is still the Extra-terrestrial Hypothesis (ETH), which holds that unexplained UFO and alien encounters represent the activities of a scientific expedition from another planet. Although some writers maintain that this explanation is among the least viable, it has become very firmly entrenched in the public psyche, and is still supported by some of the most respected UFO researchers.

To understand the reasons for this, we must go back to the early days of ufology, when humanity was just beginning to take its first tentative steps beyond the confines of Earth. As I mentioned in Chapter 9, science had enabled us to control our environment, to create a life of relative ease and prosperity, especially in the United States. In the years following World War Two, this prosperity increased with the continued advances in technology and industry, allowing America not only to improve the lives of its own citizens, but to finance the regeneration of Europe through the Marshall Plan. The atomic bombing of Hiroshima and Nagasaki had demonstrated humanity's capacity to master the secrets of matter itself, not to mention its power to extinguish all life on the planet.

Science and technology, then, constituted the apotheosis of human endeavour, in terms of both creation and destruction. While Robert Oppenheimer referred to himself as 'the destroyer of worlds', the power of the atom was also seen as the liberator of the human race, a source of abundant energy that would allow us completely to fulfill our potential as masters of this planet. These miraculous advances led us to consider science as central to our relationship with reality.

When faced with a set of mysterious events, therefore, we naturally view them within a scientific context. When Kenneth Arnold encountered nine crescent-shaped craft in the skies above Mount Rainier in Washington State on 24 June 1947, the initial assumption was that he had seen a group of high-performance aircraft secretly being tested by either the United States or some foreign government, possibly the USSR. The Air Material Command came forward with a more mundane explanation: the objects were either reflections of the Sun on low clouds, small meteorites breaking up in the atmosphere, or large, flat hailstones. However, several scientists dismissed these explanations as nonsense. As Curtis Peebles observes, this was the beginning of public suspicion of an official cover-up (Peebles, page 12).

It was also the beginning of a spate of sightings of unconventional objects displaying flight capabilities far beyond anything achievable at that time, or even today. The daylight sightings almost invariably fell into two categories: flat, disc-shaped objects, and larger cigar-shaped objects. Both types seemed to be metallic, structured craft under intelligent control, but without visible means of propulsion – no propellers, nothing that looked like a jet engine, and no wings or other stabilizing structures. Assuming that these craft were indeed of unknown origin, and neither hoaxes nor misinterpretations of mundane objects such as meteors, birds, other aircraft, and planets (all of which undeniably account for more than 90 percent of sightings), the most acceptable conclusion was that the strange craft were not built by humans; they had arrived from elsewhere. Science had already demonstrated its boundless potential in a number of different ways; it was clear that humanity was just starting its journey towards greater and greater knowledge. It was surely not too outrageous to assume that, in the far reaches of space, there might be many cultures which had progressed much further on their own journey, and that their thirst for knowledge had brought them to our planet.

When people all over the world began to report having contacted the supposed pilots of these craft, the ETH became even more firmly cemented into the public imagination, despite the exasperated protestations of both skeptics and serious ufologists, who were deeply suspicious of such alien-encounter claims. Even national newspapers, while maintaining a stance of sneering skepticism, were more than willing to publish such accounts.

At this stage, the ETH was still a relatively new theory, one which seemed perfectly logical: the history of science is littered with shattered paradigms; assertions that had seemed incontrovertible, until a new idea came along to explain observed reality in a far more successful and complete way. To the proponents of the ETH, this was (and still is) the case with UFOs. The Ptolemaic view of the universe, in which all the heavenly bodies move around the Earth, had given way to the Copernican view, in which the Sun is the centre of the universe. This in turn was modified over the centuries, until humanity realized that it occupies an insignificant sphere orbiting an insignificant star on the outskirts of an average galaxy in a medium-sized galactic cluster in a universe that may or may not be the only one.

The somewhat conceited notion that the Earth contains the only intelligent species (and probably the only life) in the universe is still a matter of intense debate; to proponents of the ETH, it is a further example of a paradigm that was made to be broken – and has been broken by the presence of UFOs and their occupants. But in view of what we have discovered about evolution and genetics, how feasible is the ETH as a theory to explain the presence of UFOs and apparently non-human creatures?

It has long been maintained by orthodox science that UFOs cannot be exploratory spacecraft from another star system. For one thing, the distances involved in interstellar travel are simply too vast. In addition to this, nothing can travel faster than the speed of light (about 300,000 km (186,000 miles) per second); indeed, nothing but light itself can travel at this speed, let alone faster. This is because, as a body approaches the speed of light, its mass increases until, at the point of light speed, it becomes infinite. So, in order to attain this speed – to cross over from a fraction under it to light speed itself – a spacecraft would need access to an infinite amount of thrust, which means using an infinite amount of fuel, which is a clear impossibility. Thus the speed of light is the absolute universal limit to how fast a spacecraft can travel. With this in mind, interstellar travel becomes an incredibly costly and time-consuming proposition, with journey times – even to the nearer stars – running into decades or even centuries. According to the skeptics, it follows that UFOs cannot be alien spacecraft, since no civilization would be either willing or able to make such an enormous investment in time and resources. In fact, this is the main rationale for SETI (the Search for Extra-terrestrial Intelligence), whose supporters argue that it would make far more sense for advanced civilizations to make contact through radio transmissions, rather than sending large, energy-hungry spacecraft.

However, science seems to be divided into those who say something can't be done, and those who go right ahead and do it anyway. As the great science-fiction writer and inventor Arthur C. Clarke has said, scientific breakthroughs tend to occur in four phases: one, it is impossible and will never be done; two, it is possible but far too expensive ever to be done; three, I always said it was entirely possible; and four, I thought of it first!

Apparently, it is the same with the concept of faster-than-light interstellar travel. Theoretical physicists are now postulating the use of gravity amplifiers to contract the space in front of a body, while elongating the space behind it, thus allowing it to cover vast distances in a tiny fraction of the time it would take a body travelling through normal space. Of course, this is just a theory, and such spacecraft haven't even reached the drawing-board yet; but today's theories sometimes turn out to be tomorrow's realities, and the skeptics can no longer cite the speed of light as confirmation that UFOs cannot come from other star systems.

While the ETH is theoretically possible, we find ourselves immediately encountering another stumbling-block: the outrageously high frequency of sightings. In his book *Revelations: Alien Contact and Human Deception*, Jacques Vallée gives an initial figure of 5,000 reported close encounters with UFOs, stretching back over the last 40 years or so. Taking account of the fact that only about one in ten close encounters are reported, together with the phenomenon's global nature, the geographic distribution of reports in terms of population density, plus the nocturnal patterns that seem so prevalent, Vallée then extrapolates the number of UFO landings that have actually occurred in the last 40 years – in other words, the actual number of reports that would be received if everyone in the world could remain in a constant observational state, without going to bed at night and so on. The total comes to approximately 14 million, (Vallée, 1991, page, 264–9).

Vallée goes on to ask what possible motive alien beings could have for landing on our planet 14 million times in four decades. He reminds us that, unlike Venus, for instance, the Earth's surface is visible from space, making mapping the planet the simplest of procedures. The visitors could also monitor our radio and television broadcasts in order to collect a colossal amount of cultural data, without interacting with us at all. Should they require physical specimens of soil, flora, etc., it would be possible to land unobtrusively and collect them. While this would probably entail making several landings, it would surely not entail making *14 million* of them.

Another very serious problem with the ETH is that of the aliens' physical appearance. Although some rather bizarre shapes have been reported over the years (including giant brains and eyeless beings with tentacles and only one leg), the vast majority have borne a striking resemblance to humans, with a recognizable head, two arms, two legs and a torso. Indeed, the so-called Grey alien has now become accepted, both in the media and by a significant number of ufologists, as the standard model of what genuine extra-terrestrials look like.

Proponents of the ETH cite this as proof that the humanoid configuration is the optimum for intelligent species throughout the universe. For example, it makes a lot of sense for the two eyes (providing stereoscopic vision) to be located on the head, as close to the brain as possible. It also makes sense for the head to be on top of the body, providing the best possible view of the being's surroundings. Two hands with opposable thumbs are best suited to the fashioning and using of tools, while two legs ensure swift and efficient locomotion, more than two would take up unnecessary processing capacity in the brain.

This sounds reasonable enough, until one remembers that the humanoid shape is a very finely tuned adaptation to conditions on this planet, and this planet alone. Also, it is the result of tens of thousands of random mutations in our genetic material, occurring over millions of years, mutations that, at any time in our history, could have occurred in a subtly different way, taking us in a markedly different evolutionary direction. Aliens originating on a distant planet would be the result of evolutionary processes within their native biosphere, which would almost certainly have different characteristics to those of Earth. For instance, it is highly unlikely, i.e. virtually impossible statistically, that the aliens' planet would have exactly the same mass as Earth, with an atmosphere of exactly the same density and with identical gases in identical proportion. As Edward Ashpole says (*The UFO Phenomena*, page 81), it is possible that beings with four limbs, a backbone, a large skull and manipulative hands could evolve on another planet, but they would still be very strikingly different from ourselves. Random genetic mutation, combined with the diverse conditions that must prevail on other worlds, makes it extremely unlikely that intelligent extra-terrestrials would look anything like us.

Of course, while the ETH cannot be made to account for unexplained close encounters in general, that does not imply that it cannot account for some of them. Take the famous case of Florida scoutmaster D.S. Desvergers, for example, who, along with his troop, witnessed a UFO landing in some nearby woods. Leaving the boys in his car, Desvergers went into the woods to investigate. He became aware of a disc-shaped object hovering above him. The object sprayed a fiery substance at him, which burned his arms. There was a turret on the object, inside which the scoutmaster reported seeing a creature so horrifying he could not bring himself to describe it. If Desvergers was telling the truth, the occupant of the UFO could conceivably qualify as a genuine, non-humanoid extra-terrestrial.

ULTRATERRESTRIAL EVOLUTIONARY CONTROL SYSTEMS

As Jacques Vallée is fond of saying, the ETH is not strange enough to account for the evidence of non-human encounters. There have been far too many landings for a planetary survey. The colossal number of UFO landings that must have occurred throughout the world is as ludicrous as the reported behaviour of the occupants, who frequently communicate with humans in absurd ways. (Vallée feels that 'absurdity' is not quite the right word to describe the non-humans' behaviour, preferring the term 'metalogic'.)

For example, in France in 1954 a man came across a UFO. The occupant asked him what time it was. The man looked at his wristwatch and replied, 'It's 2:30.' The ufonaut said, 'You lie – it is 4 o'clock.' However, the time *was* 2:30! Then the ufonaut asked, 'Am I in Italy or Germany?' (Vallée, 1988, page 177.)

These two apparently absurd questions, one about time, the other about space, don't seem quite so absurd on closer examination. Vallée wonders whether these exchanges might represent the ufonaut's attempt to instruct the human witness on relativity, to tell us that time and space are not what we think they are. There is an interesting parallel here with the Barney and Betty Hill abduction case, discussed in Chapter 4. When Betty told the ufonauts that Barney had artificial teeth because he was getting old, they didn't understand, and Betty found herself trying to explain the concept of time, with which the beings were apparently unfamiliar. When the Hills were about to leave the craft, however, the 'leader' said to Betty 'Just a minute', implying that they *were* familiar with the concept of time. Although this has been interpreted as an internal inconsistency, pointing to a shared dream as the likeliest explanation for the experience, we can speculate that there may be a deeper meaning, one that does not necessarily preclude the dream hypothesis.

It is possible that a very subtle, symbolic communication took place on board the UFO, in which the superficiality of human understanding of time was demonstrated. A close examination of these exchanges reveals our assumption that the 'aliens' do not understand the concept of time to be erroneous. They were playing a game with Betty Hill, leading her to believe something that was not true, and only giving the game away (doubtless intentionally) at the very end of the encounter. In other words, the encounter tells us that we do not know what we think we know, either about the 'aliens' or, by implication, about the universe itself.

It is this symbolic, almost playful, element to non-human contact that has led writers like Jacques Vallée and Whitley Strieber to suggest that we may be dealing with the activities of some kind of control system, which is guiding our religious, philosophical and cultural development in ways that are both immensely subtle and virtually impossible to comprehend in terms of our current scientific paradigms. Whitley Strieber has said more than once that his so-called 'Visitor Experience' could be what the forces of evolution look like when applied to a conscious mind.

Strieber has also said that the Visitors appear to be interacting with humans on a direct, one-to-one basis, completely by-passing the routes one might expect an alien expedition to follow in making contact with another culture. The leaders of our world, whether political, religious or military, do not seem to be of the slightest interest to the Visitors, who much prefer to appear before ordinary single human beings, usually at night, when they are alone and at their most vulnerable, both physically and mentally.

There is no doubt that encounters with these beings are usually extremely traumatic. Even if a percipient is spared the nightmarish medical procedures reported by so many, the simple fact that a non-human being is standing at the foot of their bed is enough to send a shudder of terror through their soul. Strieber recalls reading about stress tests carried out on rats in the 1970s. The rats were made to suffer through electrocution for long periods, with the result that they grew stronger and more intelligent: their suffering actually improved them. He goes on to say that, as he remembered this and realized that the function of the Visitors is somehow to force us to evolve, a 'tired, young voice' said, 'Thank you', acknowledging that this is indeed the case (Strieber, 1988, page 141).

If we are being forced to evolve by a higher intelligence whose true nature remains hidden from us, the question remains, what is the ultimate goal of this evolution? Many people who have claimed contact with so-called 'extra-terrestrials' have been profoundly altered by their experiences. Whether the beings are of the benign Nordic type, or the mischievous and apparently malignant Greys, the results of contact are similar. They include the acquisition of paranormal talents such as precognition, telepathy and psychokinesis, and also a sudden, consuming awareness of a wider spiritual realm, echoing the Platonist view that what we call reality is no more than a flimsy veil, hiding a far more profound yet accessible eternity. They become intimately concerned with the fate of the Earth, something which may have occurred to them only fleetingly before their experiences.

Earlier in this book, I commented on the ability of some objects to appear and vanish instantaneously, and also to plunge into and emerge from solid ground. There have been a large number of reports in which UFOs seem to change shape, as if they are not behaving according to the accepted laws of physics. One of the most famous examples of this occurred on 29 June 1954. The BOAC Stratocruiser *Centaurus* was flying from New York to Newfoundland, when the crew saw a large metallic object off the port side of the aircraft. Surrounding the large UFO were six smaller objects, apparently escorting it. The captain of the Stratocruiser began to sketch the large object which, astonishingly, seemed to be changing shape, from a delta wing, to a telephone handset, to a pear.

A Sabre jet fighter was scrambled from Goose Bay, Newfoundland, to investigate. The Sabre pilot radioed that he was in range, and that he had a radar lock on the *Centaurus* and the UFOs. As he approached, however, the six smaller objects lined up in single file and merged with the large one, which then diminished in size and suddenly disappeared.

Although this activity could indicate an extra-terrestrial understanding of physics vastly surpassing our own, when viewed in conjunction with the metalogical behaviour of the ufonauts, another, stronger implication comes to mind, one that points to a far more complex set of events and circumstances than straightforward alien visitation. The evidence seems to suggest an *extra-dimensional* rather than extra-terrestrial origin for UFOs and their occupants.

The ability of UFOs (and non-human beings, for that matter) to wink in and out of existence has some strange implications, which are increasingly being supported by our own advances in the fields of high-energy and theoretical physics. There is a distinct possibility that our strange visitors might be denizens of a superspace, in which our own universe is embedded, like a single bubble in a multi-dimensional foam.

The American researcher John A. Keel, who has been called 'the last of the great ufologists', put forward his theory of 'ultra-terrestrials' in his 1970 book *UFOs: Operation Trojan Horse*. According to Keel, it is possible that the UFOs and their occupants are natives of the Earth, not this Earth, that is, but an Earth existing at the same co-ordinates in a parallel space–time continuum. In support of this theory, Keel cites not only the capability of UFOs to appear and disappear at will, but also the colours they display when doing so. He reminds us that ultraviolet light immediately precedes the visible colour spectrum, the first visible frequencies being of purple or violet light. If UFOs have their origin in a dimension of a different electromagnetic frequency to ours, as they entered our dimension, they would appear as indistinct, purplish blobs of light. Once within this space–time continuum, they would continue to 'gear down from the higher frequencies', their colour changing from ultraviolet to violet, and then to cyan, or blue-green. Once in our continuum, they would radiate energy on all frequencies, resulting in a harsh, white glare. Keel states:

> In the majority of all landing reports, the objects were said to
> have turned orange (red and yellow) or red before descending.
> When they settle to the ground they 'solidify', and the light
> dims or goes out altogether. On takeoff, they begin to glow red
> again. Sometimes they reportedly turn a brilliant red and
> vanish. (Keel, *UFOs: Operation Trojan Horse*, page 62)

This hypothesis would seem to be supported by the observational
data that have accumulated over the years, regarding changes not
only in the colour but the shape of UFOs. However, the apparently absurd, or metalogical, behaviour of the ufonauts towards
humans implies that, although there is a physical phenomenon at
work here, it also extends into the realm of the human psyche,
and is perhaps influenced by its interactions with humanity in a
two-way exchange. In fact, this is quite probably the case, since
the phenomenon clearly takes account of the prevailing world-
view in the society with which it is interacting, and alters it surface
characteristics to appear as angels and demons, or fairies, or inno-
vative aviators, or extra-terrestrial explorers.

Although I am not qualified to write with any authority on the
field of quantum theory, I believe it is worth considering the theory that ufonauts, if they are really denizens of a realm beyond our
space–time continuum, may be a function of the Hidden Variable
theory developed by Dr David Bohm. According to this theory,
quantum events are determined by a subquantum system acting
outside space–time. And, although space and time do not exist in
this realm, to which Dr. Werner Heisenberg gave the name *poten-
tia* it is nevertheless the origin of all phenomena occurring in this
and all other universes. If the Hidden Variable is actually consciousness (as Dr Nick Herbert suggests), we can see at least a tentative link between reported interactions with a non-human intelligence, and a scientifically justifiable mechanism through which
such an intelligence could exist. Indeed, the realm of the psyche
might be the best, if not the only, theatre of interaction between
human beings and a non-human intelligence located outside this
space–time continuum.

It is becoming increasingly likely that reality is not confined to
the single universe we observe around us. A recent theory proposes that the universe itself is the intrusion into four-dimensional space–time of ten-dimensional objects called 'superstrings',
which are so small as to be beyond measurement. (Compared to

the nucleus of an atom, they are, proportionately, as small as the nucleus of the atom compared to the Sun.)

Alternatively, this 'ultraterrestrial' intelligence could have its origin in one of the infinite parallel realities predicted by Hugh Everett's Many Worlds Interpretation, according to which all of the potential outcomes of every event occurring in this universe result in a branching-off into an alternate universe. All of these universes are equally real, and 'exist in their own parts of "superspace" (and supertime)', (Gribbin, page 237). It is conceivable that a sufficiently advanced civilization might have mastered the techniques of 'jumping' between these realities in order to follow its own, unknown agenda.

If consciousness is as important as Nick Herbert proposes in his interpretation of the Hidden Variable theory, Carl Jung's theory that UFOs represent our fundamental desire for unity and wholeness might be given a new lease of life. As Vallée suggests in *Revelations* (pages 276–7), 'the human collective unconscious could be projecting ahead of itself the imagery which is necessary for our own long-term survival beyond the unprecedented crises of the twentieth century.'

VISITORS FROM THE FUTURE

An interesting alternative to the ETH, and one that is fairly acceptable to those who believe that UFOs are solid, nuts-and-bolts vehicles, is the Time Travel Hypothesis. This suggests that the ufonauts are in fact our distant descendants, who have travelled back from their own time to this era, and probably many other eras throughout the past (an idea which conveniently accounts for historical UFO reports).

The Time Travel Hypothesis also accounts for the physical similarities between ourselves and the ufonauts which, as mentioned earlier, should preclude their extra-terrestrial origin. It might also explain the occasionally reported co-operation between the diminutive, spindly Greys and the very human-like Nordics, if we accept the possibility that time travel might become practical in the relatively near future. It would then surely be feasible for humans from a few hundred years hence to engage in joint ventures with those from the distant future.

This is all very well, but is time travel actually possible, or, more to the point, will it ever be possible, even in the distant future? In his excellent and illuminating book *In Search of Schrodinger's Cat*, John Gribbin presents some intriguing insights into how time travel might be achieved by humans, without violating the laws of physics. According to Gribbin, time travel would be allowed by relativity theory if a local region of space-time could be distorted, so that the time axis, which exists at right angles to the three spatial axes, 'points in a direction equivalent to one of the three space directions in the undistorted region of space-time' (page 193). The role of time would be swapped with one of the spatial axes, which would then take on the role of time.

The American mathematician Frank Tipler has worked out the calculations which prove that such a space-time-distorting device is theoretically possible, although it would be rather large and cumbersome. It would be a cylinder measuring 100 kilometres (62 miles) in length and 10 kilometres (6.2 miles) in radius, and would have a mass equivalent to that of the Sun and the density of an atomic nucleus. It would also have to rotate at a rate of 2,000 times per second; in other words, its surface would be moving at half the speed of light.

Although Gribbin concedes that such a device would be colossally difficult to build, he informs us that similar objects exist naturally in the universe. The millisecond pulsar was discovered in 1982; it has the density of an atomic nucleus and spins once every 1.5 milliseconds, which is one-third as fast as Tipler's time cylinder.

It has long been assumed that time travel is impossible because of the paradoxical situations it might create. Gribbin cites the well-known one, in which you travel back in time to kill your grandfather before your own father has been conceived. Another involves your travelling back to perform some less dramatic action, such as filling in a lottery card with the winning numbers, which subsequently come up. This is a paradox because you would already have won the lottery when you stepped into the time machine, and there would be no need for you to travel into the past; but if you didn't make the trip, you wouldn't have won the lottery!

A number of scientists and science-fiction writers have come up with elegant solutions to this problem. For instance, in Michael Moorcock's scientific romance *The Dancers at the End of Time*, the characters are prevented from causing paradoxes by time itself: whenever they are on the point of doing so, the time in which they happen to be spits them out like pieces of bad food, hurling them unpredictably into a different time.

Stephen Hawking has speculated along similar lines, suggesting that time might conspire to prevent you from causing a paradox. For instance, if you were to travel into the past with the intention of shooting yourself in the head, the hand in which you were holding the gun would twitch at the moment you pulled the trigger. Consequently, you would miss your head and shoot yourself in the arm instead. The damage inflicted by the bullet would cause your arm to develop an occasional twitch – the very same twitch that prevented you from killing yourself.

Gribbin describes a theory of time travel in which the problem of paradoxes does not even arise, since it depends on the existence of alternative universes. So, if you did decide to travel back in time to kill your own grandfather, you would create an alternate world in which neither you nor your grandfather had ever been born. There would be no paradox, because, in your native reality you had still been born. 'Go back again to undo the mischief you have done, and all you do is re-enter the original branch of reality, or at least one rather like it' (Gribbin, page 249).

It should be mentioned that the idea of 'parallel universes', so beloved of science-fiction writers, is a somewhat misleading one, which is not borne out by the mathematics. The alternative realities of the Many Worlds Interpretation do not lie parallel to one another, like railway tracks, but at right angles to each other. It would be impossible simply to jump from one reality to another at will; instead, at the instant the relevant quantum choice was made, you would have to travel back in time to the point at which your target reality branched off at right angles to your native reality. You would then go forward in time along the alternate reality running at right angles to your native four-dimensional reality (Gribbin, page 248).

It is therefore within the bounds of possibility that the UFOs and their occupants are our own descendants. This would account for their physiological similarity to us, as discussed earlier, and it might also explain another apparent absurdity in the data on alien encounters: the harvesting of human genetic material. We can imagine a future in which the decline of human fertility (which is already giving cause for concern) will reach the point where the very survival of the species is under threat. Faced with the prospect of extinction, it might well make sense for our descendants to travel back through history to collect the materials essential to their survival. However, we are still on rather shaky ground here, since there would be no need for the time-travellers to abduct people: all they would have to do is break into a few fertility clinics, where they would find all the sperm and ova they would need to bolster their genetic stock. It is perhaps more likely that they would use their time-travelling abilities to perform historical research, in the search for knowledge that has characterized human activity throughout its history.

We must also take into account the possibility that there may be insurmountable difficulties in sending material objects through time. But sending *information* through time might be perfectly feasible, if we could make use of some of the fundamental particles that *do* travel into the past, such as tachyons (Gribbin, page 250). This might well account for the ghostly behaviour of UFOs and their occupants. Perhaps they are not physical objects and beings at all – at least, not in this time – but informational projections from holographic transmitters in the future capable of recording data from the present and then transmitting it back to their own time.

If we speculate even more wildly on this theme, we find ourselves approaching John Keel's theories again. He suggests that UFOs are composed of an energy that, once it has entered our reality, can be manipulated to 'temporarily simulate terrestrial matter' (Keel, page 62). If our remote descendants could transmit such an energy back through time – an energy that could be manipulated to simulate matter and thus interact more fully with people and objects in the 'present' – this would offer physical evidence of their visits (Hynek's Close Encounters of the Second Kind).

If a form of energy projected from the future could be made to simulate matter, it would perhaps not be constrained by the physical laws applying to that matter. This idea recalls the behaviour exhibited by the objects encountered in the Rendlesham Forest incident, the most famous alien-landing case recorded in the UK. The official report on the incident was submitted to the Ministry of Defence by Lieutenant-Colonel Charles Halt, who was deputy commander at the join USAF/RAF air base at Woodbridge, Suffolk. The report was released in 1983, under the Freedom of Information Act, to Robert Todd of the Citizens Against UFO Secrecy group in the United States, and is worth quoting here for its descriptions of both the events and the subsequent discovery of physical evidence:

Subject: Unexplained Lights
To: RAF/CC

1. Early in the morning of 27 Dec 80 (approximately 0300L), two USAF security police patrolmen saw unusual lights outside the back gate at RAF Woodbridge. Thinking an aircraft might have crashed or been forced down, they called for permission to go outside the gate to investigate. The on-duty flight chief responded and allowed three patrolmen to proceed on foot. The individuals reported seeing a strange glowing object in the forest. The object was described as being metallic in appearance and triangular in shape, approximately two to three meters [6½ to 10 feet] across the base and approximately two meters [6½ feet] high. It illuminated the entire forest with a white light. The object itself had a pulsing red light on top and a bank(s) of blue lights underneath. The object was hovering or on legs. As the patrolmen approached the object, it maneuvered through the trees and disappeared. At this time the animals on a nearby farm went into a frenzy. The object was briefly sighted approximately an hour later near the back gate.

2. The next day, three depressions 1½" [4 cm] deep and 7" [17 cm] in diameter were found where the object had been sighted on the ground. The following night (29 Dec 80) the area was checked for radiation. Beta/gamma readings of 0.1 milliroentgens were recorded with peak readings in the three depressions near the center of the triangle formed by the depressions. A nearby tree had moderate (.05–.07) readings on the side of the tree toward the depressions.

3. Later in the night a red sun-like light was seen through the trees. It moved about and pulsed. At one point it appeared to throw off glowing particles and then broke into five separate white objects and then disappeared. Immediately thereafter, three star-like objects were noticed in the sky, two objects to the north and one to the south, all of which were about 10° off the horizon. The objects moved rapidly in sharp angular movements and displayed red, green and blue lights. The objects to the north appeared to be elliptical through an 8–12 power lens. They then turned to full circles. The objects to the north remained in the sky for an hour or more. The object to

the south was visible for two or three hours and beamed down a stream of light from time to time. Numerous individuals, including the undersigned, witnessed the activities in paragraphs 2 and 3.
[Signed]
Charles I. Halt, Lt-Col, USAF
Deputy Base Commander

Several airmen subsequently came forward publicly, claiming that the military personnel had encountered not just strange, protean objects, but humanoid beings as well. Airman Lawrence Warren said that creatures were visible inside the semi-transparent, prism-like triangular UFO. The creatures allegedly put up their arms as if for protection when attempts were made to communicate with them.

The breaking up of the 'red sun-like light' into five separate objects amid a shower of 'glowing particles' is reminiscent of many previous reports, in which UFOs perform inexplicable antics like exploding into different components, or merging into a single object (as with the Stratocruiser sighting mentioned on page 203). This behaviour might be a little easier to understand if looked at it in terms of the assembly and dismantling of objects from energy that has been transmitted from a remote source, whether in space or time. It would also account for the depressions left in the ground by the Rendlesham object, and the traces of radiation that were subsequently recorded.

POWER POINTS AND PSYCHIC VORTICES

One of the favourite explanations put forward by skeptics to account for UFO sightings and encounters with non-humans is that they are 'all in the mind'. To some extent, this is a perfectly acceptable statement, since the vast majority of UFO sightings are indeed misinterpretations of mundane objects viewed under unusual conditions. For instance, an airship catching the rays of the setting sun, and seen from an odd angle, might very well resemble a strange, glowing sphere that slowly changes its shape to that of an ellipse as the wind catches it and makes its profile more visible. The human mind has a tendency to interpret visual images in a way that is understandable. This has been put forward as an explanation for the Face on Mars: (See pages 99–102): the human face is probably the single most recognizable image we know, and it is therefore only natural that our minds should interpret a structure that is vaguely reminiscent of a face *as* a face. If we see something unusual in the sky, something for which there is no immediate explanation, our minds immediately try to interpret it as something we can understand, so that even stars and planets can be seen as structured, artificial objects only a few kilometers, or even a few hundred metres, away.

In an elaborate extension of this explanation, scientists like Paul Devereux and Michael Persinger have suggested that the movements of rocks below the Earth's surface sometimes produce electromagnetic phenomena in the form of so-called 'Earth Lights', glowing balls of light which have been reported as UFOs. They add that human beings in the immediate vicinity of such phenomena might be subject to realistic hallucinations, caused by the electromagnetic stimulation of the hippocampus region of their brains, which results in an altered state of consciousness. The visions and physical sensations associated with these altered states have been duplicated under laboratory conditions, through the stimulation of the relevant structures in the brain.

'Earth Lights' often appear near power lines, transmitter towers, isolated buildings, roads and railway lines. These locations sound rather similar to the liminal zones discussed earlier in this book (see page 30), zones of transition and movement which have always been associated with encounters with anomalous phenomena such as UFOs and non-human creatures.

It seems that certain cultures have always been aware of Earth Lights, and have even incorporated them into their belief systems. According to Rosemary Ellen Guiley, the Native American Snohomish people of Washington State regarded them as doorways to other worlds, while the Yakima (also of Washington State) used them in their divination rituals. The Australian Aborigines consider Earth Lights to be the manifestation of the dead, or of evil spirits (Guiley, page 171).

The area around the town of Sedona, Arizona has gained prominence in recent years as one of the most active of these places. Situated about 65 km (40 miles) south of Flagstaff, the area is sacred to the Yavapai Native Americans, who believe that Sedona's red rocks are home to various deities. Sedona is said to contain a 'power point': a place containing supernatural energies as yet undiscovered by science, but corresponding to the planetary consciousness suggested in the Gaia Hypothesis of the British biologist James E. Lovelock.

Paranormal phenomena such as UFOs, Earth Lights and apparitions are frequently reported in the vicinity of power points. Some percipients also report acquiring psi (parapsychological) faculties, such as becoming clairvoyant, or having out-of-body experiences. Guiley sees a possible link between geomagnetic field activity and some psi activity in humans, thus suggesting that the phenomena are caused by the energies at the sites' (Guiley, page 461).

The implication here is that there is some form of interaction occurring between the energy emanating from the power points, and the so-called 'bioenergy' postulated by Wilhelm Reich. The concept of bioenergy has formed the basis of parapsychological research in Eastern Europe for many decades. Researchers in Czechoslovakia and the former Soviet Union claim that such phenomena are observable in the laboratory, and they even claim to be able to store bioenergy in generators.

Eastern Europe is not the only place where research into these subjects is taken seriously. Yoichiro Sako is a senior researcher for the Sony Corporation of Japan. Although a graduate of the prestigious Tokyo University, Sako is not quite what one would call an 'orthodox' scientist. In 1991, he was appointed director of Sony's ESP laboratory, a special research department directly approved by Sony founders Akio Morita and Masaru Ibuka. Sako describes the field of ESP as 'a new technological revolution', and although he has yet to produce any ideas as to how ESP could be incorporated into marketable products, the very fact that his department is being budgeted means that Sony believes the research has potential.

However, Sony has come under attack from some scientists for their funding of ESP research. Yohishiro Otsuki, a professor of physics at Waseda University, said he was furious at the corporation for financing an employee who believes in paranormal phenomena. Sako countered this by declaring 'We need to have a holonic and holographic vision. Our ultimate goal is to discover the "mind or consciousness" that all humanity, and the whole of creation, must possess.'

Sako claims to have obtained evidence of psychic ability. One experiment involved placing a piece of platinum in one of two black film canisters, leaving the other empty. When asked which of the canisters contained the platinum, 'normal' people guessed correctly 50 per cent of the time. But a certain 'supersensitive person' named 'T.I.' guessed right 70 per cent of the time.

Sako also echoes the idea of the 'sheep/goat effect', discovered in the 1940s by the American parapsychologist Gertrude Schmeidler, which demonstrates that people who believe in psychic abilities tend to score more highly in tests than people who are skeptical. Sako maintains that these phenomena 'never happen among the deniers, no matter how long you wait'. For that reason, he believes that only people who are predisposed to a belief in paranormal phenomena are truly qualified to conduct useful research into them.

These concepts and experiments have been drawn together under the discipline known as psychotronics, which aims to study the ways in which matter, energy and consciousness interact with each other. According to proponents of the discipline, all paranormal phenomena arise from the vital force generated by all life in the universe.

The first 'psychotronic generators' were developed by the Czech inventor and designer Robert Pavlita, who claimed to have been inspired by certain ancient manuscripts, which he refused to name. The generators were composed of bits of machinery, humanoid figures, writing utensils and Easter Island monoliths. With them, Pavlita was allegedly able to store energy collected from any biological source, which was used to enhance plant growth, purify polluted water and kill insects (Guiley, pages 488–9).

If we are prepared to allow UFOs and their occupants to slip into the world of parapsychology (something from which many ufologists would recoil with horror), we can find an intriguing correlation with the phenomenon known as 'apports'; and this might shed a little more light on the mechanisms by which they are manifested. The Hungarian psychoanalyst and paranormal researcher Nandor Fodor defined apports as 'the arrival of various objects through an apparent penetration of matter'. Although most apports are small objects such as coins, pebbles, rings and so on, and are usually manifested during spiritualist seances, larger and more complex objects, such as live animals, are occasionally reported.

Mediums say that apports appear as gifts from the realm of the spirits. While some researchers have suggested that the objects have their origin in other dimensions, from which they are taken by the medium through his or her psychic will-power, others suggest that the medium takes objects from various locations within this dimension and teleports them to the seance, disintegrating them at their initial location, and then reassembling them.

Teleportation of objects by human beings is said to be accomplished through the manipulation of universal energy (corresponding to the bioenergy of Wilhelm Reich). When spiritual adepts reach certain states of ecstasy, their bodies allegedly free themselves from the force of gravity, allowing them to levitate and sometimes move at considerable speeds. Likewise, the apports produced by mediums occasionally float and move around, a phenomenon that has been linked to some poltergeist cases.

The phenomenon of apports could thus conceivably account for reports of UFOs and their occupants, in that they are described as appearing suddenly, performing wild aerobatic maneuvers, and then disappearing as if into thin air. The objection of many ufologists that the objects sometimes leave physical traces is countered by substitution of the term 'paraphysical' for 'physical'. Air Marshal Sir Victor Goddard, who coined the term 'ufology' in 1946, while he was on the Allied Chiefs of Staff Advisory Committee in Washington, observed that physical traces such as patches of burnt grass seem 'almost never to be there the next day, when all that made them come to human consciousness of men like us has gone'.

Goddard believed this to imply that UFOs were apports, originating in:

> . . . a world pervading ours, co-incident with ours – its
> denizens created by astral mind-imagining. That which they
> create can manifest materially as apports in a transient state of
> hardware here. If so, the hardware *will* leave marks where it
> has landed on the ground, before it flies away again, or is
> again etherealized. (Goddards emphasis.)

UFO and non-human encounters may thus be an external result of interactions between the human psyche and an as-yet incomprehensible life force permeating the universe, and generated by all living entities within it. The ultimate purpose of these encounters remains unclear, but it is possible that one of their principal functions is to guide humanity towards a new phase in its evolution.

That such encounters should result in increased psi functioning in percipients should not come as a great surprise in this context. If UFOs really are apports – solid physical (or paraphysical) objects originating in the super-consciousness of the universe itself – such improvements in the psychic abilities of percipients might constitute an inevitable, and perhaps essential, alteration in consciousness as a tool with which to apprehend the universe and our place in it.

The power points mentioned above might even serve as amplifiers for these paranormal signals. If we really are constantly bathed in this bioenergy, generated by ourselves and every other living thing in the universe, we may be ill-adapted to notice it at our present stage of evolution. We might be in a similar position to someone listening to an old gramophone whose horn is missing, struggling in vain to catch the tinny fragments of music rising from the record. The power points and psychic vortices scattered all over the world might function in a similar way to an electronic amplifier, boosting the signal so that the frustrated music-lover listening to the gramophone is suddenly plunged into the ecstatic sweep of a crystal-clear symphony.

Perhaps this is what humanity has always been striving towards, without the majority even realizing it. The pursuit of knowledge in all its forms – scientific, artistic, spiritual – is an attempt to forge, or perhaps rediscover, the link between the self and the infinite universe that gave it life. Maybe the ongoing encounters between humanity and non-human beings are reassurances that someone or something, somewhere, is responding to our efforts.

Bibliography

Andrews, George C. *Extra-Terrestrials Among Us*. St Paul,
   Minnesota: Llewellyn Publications, 1993.
Ashpole, Edward. *The UFO Phenomena: A Scientific Look at the
   Evidence for Extraterrestrial Contacts*. London: Headline Books,
   1996.
Bernard, Raymond. *The Hollow Earth*. New York: Carol
   Publishing, 1991.
Blum, Howard. *Out There: The Government's Secret Quest for
   Extraterrestrials*. New York: Simon & Schuster, 1990.
Boar, Roger & Blundell, Nigel. *The World's Greatest UFO Mysteries*.
   London: Hamlyn Publishing, 1991.
Bord, Janet and Colin. *Life Beyond Planet Earth? Man's Contact With
   Space People*. London: Grafton, 1992.
Bowen, Charles, ed. *The Humanoids*. London: Futura Publications,
   1977.
Brookesmith, Peter, ed. *The Age of the UFO*. London: Orbis
   Publishing, 1984.
Bryan, C.D.B. *Close Encounters of the Fourth Kind: Alien Abduction
   and UFOs – Witnesses and Scientists Report*. London: Orion Books,
   1996.
Bulwer-Lytton. *The Coming Race*. Stroud, Gloucestershire: Alan
   Sutton Publishing, 1995.
Capra, Fritjof. *The Tao of Physics*. London: Flamingo, 1985.
Commander X. *Underground Alien Bases*. Abelard Productions,
   1990.

Drake, Frank & Sobel, Dava. *Is Anyone Out There?* London: Pocket Books, 1994.

Drury, Nevill. *The Elements of Shamanism.* Shaftesbury, Dorset: Element Books, 1992.

Edwards, Frank. *Flying Saucers – Serious Business.* Secaucus, New Jersey: Citadel Press, 1966.

Emenegger, Robert. *UFOs Past, Present and Future.* New York: Ballantine Books, 1978.

Fort, Charles. *Book of the Damned.* London: John Brown Publishing, 1995.

Freemantle, Brian. *CIA: The 'honourable' company.* London: Michael Joseph, 1983.

Fuller, John G. *The Interrupted Journey.* New York, MJF Books, 1996.

Good, Timothy. *Alien Liaison: The Ultimate Secret.* London: Arrow Books, 1992.

— *Beyond Top Secret: The Worldwide UFO Security Threat.* London: Sidgwick & Jackson, 1996.

Grey, Margot. *Return From Death: An Exploration of the Near-Death Experience.* London: Arkana, 1986.

Gribbin, John. *In Search of Schrodinger's Cat.* London: Black Swan, 1993.

Guiley, Rosemary Ellen. *Harper's Encyclopedia of Mystical & Paranormal Experience.* Edison, New Jersey: Castle Books, 1991.

Hamilton, William F. *Cosmic Top Secret: America's Secret UFO Program.* New Brunswick, New Jersey: Inner Light, 1991.

Hancock, Graham. *Fingerprints of the Gods: A Quest for the Beginning and the End.* London: Mandarin, 1996.

Harbinson, W.A. *Projekt UFO: The Case for Man-made Flying Saucers.* London: Boxtree, 1996.

Harpur, Patrick. *Daimonic Reality: A Field Guide to the Otherworld.* London: Arkana, 1995.

Hay, George, ed. *The Necronomicon.* London: Skoob Books, 1992.

Hitching, Francis. *The World Atlas of Mysteries.* London: Pan Books, 1979.

Hopkins, Budd. *Missing Time: A Documented Study of UFO Abductions.* New York: Richard Marek Publishers, 1981.

— *Intruders: The Incredible Visitations at Copley Woods.* New York: Ballantine Books, 1992.

Hynek, J. Allen. *The UFO Experience.* London: Corgi Books, 1975.

Inglis, Brian. *The Paranormal.* London: Paladin, 1986.

Jacobs, David M. *Alien Encounters: First-hand Accounts of UFO Abductions*. London: Virgin Books, 1994.

Jung, C.G. *Man and his Symbols*. London: Aldus Books, 1979.

— *Flying Saucers: A Modern Myth of Things Seen in the Sky*. London: Ark, 1987.

Keel, John A. *UFOs: Operation Trojan Horse*. London: Abacus, 1973.

Keyhoe, Donald E. *Flying Saucers From Outer Space*. London: Tandem Books, 1974.

Mack, John E. *Abduction: Human Encounters With Aliens*. London: Pocket Books, 1995.

Maclellan, Alec. *The Lost World of Agharti: The Mystery of Vril Power*. London: Souvenir Press, 1996.

Nichols, Preston & Moon, Peter. *The Montauk Project: Experiments in Time*. New York: Sky Books, 1992.

— *Montauk Revisited: Adventures in Synchronicity*. New York: Sky Books, 1994.

O'Brien, Christopher. *The Mysterious Valley*. New York: St. Martin's Press, 1996.

Peebles, Curtis. *Watch the Skies! A Chronicle of the Flying Saucer Myth*. New York: Berkley Books, 1995.

Randle, Kevin D. *A History of UFO Crashes*. New York: Avon Books, 1995.

Randle, Kevin D. & Schmitt, Donald R. *UFO Crash at Roswell*. New York: Avon Books, 1991.

—.*The Truth About the UFO Crash at Roswell*. New York: Avon Books, 1994.

Randles, Jenny. *Alien Contacts & Abductions*. New York: Sterling Publishing, 1994.

— *UFO Retrievals: The Recovery of Alien Spacecraft*. London: Blandford Press, 1995.

Sagan, Carl & Page, Thornton, eds. *UFOs: A Scientific Debate*. New York: Barnes & Noble Books, 1996.

Schnabel, Jim. *Dark White: Aliens, Abductions, and the UFO Obsession*. London: Penguin Books, 1995.

Strieber, Whitley. *Communion: A True Story*. New York: William Morrow & Co., 1987.

— *Transformation: The Breakthrough*. New York: Avon Books, 1989.

— *Breakthrough: The Next Step*. New York: HarperCollins, 1995.

Sutherly, Curt. *Strange Encounters*. St Paul, Minnesota: Llewellyn Publications, 1996.

Thompson, Keith. *Angels and Aliens: UFOs and the Mythic Imagination*. New York: Fawcett Columbine, 1993.

Thompson, Richard L. *Alien Identities: Ancient Insights into Modern UFO Phenomena*. San Diego: Govardham Hill Publishing, 1993.

Vallée, Jacques. *Anatomy of a Phenomenon*. London: Tandem Books, 1974.

— *Dimensions: A Casebook of Alien Contact*. London: Sphere Books, 1990.

— *Revelations: Alien Contact and Human Deception*. New York: Ballantine Books, 1991.

Watkins, Leslie & Ambrose, David. *Alternative 3*. London: Sphere Books, 1989.

Wilkins, Harold T. *Flying Saucers on the Attack*. New York: Ace Books, 1967.

Wilson, Robert Anton. *Cosmic Trigger: Final Secret of the Illuminati*. Phoenix, Arizona: New Falcon Publications, 1993.

— *Schrodinger's Cat Trilogy*. London: Orbit, 1990.

Index